CAMBRIDGE ENGLISH PROSE TEXTS

Burke, Paine, Godwin, and the Revolution Controversy

CAMBRIDGE ENGLISH PROSE TEXTS

General editor: GRAHAM STOREY

OTHER BOOKS IN THE SERIES
Revolutionary Prose of the English Civil War,
edited by Howard Erskine-Hill & Graham Storey
The Evangelical and Oxford Movements,
edited by Elisabeth Jay
Science and Religion in the Nineteenth Century,
edited by Tess Cosslett
American Colonial Prose: John Smith to Thomas Jefferson,
edited by Mary Ann Radzinowicz
Romantic Critical Essays, edited by David Bromwich

Burke, Paine, Godwin, and the Revolution Controversy

edited by

MARILYN BUTLER

Rector, Exeter College,
Oxford

CAMBRIDGE
UNIVERSITY PRESS

Published by the Press Syndicate of the University of Cambridge
The Pitt Building, Trumpington Street, Cambridge CB2 1RP
40 West 20th Street, New York, NY 10011–4211, USA
10 Stamford Road, Oakleigh, Melbourne 3166, Australia

First published 1984
Reprinted 1988 1989, 1991, 1993, 1994

Printed in Great Britain by
Athenæum Press Ltd, Gateshead, Tyne & Wear

Library of Congress catalogue card number: 83–15324

British Library Cataloguing in Publication Data

Burke, Paine, Godwin and the revolution controversy.
1. English prose literature – 18th century
2. Revolutions in literature
I.   Butler, Marilyn
828'.608'080358   PN6071.R43

ISBN 0 521 24386 6 hardback
ISBN 0 521 28656 5 paperback

CE

In memory of my father
Trevor Evans
1902–1981
Journalist

Contents

Contents

Contents

Acknowledgements

My debts to other scholars have been numerous. Like many other students of literature, I was introduced to the prose of the 1790s by James Boulton's *Language of Politics in the Age of Wilkes and Burke* (1963), a book from which I have been learning for a decade or more. I have incurred similar obligations, more general and pervasive than the footnotes can acknowledge, to the authors of two theses, which at the time of my book's completion are still unpublished: Olivia Smith, whose *Politics of Language, 1790–1818* (Ph.D., Birmingham, 1980) studies theories and practice concerning the democratisation of the written language, and Mark Philp, whose work on Godwin's *Political Justice* (D.Phil., University of Oxford, 1983) explores the relations between Godwin's social circle and his philosophy. G.I. Gallop introduced me to the writings of Thelwall and Spence, and lent me unpublished work on them. Paul Langford most generously read the typescript and produced many suggestions, all constructive. Deborah Quare has been unfailingly helpful in at least four roles, as friend, librarian, classical scholar, and my chief instructor in the mysteries of word processing. David Robertson prevented the same machine from consuming my introduction and notes. To Colin Matthew I owe thanks for the loan of books, and to Alison Emmitt, Daniel Butler, Edmund Butler, and above all Pamela Clemit, for checking texts and finding references. Even more than for previous books, I have drawn on the co-operation, efficiency, and knowledge of the staff of the Bodleian Library, and of Nuffield College Library, with its invaluable Cole Collection of relevant books and pamphlets. Work on the book was completed while I held a generous Readership from the British Academy. Finally, it is a special pleasure to work across a desk from a husband who breaks off from his own research to pursue problems in mine, with every appearance of enjoyment.

M.S.B.

St Hugh's College,
Oxford

Editorial note

The extracts are taken either from the first edition or, preferably, from a contemporary edition revised by the author. The original spelling and punctuation have within reason been retained. Authorial footnotes, when retained, have been included in the endnotes; editorial footnotes are indicated by letter and endnotes by number. Works excerpted below are not included in the Select Bibliography. The place of publication for the bibliographical references is London, unless otherwise stated.

Introductory essay

This book selects from the pamphlet war of the 1790s. As a public issue, the 'Revolution debate' lasted for about six years, from the first English rejoicings at France's new dawn in 1789, to December 1795, when Pitt's government introduced measures to stop the spread of radicalism by the printed and spoken word. But the questions in contention cannot be understood except in a longer perspective. When the dispute opens, the combatants are speaking of a revolution that is Britain's, not France's – the Glorious Revolution of the seventeenth century. At the close they are no longer writing of political revolution as imminent or practicable. Yet the themes and techniques of the 1790s do not disappear but go underground, to re-emerge in at least two distinct areas of nineteenth-century controversy: the working-class radical movement, and its press, of the post-Napoleonic era; and the more specialised, refined, but sometimes notionally radical body of literature known as the Romantic movement. For many of those who afterwards played a part in nineteenth-century controversy, the course taken by the Revolution debate was significant, even formative.

In 1790, Burke in his *Reflections on the Revolution in France* set out to rally English sentiment and patriotism in support of the existing aristocratic system of government. During the next three years, scores of radical writers, among whom Paine and Godwin are the most powerful, replied with critiques of monarchy and aristocracy, and with alternative proposals which include republicanism, agrarian socialism and anarchy. Alfred Cobban calls the debate 'perhaps the last real discussion of the fundamentals of politics in this country. . . . Issues as great have been raised in our day, but it cannot be pretended that they have evoked a political discussion on the intellectual level of that inspired by the French Revolution.'[1] The effect is not that of a protracted university seminar, dedicated to studying events overseas; discussion centres instead on British society, what it is like and what it ought to be like. Rather than limiting themselves, as modern academics often have them do, to theories such as 'natural rights', the participants are putting pressure on those in power, on behalf of those

I

who would like more of it, and in 1792, at least, the word 'revolution' comes to have a meaning that is close to home and practical: should Britain continue to be governed by owners of land? Why do so few own land? Even, why need individuals own land at all?

Nowadays we lack commonly accepted rules for reading books like Burke's *Reflections*, Paine's *Rights of Man*, Wollstonecraft's *Rights of Woman*, or Godwin's *Political Justice*. A philosopher sees Godwin in *Political Justice* grappling with 'perennial problems . . .: government and human progress, the power of truth and the nature of man, friendship and obligation, marriage, sex and population'.[2] A historian is concerned with its influence, which he notes 'was confined to a small and highly literate circle'.[3] Literary critics usually regard *Political Justice* as peripheral to their subject, perhaps of most interest because some greater writer, Wordsworth or Shelley, had to reject it before arriving at the more subjective, irrationalist theories appropriate to poets. If the philosopher and the literary critic collaborated, their account of the book's meaning would be enriched by the need to relate its 'perennial' matter to its method and manner, the text's subliminal ploys to win the reader's agreement. If either would consider the circumstances of the book's production, too often the concern of only the historian, they would see an unstable but more fascinating work, its matter and manner responding to the events of 1790–5, changing even in its relationship to Burke's *Reflections* (see pp. 151–2).

Study of the Revolution controversy as a whole reveals the artificiality of the practice, common among philosophers and critics, of examining an isolated book out of its context. The Revolution debate represents in its totality not discrete texts and not the *oeuvres* of autonomous authors, but a single series of works which depend for their meaning upon one another, upon the historical situation which gave them birth, and upon the different kinds of reader for whom they were designed. Perhaps two-thirds of the words in this book emerged from a community of writers, personally known to one another, stimulating and sustaining one another, at first, especially, the writer-readers of a shared project. This collective literary enterprise, and its break-up, presents the critic with a phenomenon of great methodological interest, as well as historical importance. It is so clearly focussed upon a single complex issue, and so consciously a genuinely interactive debate, that a special approach has been adopted here, and the principles of selection look rather different from those of other volumes in the present series. As usual, the main texts (which here are those by Burke, Paine, and Godwin) are given at length. But on this occasion they are accompanied by a large number of shorter extracts from other writers, including a group who carry the story from Paine and the theorists of popular language to Wordsworth. The reader can follow the successive phases of the debate, and observe how each writer responds to his predecessors, to his public, and to a European crisis of unique fascination and significance.

English radicalism encountered a severe set-back in the mid 1790s, the end of all hopes of any substantial reform legislation for well over a generation. In 1790, however, the mood on the radical side was unusually cheerful. Between 1760 and 1790, there had been a series of extra-parliamentary campaigns aimed at extending the franchise further (or much further) down the social scale, and at re-drawing parliamentary boundaries so that the new conurbations of the Midlands and the North, notably Leeds, Sheffield, Manchester, and Birmingham, were represented. The lobbying was done either by associations, hitherto run by liberal-minded gentlemen,[4] or in books, newspapers, and pamphlets. The era sees a spate of liberal writing on the Constitution, important for our purposes because it is the 'story so far' behind the radical pamphlets of the early 1790s.

We think of English eighteenth-century government as stable and broadly successful in achieving its ends; but the critique of the system was also strong, deeply rooted, and articulate, so that by the last half of the century its disparate strands had merged into what was in effect an alternative ideology. A Whig oligarchy governed with the support of City interests, controlling Parliament through its network of personal contacts and its monopoly of patronage, and maintaining an expansive, competitive, and often aggressive foreign policy in the interests of British trade. The system's natural opponents among the politicised classes included (especially early in the century) elements of the old Tory country gentry, and of the urban Old Whigs, or radicals, all of whom looked back, within their respective intellectual traditions, to the fierce doctrinaire disputes of the seventeenth century. By the second half of the eighteenth century, this opposition was generating a powerful rhetoric, heady enough to sustain the American Revolution, vague enough to manifest itself ubiquitously in the arts; for, in the poetry and painting of 1770–1800, salient themes include a sense of personal liberty and autonomy, a belief in civic virtue, and a hatred of corruption – all of which can be seen as symptomatic of a 'republican' tradition in Western European thought at least as old as Machiavelli.[5] When he applies himself more specifically to the Constitution, the late-eighteenth-century radical seeks to extend the democratic element in the system, which is notionally held to be a balance between monarch, aristocracy, and commons. Typically, then, the radical criticises the monarch, or the aristocracy, or both, and represents these institutions as encroaching upon the populace or upon its preserve, the House of Commons. He sees existing government as not truly tripartite, but aristocratic. He therefore argues for economical reform, because he believes that an oligarchic government maintains its influence through its control of patronage, or that it manipulates the economy in favour of its own small class, the 'landed interest'. The radical opposes war because, again, he thinks wars tend to profit certain wealthy interests (like the aristocratic owners of West Indian plantations), while they entail loss to ordinary commerce, and hardship to the population at large.

This is the common currency of radical writing at almost any point in the closing decades of the century, as familiar to the literary reader from the poetry of Cowper or Blake as to the historian from news-papers and parliamentary speeches. But, though the principles are much repeated, the ideas evolve during the 1770s and 1780s, becoming larger and more insistently radical; arguably the ideas, and the language in which they are couched, begin to run ahead of real reformist sentiment. It was in 1780, during the American war, that English radicals adopted a platform of demands which would remain unsatisfied until the middle of the next century, like universal adult male suffrage and the redistribution of parliamentary seats according to population; perhaps, indeed, liberal sentiments were more widely found among the educated classes in 1780 than a decade later.

The most public, overt agency of reform in the period – the lobbying, petitioning political association – was not much in evidence in the 1780s: the important groups had to be founded or re-founded early in the next decade. Instead the most coherent group among the reformers, the rational Dissenters, relied on the support of friendly liberal Whigs to bring up in Parliament their special cause, the repeal of the Test and Corporation Acts, the seventeenth-century legislation which prevented non-Anglicans from holding public office: bills which would have given them these civic rights were introduced and defeated in 1787, 1789, 1790, and 1791. But in the era of the American Revolution, the general case for reform had already been eloquently made by the two leading spokesmen for the Dissenters, Richard Price, author of *Observations on the Nature of Civil Liberty, the Principles of Government, and the Justice and Policy of the War with America* (1776), and Joseph Priestley, whose prolific works include *An Essay on the First Principles of Government* (1768). In intention, these two leading radicals have limited objectives, and are hardly (by modern standards) democrats: Priestley, for example, does not advocate any redistribution of property and certainly does not envisage handing over power to the masses, for he expects the enfranchised common man to choose an educated representative.[6] Yet Priestley and other Dissenting intellectuals are all along in a false position, cut off both from the governmental process and from meaningful political discussion with members of other social groups. The result is that during the 1780s and early 1790s they and those like them evolve a rhetoric of liberty which is international rather than patriotic, 'levelling' rather than hierarchical, and above all misleadingly unconstrained, since it puts its claims in respect of the individual conscience, which has no class accent. The message that comes across, unspecific yet unmistakable, is *insubordination*. A phrase like 'the sovereignty of the people' acquires almost indefinite implications, including, for Richard Price, the concept that the people can dismiss their monarch (see p. 29). The extremist tone of the Dissenters' rhetoric may have helped to lose gentry and middle-class support for reform in 1792–5 – if, indeed, widespread reformist sentiment was still there to lose. Extremism, out of step with real sentiment in the country, is the main characteristic of this body of writing, perhaps insufficiently noticed because modern historians of these events are prone to discuss the class affiliations of the writers, their conscious intentions and their careful caveats, rather than their subliminal impact.

Fired by enthusiasm at events in France, and by the too-ready sympathy of a likeminded, pre-selected circle of readers, the leading London radicals produce between 1791 and early 1793 a series of innovative and utopian proposals. Paine, Godwin, and Wollstonecraft envisage, for example, the establishment of a humane welfare state; or the ultimate withering away of the centralised state; or a new egalitarianism in inter-personal relations which would do away with the employee's subservience to the employer or the woman's to a man.

But these are the celebrated performances, preserved for us perhaps by their extremism; the debate, as it evolved after 1790, was often more humdrum or more practical. Most of the excerpts I have chosen originate as pamphlets, published at prices varying from one penny (Thomas Spence's *Meridian Sun of Liberty*) to three shillings (Burke's *Reflections*): the price is an indicator of the public aimed at. A few came out in books, in one volume or more, and costing at least a pound (Wollstonecraft, Young, Godwin). Rather more were not independently published, but contributions to journals or newspapers. The writers involved in the debate chose different ways to reach the public or rather, in each case, a section of the public, defined by the price it would be willing to pay.

A publishing industry with discriminating techniques of marketing already existed in London (and almost everything in the present selection emanated from London). It was largely run by Dissenters, of whom two of the most influential were the Unitarian Joseph Johnson, publisher, bookseller, and owner-editor of the *Analytical Review*, and Ralph Griffiths, proprietor of the *Monthly Review*. Though these were the two best reviews in 1791–3, their only competitors, the *Critical* and the *English*, were also sympathetic to the Dissenters and to the cause of reform.[7] It became a matter of conservative comment, indeed scandal, that early in the decade 'informed opinion' was in the hands of a closely knit circle for which Johnson's dinner table in particular served as a focus, since Johnson was the publisher, friend, at times the host of Joseph Priestley, John Aikin, Anna Laetitia Barbauld, Joel Barlow, William Blake, Erasmus Darwin, R. L. and Maria Edgeworth, Henry Fuseli, William Wordsworth, Thomas Christie, William Godwin, Tom Paine, John Horne Tooke, Mary Wollstone-craft, Thomas Beddoes, and Humphry Davy.

The emergence of this group of interconnected radical intellectuals looked dangerous in a period when the political importance of 'public opinion' was becoming recognised. Even oligarchies cannot govern without a basis of support, or acquiescence; the proliferation of comment in books and newspapers, much of it hostile, brought the extent of that support into question, and made Pitt's Administration nervous. By the early nineteenth century, it could be claimed that British governments might fall if the press turned against them. Though this state of affairs shocked many members of the Adminis-tration and its supporters, who tended to think of radical journalists as irresponsible, ignorant, and scurrilous, the liberty of the press was also widely treasured in England, even by spokesmen for the upper orders, and perceived as a valuable element in the constitution. It was 'the great palladium of British freedom' and 'essential to the nature of a free state', according to the constitutional lawyer Blackstone, while parliamentary liberal Whigs went further. 'Against despotism of any kind or in any shape', cried Sheridan in a celebrated speech, 'let me but array a free Press, and the liberties of England will stand unshaken'.[8] To its friends and its enemies, the press could be seen as a new fourth estate of the realm. A more cynical view of the real influence of opinion-mongering intellectuals in pre-Reform England would be that they operated as a safety valve for the Establishment; they might not often change government policy, but they gave an illusion of effectiveness to writers and readers, so that as a whole this class failed to take up the option of organised political action.[9] The view at the time, however, was that the more vociferous reformist writing *was* part of the political action, and it was upon this premise that the radicals and their antagonists in the government acted.

The twelve-month period beginning in February 1792 was the *annus mirabilis* of eighteenth-century radicalism, for it saw not only the appearance of its classic texts, but the peak activity of radical associations, in London and in the provinces, which were now for the first time not merely joined but run by working men. The London Society for Constitutional Information was, it is true, led by intellectuals: The S.C.I. was John Horne Tooke's revival, in 1790, of a society founded ten years earlier by Major John Cartwright, R. B. Sheridan, Thomas Day, and others 'to revive in the minds of their fellow-citizens, THE COMMONALTY AT LARGE, a knowledge of their lost rights'.[10] Occasionally in the provinces educated men took the initiative while working men stood aloof: in Derby and Belper in 1792, the manufacturer William Strutt and the doctor Erasmus Darwin met opposition from workpeople when they attempted to distribute the Painite propaganda sent them by the S.C.I. Much more commonly, gentlemen continued to meet in their Literary and Philosophical societies, in order to debate revolution in its various aspects at a safely general level.

For many modern historians, the most significant feature of the reform agitation of the 1790s is the spontaneous growth, in London and in cities like Sheffield and Manchester, of associations dominated by working men. Their point of contact in London, indeed the society specially founded to provide the organisational link between radicals, was the London Corresponding Society, founded in January 1792 by the shoemaker Thomas Hardy, with unlimited membership and a subscription of a penny a week. As a political phenomenon, the L.C.S., with its discussions, its support for radicals in the Midlands, the North, and Scotland, its links with the French National Convention, its mass meetings, was undoubtedly the single most important organisation in the radical campaign. But the written word remained the other crucial weapon, one on which the popular societies were, in the long run, dependent. Here it was the S.C.I. which took the decisive step, a step which temporarily bonded the middle-class intellectuals to the mass movement, when in May 1792 it determined to print as a pamphlet and distribute nationwide Tom Paine's *Rights of Man*.

No other production of the pamphlet war achieved the impact or the notoriety of Paine's. While the London intellectuals were self-evidently addressing one another, or similar members of the propertied classes in the provinces, they represented no threat to established order. But the combination of rapidly spreading political organisations with a supply of eloquent radical writings to politicise the masses was another thing entirely. Late 1792 sees the build-up of the antijacobin backlash, a largely spontaneous campaign to silence agitation and to ensure the loyalty of the common people. The gentry organised tenants into groups of yeomanry, a kind of Home Guard which could not have stood up to the French army, but imbibed sound patriotic principles along with its drill. A recently returned Chief Justice of Newfoundland, John Reeves, founded an Association for Preserving Liberty and Property against Republicans and Levellers, which commissioned and then circulated a spate of popularly written pamphlets – religious, loyalist, and soon far more numerous than radical reading-matter aimed at the same audience.

In the second half of 1792, Pitt's Administration began its series of moves to stop the spread of radicalism through the written word. Paine left in September for France, but in December 1792 he was tried and sentenced in his absence for his authorship of a seditious libel, *The Rights of Man*. In court the Attorney-General made it clear that Paine's crime could not be estimated by considering his book as so many mere words on the page, or as abstract ideas. Its being placed in the hands of the masses made it a political tool; the cheapness was an essential part of the offence. From this point, the government kept up a steady pressure against the popular side of radical publishing, and regularly pulled in not so much the writers, but the publishers and distributors of Painite literature, such as the booksellers Symonds, Eaton, and Spence in London (see pp. 244 n.12, 185, 190) and Richard Phillips in Leicester, and the editor James Montgomery in Sheffield.

By contrast, the intellectual leaders and writers remained for a while relatively safe, because their role was perceived as in some sense gentlemanly, and thus privileged, unlike that of the commercial bookseller or political organiser. Although the parliamentary Whigs, headed by Charles James Fox, and their association the Friends of the People, were considered faint allies by the radicals of the L.C.S. and S.C.I., they were of one mind, and practically helpful, on the principle of the free expression of opinion. In 1792 Fox got a Libel Act through Parliament which ensured that the jury, not the judge, would be charged with determining whether or not a particular article amounted to libel. English juries over the next few years were to prove notably reluctant to find for the government, as they demonstrated when they threw out the charges of treason against the London radical leaders Hardy, Tooke, and Thelwall in November 1794 (see p. 169). Scottish law left more to the judge, a difference which in 1793–4 sent five prominent middle-class radicals to Botany Bay for either seven or fourteen years. The parliamentary Whigs became a fully motivated Opposition again in late 1795, when Pitt forced new repressive laws through Parliament (see p. 198). At this point pamphleteers of the extra-parliamentary movement, like Godwin and Coleridge, seem indistinguishable from aristocratic parliamentary Whigs like Fox and Sheridan.

But by 1795 the freedom they were claiming was to express their minds as individuals, not as a group. The growing importance, the respectable, consensual popularity, of the issue of free expression, must have worked to detach the leading writers from the reform movement in which they began. The dignity they perceive in writing increases in proportion to its intricacy and individuality, and is compromised (says Godwin in 1796) if the writing aims to express the views of a group (see p. 162). In fact, the uproar over Paine now looks like the crucial moment of the controversy, as decisive a turning-point in the psychology of the radical intellectual as in general political opinion. Paine forced his friends and colleagues to see themselves for the first time as activists – in, moreover, what was now a mass movement rather than a coterie or a middle-class 'interest'. The re-thinking which had to follow this development drove some prominent reformers, like Mackintosh (p. 90) and Bishop Watson (p. 145), out of the radical camp, and forced painful, protracted revisions on the more heavily committed, very well exemplified in the defensive strategies of Godwin. The shock and anxiety felt by intellectuals was all the greater because their prestige in the late eighteenth century had risen so extraordinarily high. Godwin's novel about a man subjected to witch-hunting when he tries to tell the truth, *Caleb Williams* (1794), expresses the fears of every critic of the system, once he finds Paine being described by politicians, judges, churchmen, and fellow-journalists as a fugitive and a criminal.

Even without Painite incendiarism and the backlash provoked by it, nothing could stop the ebbing of the radical tide once England began to move towards total war with France. These two most powerful European nations had been rivals, and intermittently at war, for over a century; once the French government was not merely revolutionary, but aggressively bent on exporting revolution, external pressure forced English opinion towards conservatism. Before war broke out, during 1792, the French Revolution became much more radical. In November the Convention issued a decree of 'fraternity and assistance' to all peoples, threatening every conservative European government with a fifth column within the state.

For the time being many English radicals nevertheless tried to maintain their links with the Convention in Paris; Paine in his exile became a deputy. After war was declared between France and England in February 1793, fairly moderate members of the opposition, in and out of Parliament, believed it to be the ploy of an aggressive, aristocratic English government against the peace-loving, humane, and united people of France. It was not altogether easy for English critics of Pitt's government to maintain a rosy view of the new French republic. They had to contend with disconcerting news: the September Massacres of 1792, the execution of first the King and then the Queen in 1793, the Terror of 1794 and the royalist rebellion in the Vendée of 1793–5. Yet some radicals and liberal Whigs saw the war, to the end, as England's 'fault'; Godwin claimed that no one who had once favoured the French deserted them, at least until in 1797 the government across the Channel became unmistakably a military dictatorship, and French armies had marched into the Low Countries, Switzerland, and Italy.[11]

Insidiously, however, even the most stalwart radical was caught up in the powerful change of feeling which begins with the mass distribution of *The Rights of Man*. With the publication of *Political Justice* in February 1793, the month the war began, the heroic age of the *expansion* of radical thinking comes to an end. After this, the pamphlets drop away sharply in number, and the new ones are less innovatory. Rather than attempting new theories, or new applications of old theories, they repeat familiar principles and make the kind of broad humanitarian points that are calculated to hold, and reassure, the right-minded reader.[12] The years 1793–6 see the emergence of John Thelwall, sentimental poet and novelist, journalist, lecturer, and orator rather than original thinker, as the leading figure among the radicals.

Many brave and risky efforts to both organise radicals and write for them occur in these post-Paine years. The political objective now is to attract and hold the widest possible support for an anti-government platform; activists no longer use the self-sustaining discourse of a closed clique of convinced reformers. We are judging from the viewpoint of professional intellectuals when we object that the journals and pamphlets that follow Paine, a more working-class phase of the movement, seem (if Thomas Spence is excepted) less innovatory and bold than the work of the middle-class reformers in the climactic year 1792. Perhaps the most remarkable populariser for the masses was Joseph Gales of Sheffield, a Unitarian master-printer and book-seller, who ran two journals, the weekly *Sheffield Register* (from 1787) and the fortnightly *Patriot* (from 1792), both designed to disseminate radical opinion and information to a readership which would include working men. The *Register* cost only one and a half pence for a weekly copy; the *Patriot*, which Albert Goodwin calls 'the most original and significant radical publication to issue from the provincial press',[13] contained accounts of radical politics at home and of events in France, and selections from the classics of radical political theory – Locke, Bolingbroke, Montesquieu, Junius, Rousseau, David Williams, Obadiah Hulme, Volney. In 1794 the *Register* became the *Iris*, under the editorship of the Moravian James Montgomery, a minor poet and man of letters, and a literary patron and focus of intellectual life in Sheffield throughout the war. Other important newspapers in the Midlands and the North included the fiery radical *Manchester Herald*, the Methodist William Ward's *Derby Mercury*, and Richard Phillips's moderate *Leicester Herald*. Meanwhile Norwich was rather a different case, a city with a flourishing literary life which included the neigh-bouring gentry but was dominated by Dissenters. Its *Cabinet* (1794–5) is an anonymous collective enterprise which shows that genteel radicals were still willing to emit libertarian principles in public, at least when they had the encouragement of a sympathetic audience. But thinking in the *Cabinet*, though sometimes unselfishly critical of property, is not new; nor is it in the provincial lecturing and journalism of Samuel Taylor Coleridge, who in 1796 tries with his *Watchman* to reach the rational Dissenting public of Bristol, the Midlands, and the North-west (pp. 195–202).

In the second half of the present book intellectual radicalism can be observed going underground. The 1793 version of Godwin's *Political Justice* well exemplifies the early positive phase of radical writing, with its large horizons, optimism, extremism, and impracticality. In 1795, Godwin embarked on the first of two large-scale revisions of *Political Justice*, in the course of which he made significant alterations to the 1793 version. These are not, as legend has it, simple political retrac-tions. In fact, Godwin now develops a more subtle, hostile, and profound account of how 'Aristocracy' really functions, and he develops those passages which suggest how it victimises its intelligent dissidents (see p. 151). Yet to make a book more subtle and individual is also perhaps to make its appeal more specialised; and the new insistence upon a refined reader is further signalled when Godwin stresses that revolution will come first by means of enlightened thinking. In the preface to his next work, *The Enquirer* (1797), a miscellany of essays on neutral subjects like education and an educated style, Godwin apologises both for his early precipitancy over the French Revolution, and for the ambitious, systematic format of *Political Justice*. His new book will be far more cautious. Its 'recurrence to experiment and actual observation', 'only a short excursion at a time', not dicta, but 'materials of thinking', together prove its humbler aspirations, and its intended appeal to those committed to a life of thought rather than of action.[14]

Godwin did not show others how to retreat; it is one of the characteristics of a community that its members react similarly, though independently. By 1800, he found himself a member of a reconstituted circle of radicals or ex-radicals, a more strictly literary 'literary London', which included Coleridge, Charles Lamb, William Hazlitt, George Dyer, and Joseph Cottle, and his thinking came to coincide with theirs:

In my forty-fourth year I ceased to regard the name of Atheist with the same complacency I had done for several preceding years . . . My theism, if such I may be permitted to call it, consists in a reverent and soothing contemplation of all that is beautiful, grand or mysterious in the system of the universe . . . into this train of thinking I was first led by the conversations of S. T. Coleridge.[15]

Godwin's earlier work, now much more inflammatory than its author, continued to suggest to later radicals, like Shelley, that the intellectual might usefully aim for revolution in the minds of his readers, if not on the streets, in the taverns, or at the barricades.[16] The tone of the circle after 1800 was better caught by Charles Lamb, who that year professed an inability to interest himself in the French Revolution at all. 'As to France and Frenchmen, and the Abbé Sieyès and his constitutions, I cannot make these present times present to me.'[17]

The polarisation of literature and politics around 1800, the writers' own developing insistence that these are two different kinds of interest, comes as an ironic ending to half a century in which the arts are impregnated with politics. In painting, especially, the 'alternative' ideology expressed in so much directly political writing (see p. 3) finds an expressive language and iconography. From the era of the American war, painters such as Barry, West, Morland, Fuseli, Banks, and Blake are firmly identified with the radical camp. The poets who rise to prominence in the 1780s are headed by Cowper, Crabbe, Burns – and Blake once more. A pro-French and freethinking strain common in some circles of pre-Revolution aristocracy is reflected in long poems on esoteric but controversial subjects, like Erasmus

Darwin's *Botanic Garden* (1789–91), which portrays a universe governed by the sexual principle, Richard Payne Knight's *The Landscape* (1794), which views landscape gardening with an egalitarian eye, and the same author's *Progress of Civil Society* (1796), a primitivist critique of its subject.[18] But by 1797, when George Canning and his friends found *The Antijacobin*, they are able to point to more middle-class styles of poetic subversion, which they evidently feel to be more of a threat than the long philosophic poem – the German sentimental drama, which is now all the theatrical rage, and the sentimental humanitarian ballad or sonnet of Southey, Coleridge, and their Bristol circle. *The Antijacobin* even acknowledges that most good new poetry is of this democratic kind (see p. 217) – a case which would have more cogency if Canning had included Wordsworth's *Salisbury Plain* or Thelwall's miscellaneous verse and *Peripatetic* (1793), or extended his argument to prose, to include jacobin novels such as Charlotte Smith's *Desmond* (1792), Robert Bage's *Man As He Is* (1792) and *Hermsprong* (1796), Holcroft's *Anna St Ives* (1792) and *Hugh Trevor* (1794–7), Godwin's *Caleb Williams* (1794), Elizabeth Inchbald's *Nature and Art* (1796), Mary Hays's *Memoirs of Emma Courtney* (1796), and Mary Wollstonecraft's *Maria, or the Wrongs of Woman* (1798).

The literary London of such writers no longer depended upon upper-class leadership and patronage. Painters and sculptors, like musicians, had a more problematic and potentially humiliating relationship to the wealthy, which is no doubt why Morland for one tried to use go-betweens to market his work, so that the buyer would have no direct say in subject-matter or treatment.[19] Engravers, on the other hand, shared many of the economic opportunities of writers, who were able to reach out through the booksellers, with their networks of journals and libraries, to an increasingly large and ill-defined middle-class public. Given the circumstances of production in the late eighteenth and early nineteenth centuries, it is no wonder if writers' and artists' self-images begin to assume a new dignity, an insistence on sturdy independence of the wealthy and powerful. The same confidence is expressed in works of scholarship, which also share the tendency of the arts and of journalism to convey oppositional opinion. Hume's Tory version of England's recent past is challenged by the Whig Catherine Macaulay, who ends her story triumphantly at the 1688 Revolution.[20] In his *Historical View of the English Government* (1787), the Scotsman John Millar gives a sweeping, scientific account of the evolution of government which lends historical sophistication and respectability to the sentimental primitivism beloved of radical polemicists, that myth – common to Cartwright, Priestley and Paine – that Anglo-Saxon liberties were lost under a Norman yoke.[21] Burke's medievalist, Catholic vision counters such values, to be opposed in turn by a yet more aggressive version of popular history, Joseph Ritson's claim that by using an oral form, the ballad, the people have kept a record distinct from that of their rulers and from monkish chroniclers (see p. 204).

To claim that learned arguments may not be merely on the side of the people but written for the people and by the people is of course to go further than to write Whiggish history. One of the most significant innovatory themes illustrated in this volume is the attempt to democratise language, to find a written style appropriate for the literate but not classically educated lower middle and upper working class.[22] Some of the efforts to de-mystify learning were doomed to failure, like schemes by Ritson and Spence to simplify spelling (see pp. 203 and 189). Others, like Tooke's attack on the obfuscations built into learned language by the self-interested upper orders (p. 18), had a prolonged influence. But as a whole the fate of these fundamentalist experiments depended upon the fate of radicalism, which means that in the short term they met defeat. When mass education got under way, with the late-eighteenth-century Sunday School movement and the early-nineteenth-century national systems, it did without theories about popular poetry and alternative history. Wordsworth's Preface to the *Lyrical Ballads* (see p. 226) reiterates the case for the dignity of the language of simple, uneducated people, along with the truth and profundity of their experience. But these pages were singled out for attack by Coleridge and Jeffrey, critics relatively sympathetic to Wordsworth and to liberalism (see p. 228). Instead of providing a manifesto for nineteenth-century literature, they mark the end of the eighteenth-century dream of universal culture.

The notion of a poetry (or prose, or grammar) for the people was profoundly in conflict with that other theme emerging in ex-radical literary London, that Literature should be guaranteed immunity from prosecution because, by definition, it did not threaten the state. The excerpts which follow here begin with a series of thumbnail sketches of intellectuals written by themselves: for Tooke, the writer is the brave, persistent challenger of authority (p. 21), for Price he is a wise enlightener (pp. 26–7), and for both he belongs in a public tradition of nonconformity going back to the Civil War. But these self-idealisations – for that is what they are – come under increasingly fierce challenge. Burke in the *Reflections* deprives his opponents of their history, and puts them prosily behind the shop counter, as economists, calculators, and tallow-chandlers (pp. 44, 47); in his *Letter to a Noble Lord* (1796), he makes the radicals seem more dangerous than this, the same breed as 'the cannibal philosophers' of France (p. 56).

The campaign against radical intellectuals grows greatly in volume in the second half of the decade, and it is fought in newspapers and journals, in the cartoons of Gillray, and in scores of 'antijacobin' satirical novels. Thelwall is at last driven out of politics, though not before he has replied to Burke with a glowing defence of enlightened intellectuals in general, and of himself in particular (see p. 212). In October 1797 he writes a sad cradle poem to his baby son, named John Hampden after the Civil War patriot, who has been born into a 'wilderness of wrongs', where his father 'in his native land / Wanders an exile'.[23] Four months later Thelwall's friend Coleridge writes *his* cradle poem, 'Frost at Midnight', to a baby son named pointedly after a philosopher, Hartley, and destined, his father hopes, to a calm life lived at one with Nature and receptive to God's eternal language. Coleridge's poetic subjects over the next few years include nature and religion, the inner life, friendship, the home. Gradually he turns in his prose to abstruser subjects, philosophy and theology, to produce, eventually, a sophisticated theory of literature which associates it with a pious and responsible class, the 'clerisy'. Wordsworth remains for the time being more ambivalent, at his most radical in the version of the Preface to the *Lyrical Ballads* that appeared in 1802, but already a philosophical poet, in the Coleridgean sense, in *The Borderers* (1796–7), and in the great series of poems, including *The Prelude*, in which, before the turn of the century, he ponders the experiences of recluses and private men.

In the years 1798–9 Joseph Johnson, doyen of publishers, spent nine months in jail for selling Gilbert Wakefield's anti-war pamphlet, while Wakefield himself, an elderly Dissenting minister and classical scholar, received a two-year sentence from which he emerged a dying man. That pamphlet does indeed seem actionable by the modern conventions of war (see p. 220), but eighteenth-century England had no tradition of wartime censorship in the national interest. The government's treatment of Johnson and Wakefield was taken to be unprecedented aggression, the end of the truce against scholars with no defence except pure motives and a small readership. Fox at the time considered the case 'a death blow to the liberty of the press';[24] Wordsworth remembered Wakefield nervously a decade later, while he was preparing his hardly disloyal pamphlet on the Convention of Cintra. In their demoralisation, it is not surprising that literary men began to emphasise their intention to be of good behaviour and keep the peace.

The new literary dispensation after about 1800 puts serious difficulties in the way of the critic who approaches the prose of the 1790s. In theory it is not hard to specify a suitable method for criticising political rhetoric. Polemicists are in the business of selling something, so that approaching them intelligently means approaching them sceptically. Do they claim to be discussing principles, rather than their own material advantage? Do they describe themselves as moderates, or as disinterested bystanders? The more dignified the posture, sonorous the rhetoric, enhancing the ideals, the more persuasive a writer is likely to be; we should not be gullible, any more than when seeing an advertisement, or listening to a politician. Analysing polemical prose will include identifying the author's self-characterisation (sane, tolerant, public-spirited, harmless), and noting his devices (such as Burke's emotive imagery, or Paine's vulgarisms), and then considering how the persona and the devices function on behalf of his chosen cause.

In practice, our approach to political prose is bedevilled because we are ourselves Romantics or post-Romantics; we have been taught the primarily aesthetic values adopted by literary men after their political defeat. So we tend to ask questions which already pre-judge the issue, by smuggling in aesthetic and individualistic values – such as 'who wrote the best prose?' or 'which are the masterpieces?' If these are really the right questions, the answers follow without much room for dispute. Burke is the pre-eminent prose writer of the decade, for he has a range, inventiveness, wit, and personal feeling which no one else matches. Burke makes a highly subtle appeal, using the stick and the carrot: on the one hand he frightens the reader with a prospect of social breakdown and with biblical tones reminiscent of paternal authority, while on the other he cajoles him into loyalty with reminders of home and a tightly drawn family. By the end of the century, with European societies de-stabilised and Burke's fears apparently realised, these themes and rhythms seem to enter into the prose and verse of many imaginative writers, notably of Wordsworth and Coleridge. Though no match for Burke in skill, Godwin among the Revolution debaters proper is sensitive to some of the same insecurities.

To single out these two is, however, to concur with the position being reached in 1800 – that good writing should be about personal experience, not public problems. It is to reject the 'alternative' tradition which the reader of this book will also find advocated, the radical goal of communicating with a wider audience in a common language. The 'highbrow', specialist discourse of the educated classes, in which Godwin and Coleridge not only wrote, but gradually helped to define and defend,[25] was challenged in the period by an idealised concept of the vernacular, which could be a suitable medium for intellectual debate and even for art. Here it is the two writers returning to England with American experience, Paine and Cobbett, who use popular vocabulary and rhythms, and draw on popular suspicion of rulers, and thus pragmatically establish that politics is the people's business. No contemporary prose writer matches these two in their capacity to make a simple uncluttered point. Their only challenger, Spence, never achieves their command of language, and succeeds, when he succeeds, with the boldness of his radical vision. For this group of writers, the prose pamphlet was related to the newspaper, and the criterion of excellence was not to stimulate the reader's introversion, not to address his private fears, but to encourage notions large enough, and common enough, to become a basis for collective political action. In the search for a plain comprehensible style, the defeat of radicalism in the mid 1790s was a set-back, but it was temporary. By the early 1800s, Cobbett was taking up the natural position of the political journalist in unreformed England, that of a spokesman for the extra-parliamentary opposition. When the next radical opportunity came, in 1816, Cobbett did with his *Political Register* what had been done with Paine's *Rights of Man* in 1792 – he sold it direct to the mass public at two pence a time. Where the after-history of poetry is ultimately that of the private theme and the small, highly educated audience, in prose the experiences of the 1790s set a pattern for the future.

John Horne Tooke

(1736–1812)

1. ΕΠΕΑ ΠΤΕΡΟΕΝΤΑ or *The Diversions of Purley* (1798),

(vol. I, 1786, 2nd rev. edn, 1798; vol. II, 1805),

vol. I (1798), pp. 3–15

The career of John Horne Tooke (born, and until 1782 known as, John Horne) actively involves him in all the major reform agitations for half a century. He was a supporter and pamphleteer on behalf of John Wilkes in the 1760s, and was jailed during the American Revolution for soliciting subscriptions for 'our beloved American fellow-subjects . . . inhumanly murdered by the king's troops at or near Lexington'. Tooke acted as both a source of ideas and a skilful political organiser over four decades. His groups included the Society for Supporting the Bill of Rights and the Constitutional Society, of Wilkesite days, and the important Society for Constitutional Information, which he revived in 1790 and which played a key part in distributing *The Rights of Man* (see above, p. 7). When twelve London radicals were arrested for treason in 1794, Tooke was one of three brought to trial, a fact which illustrates his dangerousness in the eyes of the government. During the 1790s and the first decade of the next century, he regularly entertained to Sunday dinner at his house in Wimbledon liberal peers, Foxite M.P.s, radicals, and men of letters. The closest political ally of his last years was the radical Whig M.P. Sir Francis Burdett, one of his interlocutors in *The Diversions of Purley*.

For so central a figure, Tooke's political writings seem few in number and oddly coded. His major work, *The Diversions,* a Socratic dialogue about philology, has been taken as two very different kinds of book, each of them censurable. For the modern historian of ideas Hans Aarsleff, Tooke was right to insist upon the derivation of English vocabulary from Anglo-Saxon, but wrong about much else, and he put the comparative study of language on an eccentric course in England just when philology was taking off in Germany.[1] For contemporaries, however, *The Diversions* was not an academic but a political book. Its influence can be felt pervasively in Godwin's subtle arguments in *Political Justice* about aristocratic imposture. A link with Wordsworth's Preface to the *Lyrical Ballads,* though hard to substantiate, seems very probable (see below, p. 227). T. L. Peacock admired it immensely, and imitated its dialectical form and its iconoclasm.[2] For Hazlitt and for

1. *The Diversions of Purley*

Cobbett, who were both radical grammarians, Tooke was the pioneer. The fault these and other contemporaries were likely to find with him was over-subtlety, which some put down to political caution.[3] It was odd, as a hostile pamphleteer was already suggesting in 1790, to bestow upon a polemic in favour of a plain English a Greek title which, when translated, left no one the wiser, along with a subtitle that also needed explaining.[4] Tooke's esotericism and his reluctance, even while making a 'levelling' case, to descend to vulgarity of manner, seem in fact very characteristic of the aristocratic radical in this age, from Erasmus Darwin and R. P. Knight to Byron, Shelley, and Peacock.

Nevertheless, *The Diversions of Purley* takes to a polemical extreme those efforts to democratise language which are specially characteristic of the last three decades of the century (see p. 14). Tooke traces individual words back to Anglo-Saxon instead of to Latin, thus heartening non-learned speakers of the vernacular. The organic, evolutionary picture of the English language which emerges echoes the conception of English history favoured by radical polemicists and historians (see above, pp. 4, 13–14). He gives a drastically simplified account of the parts of speech and of the meaning of individual words, in defiance of the orthodoxies of grammarians and lawyers, which function, he says, to mystify or intimidate the populace. His political critique is applied to most theorists of language, including the Tory dictionary-maker Samuel Johnson, the idealist metaphysician Lord Monboddo, and the Treasury minister and courtier James Harris, author of *Hermes, or a Philosophical Inquiry concerning Universal Grammar* (1751). Harris, a favourite target of Tooke's, argued that language represented 'COMPREHENSIVE AND PERMANENT IDEAS, the genuine perceptions of pure mind'.[5] For Tooke, such a theory was an ideological device, resembling the Burkean myth of history, to uphold the present order in perpetuity.

T*[ooke]*.[6]

I will tell you on what we were discoursing yesterday when you came in; and I believe you are the fittest person in the world to decide between us. He insists, contrary to my opinion, that all sorts of wisdom and useful knowledge may be obtained by a plain man of sense without what is commonly called Learning. And when I took the easiest instance, as I thought, and the foundation of all other knowledge, (because it is the beginning of education, and that in which children are first employed) he declined the proof of his assertion in this instance, and maintained that I had chosen the most difficult: for, he says, that, though Grammar be usually amongst the first things taught, it is always one of the last understood.

John Horne Tooke (1736–1812)

B[urdett].[7]

I must confess I differ from Mr. H. concerning the difficulty of grammar: if indeed what you have reported be really his opinion. But might he not possibly give you that answer to escape the discussion of a disagreeable, dry subject, remote from the course of his studies and the objects of his inquiry and pursuit? By his general expression of *what is commonly called Learning* – and his declared opinion of that, I can pretty well guess what he thinks of grammatical learning in particular. . . .

H[orne].[8]

Indeed I spoke my real sentiments. I think Grammar difficult, but I am very far from looking upon it as foolish: indeed so far, that I consider it as absolutely necessary in the search after philosophical truth; which if not the most useful perhaps, is at least the most pleasing employment of the human mind. And I think it no less necessary in the most important questions concerning religion and civil society. . . .

B.

Have you tried any other of our English authors on the subject?

H.

I believe all of them, for they are not numerous; but none with satisfaction. . . .

B.

You must then give up one at least of your positions. For if, as you make it out, Grammar is so difficult that a knowledge of it cannot be obtained by a man of sense from any authors in his own language, you must send him to what is commonly called Learning, to the Greek and Latin authors, for the attainment of it. . . .

H.

On the contrary, I am rather confirmed by this instance in my first position. I acknowledge philosophical Grammar (to which only my suspected compliment was intended) to be a most necessary step towards wisdom and true knowledge. From the innumerable and inveterate mistakes which have been made concerning it by the wisest philosophers and most diligent inquirers of all ages, and from the thick darkness in which they have hitherto left it, I imagine it to be one of the most difficult speculations. Yet, I suppose, a man of plain common sense may obtain it, if he will dig for it; but I cannot think that what is commonly called Learning, is the mine in which it will be found. Truth, in my opinion, has been improperly imagined at the bottom of a well: it lies much nearer to the surface; though buried indeed at present under mountains of learned rubbish; in which there is nothing to admire but the amazing strength of those vast giants of literature who have been able thus to heap Pelion upon Ossa. . . . I acknowledge then that the subject is not intirely new to my thoughts: for, though languages themselves may be and usually are acquired without any regard to their principles; I very early found it, or thought I found it, impossible to make many steps in the search after *truth* and the nature of *human understanding*, of *good* and *evil*, of *right* and *wrong*, without well considering the nature of language, which appeared to me to be inseparably connected with them. I own therefore I long since formed to myself a kind of system, which seemed to me of singular use in the very small extent of my younger studies to keep my mind from confusion and the imposition of words. . . . Whilst I was thus amusing myself the political struggle commenced; for my share in which you so far justly banter me, as I do acknowledge that, both in the outset and the progress of it, I was guilty of two most egregious blunders; by attributing a much greater portion of virtue to individuals and of understanding to the generality than any experience of mankind can justify.[9]. . .

B.

You will begin then either with *things* or *ideas*: for it is impossible we should ever thoroughly understand the nature of the *signs*, unless we first properly consider and arrange the *things signified*. Whose system of philosophy will you build upon?

H.

What you say is true. And yet I shall not begin there. Hermes, you know, put out the eyes of Argus: and I suspect that he has likewise blinded philosophy:[10] and if I had not imagined so, I should never have cast away a thought upon this subject. If therefore Philosophy herself has been misled by Language, how shall she teach us to detect his tricks?

B.

Begin then as you please. Only begin.

Richard Price

(1723–1791)

2. *A Discourse on the Love of our Country*, Delivered on November 4, 1789, at the Meeting-House in the Old Jewry, to the Society for Commemorating the Revolution in Great Britain (3rd edn, 1790),[1]

pp. 1–5, 10–15, 20–6, 29–42, 48–51

Richard Price was a Dissenting preacher first at Newington and later at Hackney (outer London), and one of the intellectual leaders of rational Dissent. As a moral philosopher he is best known for *A Review of the Principal Questions in Morals* (1756). He was also a mathematician, an expert in insurance and an advisor to Shelburne and Pitt on financial reform. He was one of the leaders of the Dissenting campaigns to extend the rights of freedom of worship and of civic equality, and his pamphlet against the American war in 1776, a best-seller, led to an invitation from Congress to go to America. As the doyen of Dissenting ministers and campaigners, he was originally meant to give the commemorative sermon at the Presbyterian chapel in London's Old Jewry the previous year, which was the one-hundredth anniversary of the Glorious Revolution of 1688. Delivering it a year later, after the Fall of the Bastille and shortly before the renewed effort in the winter of 1790 to get the Test Acts repealed by Parliament (see above, p. 4) he attracted the attention of Edmund Burke, whose *Reflections on the Revolution in France* (November 1790) is a direct reply to Price's *Discourse*.

The sermon contains little that Price had not already written or spoken elsewhere. His fellow-reformer Christopher Wyvill placed Price among the moderates of the movement.[2] He did not wish to abolish the monarchy, and he preferred the existing 'mixed' form of government to a democracy; he could claim that he merely wished to 'restore' the constitution by 'establishing that independence of the three [e]states on one another in which its essence consists'.[3] Nevertheless, in some of the phrasing of his *Discourse* – for example, in the trenchant claim that the monarch is no more than the first servant of the public, who can be cashiered for misconduct – Price displays that reckless expansive spirit which was typical of the radicalism of about 1790. In a similar mood a year later, at a dinner of the Revolution Society on 4 November 1790, he proposed a toast, 'The Parliament of Britain, may it become a National Assembly', which gave his enemies the impression that the revolution he wished to see in Britain was more total and more alien than it was.[4] The reader might be similarly misled by the sonorous pulpit oratory at the close of the *Discourse*, a reminder that Price was, after all, a Welshman.

Price's sermon compares instructively with Burke's attack upon it (pp. 36ff.) After favouring the claims of Dissenters early in his career,[5] Burke had steadily developed a case against theoretical moves to rewrite the Constitution. Some of his reiterated preference for 'experience' is the practising politician's contempt for the academic, a not unnatural defensive reaction at a time when the real, formidable opposition to the Administration was functioning outside Parliament. Burke has a strong feeling for the Established Church, to which his family tradition of Catholicism gives a special colouring, and a consequent dislike for Price's Puritan stress on freedom of conscience, as opposed to 'priestcraft' and 'superstition'; he senses in British rational Dissenters a taint of the atheism of their friends the French *philosophes*. The character-sketch Burke gives of Price in the *Reflections* is aimed not at the man but at the ideas. Price becomes a social upstart, ridiculous in his claim to be a 'Spiritual Doctor of Politics'; a prosy figure, limited by cold rationalism in his comprehension of human life. But his priestly function also prompts more sinister hints concerning this pagan presider over 'Babylonian pulpits', this magician 'in whom the fumes of his oracular tripod were not entirely evaporated', or 'this archpontiff of the *rights of men*' (see p. 38). Burke's Price is the first of those travesties of Enlightenment intellectuals – conspirators, freemasons, Illuminati, mad, bad scientists, and philosophers – which turn-of-the-century counter-revolutionaries conjure up in order to discredit reform movements and their leaders.

PSALM cxxii. 2d, and following verses.

Our feet shall stand within thy gates, O Jerusalem, whither the tribes go up; the tribes of the Lord unto the testimony of Israel. . . . Pray for the peace of JERUSALEM. . . . They shall prosper that love thee. . . .

In these words the Psalmist expresses, in strong and beautiful language, his love of his country, and the reasons on which he founded it; and my present design is, to take occasion from them to explain the duty we owe to our country, and the nature, foundation, and proper expressions of that love to it which we ought to cultivate.

I reckon this a subject particularly suitable to the services of this day, and to the Anniversary of our deliverance at the Revolution from the dangers of popery and arbitrary power; and should I, on such an occasion, be led to touch more on political subjects than would at any other time be proper in the pulpit, you will, I doubt not, excuse me.

The love of our country has in all times been a subject of warm commendations; and it is certainly a noble passion; but, like all other passions, it requires regulation and direction. There are mistakes and prejudices by which, in this instance, we are in particular danger of being misled. – I will briefly mention some of these to you and observe,

First, That by our country is meant, in this case, not the soil or the spot of earth on which we happen to have been born; not the forests and fields, but that community of which we are members; or that body of companions and friends and kindred who are associated with us under the same constitution of government, protected by the same laws, and bound together by the same civil polity.[6]

Secondly, It is proper to observe, that even in this sense of our country, that love of it which is our duty, does not imply any conviction of the superior value of it to other countries, or any particular preference of its laws and constitution of government. Were this implied, the love of their country would be the duty of only a very small part of mankind; for there are few countries that enjoy the advantage of laws and governments which deserve to be preferred. To found, therefore, this duty on such preference, would be to found it on error and delusion. It is, however, a common delusion. There is the same partiality in countries, to themselves, that there is in individuals. All our attachments should be accompanied, as far as possible, with right opinions. – We are too apt to confine wisdom and virtue within the circle of our own acquaintance and party. Our friends, our country, and in short every thing related to us, we are disposed to overvalue. A wise man will guard himself against this delusion. He will study to think of all things as they are, and not suffer any partial affections to blind his understanding. In other families there may be as much worth as in our own. In other circles of friends there may be as much wisdom; and in other countries as much of all that deserves esteem; but, notwithstanding this, our obligation to love our own families, and country, and to seek, in the first place, their good, will remain the same.

Thirdly, It is proper I should desire you particularly to distinguish between the love of our country and that spirit of rivalship and ambition which has been common among nations. – What has the love of their country hitherto been among mankind? What has it been but a love of domination; a desire of conquest, and a thirst for grandeur and glory, by extending territory, and enslaving surrounding countries? What has it been but a blind and narrow principle, producing in every country a contempt of other countries, and forming men into combinations and factions against their common rights and liberties? . . .

In pursuing particularly the interest of our country, we ought to carry our views beyond it. We should love it ardently, but not exclusively. We ought to seek its good, by all the means that our different circumstances and abilities will allow; but at the same time we ought to consider ourselves as citizens of the world, and take care to maintain a just regard to the rights of other countries. . . . Our first concern, as lovers of our country, must be to *enlighten* it. – Why are the nations of the world so patient under despotism? – Why do they crouch to tyrants, and submit to be treated as if they were a herd of cattle? Is it not because they are kept in darkness, and want knowledge? Enlighten them and you will elevate them. Shew them they are *men*, and they will act like *men*. Give them just ideas of civil government, and let them know that it is an expedient for gaining protection against injury and defending their rights,[7] and it will be impossible for them to submit to governments which, like most of those now in the world, are little better than contrivances for enabling the *few* to oppress the *many*. Convince them that the Deity is a righteous and benevolent as well as omnipotent being, who regards with equal eye all his creatures, and connects his favour with nothing but an honest desire to know and do his will; and that zeal for mystical doctrines which has led men to hate and harass one another will be exterminated. Set religion before them as a rational service, consisting not in any rites and ceremonies, but in worshipping God with a pure heart and practising righteousness from the fear of his displeasure and the apprehension of a future righteous judgment, and that gloomy and cruel superstition will be abolished which has hitherto gone under the name of religion, and to the support of which civil government has been perverted. . . . Happy is the Scholar or Philosopher who at the close of life can reflect that he has been made this use of his learning and abilities: but happier far must he be, if at the same time he has reason to believe he has been successful, and actually contributed, by his instructions, to disseminate among his fellow-creatures just notions of themselves, of their rights, of religion, and the nature and end of civil government. Such were *Milton*, *Locke*, *Sidney*,[8] *Hoadley*,[9] &c. in this country; such were *Montesquieu*,[10] *Fénelon*,[11] *Turgot*,[12] &c. in France. They sowed a seed which has since taken root, and is now growing up to a glorious harvest. To the information they conveyed by their writings we owe those revolutions in which every friend to mankind is now exulting. – What an encouragement is this to us all in our endeavours to enlighten the world! Every degree of illumination which we can communicate must do the greatest good. It helps to prepare the minds of men for the recovery of their rights, and hastens the overthrow of priestcraft and tyranny.– In short, we may, in this instance, learn our duty from the conduct of the oppressors of the world. They know that light is hostile to them, and therefore they labour to keep men in the dark. With this intention they have appointed licensers of the press; and, in Popish countries, prohibited the reading of the Bible. Remove the darkness in which they envelope the world, and their usurpations will be exposed, their power will be subverted, and the world emancipated. . . .

The observations I have made include our whole duty to our country; for by endeavouring to liberalize and enlighten it, to discourage vice and to promote virtue in it, and to assert and support its liberties, we shall endeavour to do all that is necessary to make it great and happy. – But it is proper that, on this occasion, I should be more explicit, and exemplify our duty to our country by observing farther, that it requires us to obey its laws, and to respect its magistrates.

Civil government (as I have before observed) is an institution of human prudence for guarding our persons, our property, and for securing to the members of a community that liberty to which all have an equal right, as far as they do not, by any overt act, use it to injure the liberty of others. Civil laws are regulations agreed upon by the community for gaining these ends;[13] and civil magistrates are officers appointed by the community for executing these laws, Obedience, therefore, to the laws and to magistrates, are necessary expressions of our regard to the community; and without this obedience the ends of government cannot be obtained, or a community avoid falling into a state of anarchy that will destroy those rights and subvert that liberty which government is instituted to protect.

I wish it was in my power to give you a just account of the importance of this observation. It shews the ground on which the duty of obeying civil governors stands, and that there are two extremes in this case which ought to be avoided. – These extremes are adulation and servility on one hand; and a proud and licentious contempt on the other. The former is the extreme to which mankind in general have been most prone; for it has oftener happened that men have been too passive than too unruly; and the rebellion of Kings against their people has been more common, and done more mischief, than the rebellion of people against their Kings.

Adulation is always odious, and when offered to men in power it corrupts *them*, by giving them improper ideas of their situation; and it debases those who offer it, by manifesting an abjectness founded on improper ideas of *themselves*. I have lately observed in this kingdom too near approaches to this abjectness. In our late addresses to the King, on his recovery from the severe illness with which God has been pleased to afflict him,[14] we have appeared more like a herd crawling at the feet of a master, than like enlightened and manly citizens rejoicing with a beloved sovereign, but at the same time conscious that he derives all his consequence from themselves. . . .

Civil governors are properly the servants of the public; and a King is no more than the first servant of the public, created by it, maintained by it, and responsible to it: and all the homage paid him, is due to him on no other account than his relation to the public. His sacredness is the sacredness of the community. His authority is the authority of the community; and the term MAJESTY, which it is usual to apply to him, is by no means *his own* majesty, but the MAJESTY OF THE PEOPLE. For this reason, whatever he may be in his private capacity; and though, in respect of personal qualities, not equal to, even far below many among ourselves – For this reason, I say (that is, as representing the community and its first magistrate), he is entitled to our reverence and obedience. The words MOST EXCELLENT MAJESTY are rightly applied to him; and there is a respect which it would be criminal to withhold from him. . . .

Had I been to address the King on a late occasion, I should have been inclined to do it in a style very different from that of most of the addressers, and to use some such language as the following: –

I rejoice, Sir, in your recovery. I thank God for his goodness to you. I honour you not only as my King, but as almost the only lawful King in the world, because the only one who owes his crown to the choice of his people. May you enjoy all possible happiness. May God shew you the folly of those effusions of adulation which you are now receiving, and guard you against their effects. May you be led to such a just sense of the nature of your situation, and endowed with such wisdom, as shall render your restoration to the government of these kingdoms a blessing to it, and engage you to consider yourself as more properly the *Servant* than the *Sovereign* of your people. . . .

We are met to thank God for that event in this country to which the name of THE REVOLUTION has been given; and which, for more than a century, it has been usual for the friends of freedom, and more especially Protestant Dissenters, under the title of the REVOLUTION SOCIETY, to celebrate with expressions of joy and exultation. . . . By a bloodless victory, the fetters which despotism had been long preparing for us were broken; the rights of the people were asserted, a tyrant expelled, and a Sovereign of our own choice appointed in his room. Security was given to our property, and our consciences were emancipated. The bounds of free enquiry were enlarged; the volume in which are the words of eternal life, was laid more open to our examination; and that æra of light and liberty was introduced among us, by which we have been made an example to other kingdoms, and became the instructors of the world. . . . We have particular reason, as Protestant Dissenters, to rejoice on this occasion. It was at this time we were rescued from persecution, and obtained the liberty of worshipping God in the manner we think most acceptable to him. It was then our meeting-houses were opened, our worship was taken under the protection of the law, and the principles of toleration gained a triumph. We have, therefore, on this occasion, peculiar reasons for thanksgiving – But let us remember that we ought not to satisfy ourselves with thanksgivings. Our gratitude, if genuine, will be accompanied with endeavours to give stability to the deliverance our country has obtained, and to extend and improve the happiness with which the Revolution has blest us – Let us, in particular, take care not to forget the principles of the Revolution. This Society has, very properly, in its Reports, held out these principles, as an instruction to the public. I will only take notice of the three following:

First; The right to liberty of conscience in religious matters.

Secondly; The right to resist power when abused. And,

Thirdly; The right to chuse our own governors; to cashier them for misconduct; and to frame a government for ourselves.

On these three principles, and more especially the last, was the Revolution founded. Were it not true that liberty of conscience is a sacred right; that power abused justifies resistance; and that civil authority is a delegation from the people – Were not, I say, all this true; the Revolution would have been not an ASSERTION, but an INVASION of rights; not a REVOLUTION, but a REBELLION. Cherish in your breasts this conviction, and act under its influence; detesting the odious doctrines of passive obedience, non-resistance, and the divine right of kings[15] – doctrines which, had they been acted upon in this country, would have left us at this time wretched slaves – doctrines which imply, that God made mankind to be oppressed and plundered; and which are no less a blasphemy against him, than an insult on common sense.

I would farther direct you to remember, that though the Revolution was a great work, it was by no means a perfect work; and that all was not then gained which was necessary to put the kingdom in the secure and complete possession of the blessings of liberty. – In particular, you should recollect, that the toleration then obtained was imperfect. It included only those who could declare their faith in the doctrinal articles of the church of England. It has, indeed, been since extended, but not sufficiently; for there still exist penal laws on account of religious opinions, which (were they carried into execution) would shut up many of our places of worship, and silence and imprison some of our ablest and best men. – The TEST LAWS are also still in force; and deprive of eligibility to civil and military offices, all who cannot conform to the established worship. It is with great pleasure I find that the body of protestant dissenters, though defeated in two late attempts to deliver their country from this disgrace to it, have determined to persevere. Should they at last succeed, they will have the satisfaction, not only of removing from themselves a proscription they do not deserve, but of contributing to lessen the number of our public iniquities. For I cannot call by a gentler name, laws, which convert an ordinance appointed by our Saviour to commemorate his death, into an instrument of oppressive policy, and a qualification of rakes and atheists for civil posts.[16] – I have said, *should* they succeed – but perhaps I ought not to suggest a doubt about their success.[17] And, indeed, when I consider that in SCOTLAND the established church is defended by no such test – that in IRELAND it has been abolished – that in a great neighbouring country it has been declared to be an indefeasible right of all citizens to be equally eligible to public offices – that in the same kingdom a professed Dissenter from the established church holds the first office of the state[18] – that in the Emperor's dominions *Jews* have been lately admitted to the enjoyment of equal privileges with other citizens – and that in this very country, a Dissenter, though excluded from the power of *executing* the laws, yet is allowed to be employed in *making* them. – When, I say, I consider such facts as these, I am disposed to think it impossible that the enemies of the repeal of the Test Laws should not soon become ashamed, and give up their opposition.

But the most important instance of the imperfect state in which the Revolution left our constitution, is the INEQUALITY OF OUR REPRE-SENTATION. I think, indeed, this defect in our constitution so gross and so palpable, as to make it excellent chiefly in form and theory. You should remember that a representation in the legislature of a kingdom is the *basis* of constitutional liberty in it, and of all legitimate govern-ment; and that without it a government is nothing but an usurpa-tion.[19] When the representation is fair and equal, and at the same time vested with such powers as our House of Commons possesses, a kingdom may be said to govern itself, and consequently to possess true liberty. When the representation is partial, a kingdom possesses liberty only partially; and if extremely partial, it only gives a *semblance* of liberty; but if not only extremely partial, but corruptly chosen, and under corrupt influence after being chosen, it becomes a *nuisance* and produces the worst of all forms of government – a government by corruption – a government carried on and supported by spreading venality and profligacy through a kingdom. May heaven preserve this kingdom from a calamity so dreadful! It is the point of depravity to which abuses under such a government as ours naturally tend, and the last stage of national unhappiness. We are, at present, I hope, at a great distance from it. But it cannot be pretended that there are no advances towards it, or that there is no reason for apprehension and alarm.

The inadequateness of our representation has been long a subject of complaint. This is, in truth, our fundamental grievance; and I do not think that any thing is much more our duty, as men who love their country, and are grateful for the Revolution, than to unite our zeal in endeavouring to get it redressed. At the time of the American war, associations were formed for this purpose in LONDON, and other parts of the kingdom; and our present Minister himself has, since that war, directed to it an effort which made him a favourite with many of us.[20] But all attention to it seems now lost, and the probability is that this inattention will continue, and that nothing will be done towards gaining for us this essential blessing, till some great calamity again alarms our fears, or till some great abuse of power again provokes our resentment; or, perhaps, till the acquisition of a pure and equal representation by other countries (while we are mocked with the shadow[21]) kindles our shame.

Such is the conduct by which we ought to express our gratitude for the Revolution. . . .

You may reasonably expect that I should now close this address to you. But I cannot yet dismiss you. I must not conclude without recalling, particularly, to your recollection, a consideration to which I have more than once alluded, and which, probably, your thoughts have been all along anticipating: A consideration with which my mind is impressed more than I can express. I mean, the consideration of the favourableness of the present times to all exertions in the cause of public liberty.

What an eventful period is this! I am thankful that I have lived to it; and I could almost say, *Lord, now lettest thou thy servant depart in peace, for mine eyes have seen thy salvation.* I have lived to see a diffusion of knowledge, which has undermined superstition and error – I have lived to see the rights of men better understood than ever; and nations panting for liberty, which seemed to have lost the idea of it. – I have lived to see THIRTY MILLIONS of people, indignant and resolute, spurning at slavery, and demanding liberty with an irresistible voice; their king led in triumph,[22] and an arbitrary monarch surrendering himself to his subjects. – After sharing in the benefits of one Revolution, I have been spared to be a witness to two other Revolutions, both glorious. – And now, methinks, I see the ardour for liberty catching and spreading; a general amendment beginning in human affairs; the dominion of kings changed for the dominion of laws, and the dominion of priests giving way to the dominion of reason and conscience.

Be encouraged, all ye friends of freedom, and writers in its defence! The times are auspicious. Your labours have not been in vain. Behold kingdoms, admonished by you, starting from sleep, breaking their fetters, and claiming justice from their oppressors! Behold, the light you have struck out, after setting AMERICA free, reflected to FRANCE, and there kindled into a blaze that lays despotism in ashes, and warms and illuminates EUROPE!

Tremble all ye oppressors of the world! Take warning all ye supporters of slavish governments, and slavish hierarchies! Call no more (absurdly and wickedly) REFORMATION, innovation. You cannot now hold the world in darkness. Struggle no longer against increasing light and liberality. Restore to mankind their rights; and consent to the correction of abuses, before they and you are destroyed together.

Edmund Burke

(1729–1797)

3. *Reflections on the Revolution in France* (1790)

pp. 7–21, 47–65, 111–20, 143–8, with cuts

The great literary genius of the Revolution controversy, Burke was sixty when the Bastille fell, and had for many years been the eloquent pamphleteer and parliamentary orator of the liberal wing of the dominant Whigs. As a long-established critic of the power of the monarchy, an opponent of the American war, and a stern investigator of suspect financial dealings in India, he was thought of as an ally by most of those on the reform side.[1]

Burke's writings are almost all pamphlets: occasional pieces, written in specific circumstances and towards political ends. The selection which appears here fails to do justice to his range and variety of tone, since he wrote on history, aesthetics, and philosophy as well as on politics. Even on politics, to represent Burke adequately we should need him on a range of topics other than the French Revolution – such as the *Letter to Sir Hercules Langrishe* (1792), which urges that toleration should be extended to Irish Catholics, and is written in the rational and civilised tone so characteristic of the eighteenth-century Whig tradition. The tough-mined *Thoughts and Details on Scarcity* does display him in another mood, and it has sometimes been hailed as particularly modern-minded – here is Burke, so the story goes, expounding the principles of capitalism to his party in terms that anticipate pragmatic modern British conservatism. But this is perhaps to underestimate the consistency of his social and economic thinking, as it is manifest throughout, in the *Reflections* too. Burke sees Whig government founded on an identity of interest between the hereditary landed gentry and the commercial classes, but there is something distinctive, and peculiar to times of crisis, in his insistence that the reins of power should be left in the hands of aristocrats.

The *Reflections on the Revolution in France* has a unique historical import-ance, while the even more emotional *Letter to a Noble Lord* seems to have played a special part in whipping up hysteria against reformers and their alleged subversions. Burke began the *Reflections* in response to a young *conseiller* of the Parlement of Paris, C.-J.-F. De Pont, who respectfully sought from the champion of English liberties advice on how the French could acquire a similar constitution. De Pont was not pleased with the answer he got,[2] but Burke neither knew in detail about events in France, nor essentially cared about them. His detail, tone, and method show that he was trying to influence politics at home, not through reasoning with his enemies the

Dissenters, but through dissuading his natural friends, Fox and the liberal Whigs, from espousing their cause in Parliament.

Burke's *Philosophical Enquiry into the Origin of our Ideas of the Sublime and Beautiful* (1757) is a study in aesthetics and psychology: the effect of works of art, what impresses us and how. Large inexact notions convey ideas best, and the sensation of grandeur, though curiously pleasing, is never far from the sensation of fear. Burke sets out to evoke uneasiness about the ideas which Dr Price and the radicals have greeted with joy. His methods are indirect and unsettling. The skills are architectonic, yet (in the newer architectural taste) irregularly so: the main 'feature' of the *Reflections*, what in a more formal composition one might call the centrepiece, is Burke's lyrical eulogy of Louis XVI of France, depicted as the wronged father of his family of twenty-five million, who came near to being the victim of parricide when the mob attacked Versailles on 6 October 1789. Marie Antoinette is portrayed as all that is delicate and feminine, semi-divine and yet vulnerable, Woman as seen in the chivalric tradition, calling upon men for protection.

The vignette of Versailles is flanked with passages in two contrasting styles. Both before and after his elevated portraits of the King and Queen, Burke reduces and lampoons the meddlesome upstarts of the Revolution Society and their spokesman, Dr Price. Here the language is idiomatic, even slangy. According to Price, Burke says racily, the King of Great Britain is no 'better than the rest of the gang of usurpers, who reign, or rather rob, all over the face of this our miserable world'; though Burke is amused to imagine his quietly holding his crown 'in contempt of the choice of the Revolution Society, who have not a single vote for a king amongst them' (p. 38). In France he views the pathetic spectacle of the commercial classes and *gens de lettres* usurping the reins of government, which under the old régime, as still in Britain, were held by the gentry supported by the Church. This is not quite the sinister conspiracy of intellectuals he envisages in his last works (see pp. 49–60), but the life of the French state is already denatured, thin as its paper currency and its paper rights of man. Burke arranges his portraits of gallant aristocrats and mundane burgesses to offset one another, and pays little attention to the masses, except for one insulting expression, when he alludes in passing to the mob as 'a swinish multitude' (p. 46).

Among these lighter moments, Burke places occasional rhetorical set-pieces to convey his positive political vision. Since the reformers were often primitivists, who thought of the institutions of advanced society as corruptions of man's primal freedom and equality, Burke suggests that, on the contrary, centuries of living in society have brought accumulating comforts and benefits. In a brilliant passage he couples legal words with visions of the simple life, 'entailed inheritance' with 'the happy effect of following nature'. It is an advantage to be 'locked fast as in a sort of family settlement; grasped as in a kind of mortmain for ever' (p. 40). Learning and the arts are detached from the new intellectuals, with their individualistic, arbitrary, abstract theories, and restored to the educated élite of unchanging, traditional society. Here, as in the second of his flights about the true nature of the state, the passage beginning 'Society is indeed a contract' (p. 47), Burke makes society seem both cohesive and all-welcoming – 'a partnership in every virtue, and in all perfection' (p. 48). But the *Reflections* is a political tract, cunningly adapted to circumstances, though reworked over nearly a year to look spontaneous. The ideals that Burke celebrates are not comprehensive but sectarian, the aristocratic concepts of paternalism, loyalty, chivalry, the hereditary principle, bonding to the land through ownership of it. Burke, though inaccurate about some recent events in France, correctly analyses what in fact has taken place, a bourgeois revolution. He responds with a vision of the ideal society which keeps the bourgeoisie in their place, and makes the great social institutions – the Church, the Law, even the family – validate the aristocracy as the class of government, and the protectors of the world as we know it.

The *Reflections* achieved instant popularity, or notoriety, together with large sales. Priced at three shillings, it appears to have sold thirty thousand copies in two years, a prodigious number unless it is compared with Paine's *Rights of Man* (see p. 108). Its phrasing passed immediately into English political discourse, with notions of chivalry and of rich, organic nationhood duly emerging in the parliamentary rhetoric of Pitt, Windham, and also Fox, while reformers parodied the celebrated passages (see pp. 93, 197n.), or jokily and often tediously depicted themselves and their readers as swine (see pp. 185, 189). Rapidly translated into French by Pierre-Gaeton Dupont and into German by Friedrich von Gentz, Burke's arguments made their way into the configurations of European ideological warfare. They are felt in imaginative literature too, with most of the bitterly divisive class bias discreetly filtered out. (Coleridge, whose social theories in the *Lay Sermons*, 1816–17, and *On the Constitution of the Church and State,* 1830, are strongly Burkean, nevertheless divests himself of Burke's stress on property and the hereditary principle.) In the work and correspondence of poets and novelists, many of the penetrative features of the *Reflections* – its irrationalism, its hatred of system and argument, its reverence for the family, neighbourhood, and native country – recur in English and German literature around 1800, at the point when 'Romanticism' first makes a distinct appearance.

I flatter myself that I love a manly, moral, regulated liberty as well as any gentleman of that society,[a] be he who he will; and perhaps I have given as good proofs of my attachment to that cause, in the whole course of my public conduct. I think I envy liberty as little as they do, to any other nation. But I cannot stand forward, and give praise or blame to any thing which relates to human actions, and human concerns, on a simple view of the object, as it stands stripped of every relation, in all the nakedness and solitude of metaphysical abstraction. Circumstances (which with some gentlemen pass for nothing) give in reality to every political principle its distinguishing colour, and

---

[a] The Revolution Society.

discriminating effect. The circumstances are what render every civil and political scheme beneficial or noxious to mankind. Abstractedly speaking, government, as well as liberty, is good; yet could I, in common sense, ten years ago, have felicitated France on her enjoyment of a government (for she then had a government) without enquiry what the nature of that government was, or how it was administered? Can I now congratulate the same nation upon its freedom? . . . I must be tolerably sure, before I venture publicly to congratulate men upon a blessing, that they have really received one. Flattery corrupts both the receiver and the giver; and adulation is not of more service to the people than to kings.[3] I should therefore suspend my congratulations on the new liberty of France, until I was informed how it had been combined with government; with public force; with the discipline and obedience of armies; with the collection of an effective and well-distributed revenue; with morality and religion; with the solidity of property; with peace and order; with civil and social manners. All these (in their way) are good things too: and, without them, liberty is not a benefit whilst it lasts, and is not likely to continue long. The effect of liberty to individuals is, that they may do what they please: We ought to see what it will please them to do, before we risque congratulations, which may be soon turned into complaints. . . .

All these considerations however were below the transcendental dignity of the Revolution Society. Whilst I continued in the country, from whence I had the honour of writing to you, I had but an imperfect idea of their transactions. On my coming to town, I sent for an account of their proceedings, which had been published by their authority, containing a sermon of Dr. Price, with the Duke de Rochefaucault's and the Archbishop of Aix's letter, and several other documents annexed. The whole of that publication, with the manifest design of connecting the affairs of France with those of England, by drawing us into an imitation of the conduct of the National Assembly, gave me a considerable degree of uneasiness. . . .

On the forenoon of the 4th of November last, Doctor Richard Price, a non-conforming minister of eminence, preached at the dissenting meeting-house of the Old Jewry, to his club or society, a very extraordinary miscellaneous sermon, in which there are some good moral and religious sentiments, and not ill expressed, mixed up in a sort of porridge of various political opinions and reflections: but the revolution in France is the grand ingredient in the cauldron. I consider the address transmitted by the Revolution Society to the National Assembly, through Earl Stanhope,[4] as originating in the principles of the sermon, and as a corollary from them. It was moved by the preacher of that discourse. It was passed by those who came reeking from the effect of the sermon, without any censure or qualification, expressed or implied. If, however, any of the gentlemen concerned shall wish to separate the sermon from the resolution, they know how to acknowledge the one, and to disavow the other. They may do it: I cannot.

For my part, I looked on that sermon as the public declaration of a man much connected with literary caballers, and intriguing philosophers; with political theologians, and theological politicans, both at home and abroad. I know they set him up as a sort of oracle; because, with the best intentions in the world, he naturally *philippizes*,[a] and chaunts his prophetic song in exact unison with their designs.

That sermon is in a strain which I believe has not been heard in this kingdom, in any of the pulpits which are tolerated or encouraged in it, since the year 1648, when a predecessor of Dr. Price, the Reverend Hugh Peters, made the vault of the king's own chapel at St. James's ring with the honour and privilege of the Saints, who, with the 'high praises of God in their mouths, and a *two*-edged sword in their hands, were to execute judgement on the heathen, and punishments upon the *people*; to bind their *kings* with chains, and their *nobles* with fetters of iron'.[5] Few harangues from the pulpit, except in the days of your league in France, or in the days of our solemn league and covenant in England, have ever breathed less of the spirit of moderation than this lecture in the Old Jewry. Supposing however, that something like moderation were visible in this political sermon; yet politics and the pulpit are terms that have little agreement. No sound ought to be heard in the church but the healing voice of Christian charity. The cause of civil liberty and civil government gains as little as that of religion by this confusion of duties. Those who quit their proper character, to assume what does not belong to them, are, for the greater part, ignorant both of the character they leave, and of the character they assume. Wholly unacquainted with the world in which they are so fond of meddling, and inexperienced in all its affairs, on which they pronounce with so much confidence, they have nothing of politics but the passions they excite. Surely the church is a place where one day's truce ought to be allowed to the dissensions and animosities of mankind.

This pulpit style, revived after so long a discontinuance, had to me the air of novelty, and of a novelty not wholly without danger. . . .

---

[a] *Philippizes*: to favour, or take the side of, Philip of Macedon; to speak or write as one corruptly inspired or influenced (*O.E.D.*).

Edmund Burke (1729–1797)

[Dr Price's] doctrines affect our constitution in its vital parts. He tells the Revolution Society, in this political sermon, that his majesty 'is almost the *only* lawful king in the world, because the *only* one who owes his crown to the *choice of his people*'. As to the kings of the *world*, all of whom (except one) this archpontiff of the *rights of men*, with all the plenitude, and with more than the boldness of the papal deposing power in its meridian fervour of the twelfth century, puts into one sweeping clause of ban and anathema, and proclaims usurpers by circles of longitude and latitude, over the whole globe, it behoves them to consider how they admit into their territories these apostolic missionaries, who are to tell their subjects they are not lawful kings. That is their concern. It is ours, as a domestic interest of some moment, seriously to consider the solidity of the *only* principle upon which these gentlemen acknowledge a king of Great Britain to be entitled to their allegiance.

This doctrine, as applied to the prince now on the British throne, either is nonsense, and therefore neither true nor false, or it affirms a most unfounded, dangerous, illegal, and unconstitutional position. According to this spiritual doctor of politics, if his majesty does not owe his crown to the choice of his people, he is no *lawful* king. Now nothing can be more untrue than that the crown of this kingdom is so held by his majesty. Therefore if you follow their rule, the king of Great Britain, who most certainly does not owe his high office to any form of popular election, is in no respect better than the rest of the gang of usurpers, who reign, or rather rob, all over the face of this our miserable world, without any sort of right or title to the allegiance of their people. . . .

At some time or other, to be sure, all the beginners of dynasties were chosen by those who called them to govern. There is ground enough for the opinion that all the kingdoms of Europe were, at a remote period, elective, with more or fewer limitations in the objects of choice; but whatever kings might have been here or elsewhere, a thousand years ago, or in whatever manner the ruling dynasties of England or France may have begun, the King of Great Britain is at this day king by a fixed rule of succession, according to the laws of his country; and whilst the legal conditions of the compact of sovereignty are performed by him (as they are performed) he holds his crown in contempt of the choice of the Revolution Society, who have not a single vote for a king amongst them, either individually or collectively; though I make no doubt they would soon erect themselves into an electoral college, if things were ripe to give effect to their claim. His majesty's heirs and successors, each in his time and order, will come to the crown with the same contempt of their choice with which his majesty has succeeded to that he wears.

Whatever may be the success of evasion in explaining away the gross error of *fact*, which supposes that his majesty (though he holds it in concurrence with the wishes) owes his crown to the choice of his people, yet nothing can evade their full explicit declaration, concerning the principle of a right in the people to choose, which right is directly maintained, and tenaciously adhered to. All the oblique insinuations concerning election bottom in this proposition, and are referable to it. Lest the foundation of the king's exclusive legal title should pass for a mere rant of adulatory freedom, the political Divine proceeds dogmatically to assert, that by the principles of the Revolution the people of England have acquired three fundamental rights, all which, with him, compose one system, and lie together in one short sentence; namely, that we have acquired a right

1. "To choose our own governors."
2. "To cashier them for misconduct."
3. "To frame a government for ourselves."

This new, and hitherto unheard-of bill of rights, though made in the name of the whole people, belongs to those gentlemen and their faction only. The body of the people of England have no share in it. They utterly disclaim it. They will resist the practical assertion of it with their lives and fortunes. They are bound to do so by the laws of their country, made at the time of that very Revolution, which is appealed to in favour of the fictitious rights claimed by the society which abuses its name. . . .

You will observe, that from Magna Charta to the Declaration of Right,[6] it has been the uniform policy of our constitution to claim and assert our liberties, as an *entailed inheritance* derived to us from our forefathers, and to be transmitted to our posterity; as an estate specially belonging to the people of this kingdom without any reference whatever to any other more general or prior right. By this means our constitution preserves an unity in so great a diversity of its parts. We have an inheritable crown; an inheritable peerage; and an house of commons and a people inheriting privileges, franchises, and liberties, from a long line of ancestors.

This policy appears to me to be the result of profound reflection; or rather the happy effect of following nature, which is wisdom without reflection, and above it. A spirit of innovation is generally the result of a selfish temper and confined views. People will not look forward to posterity, who never look backward to their ancestors. Besides, the people of England well know, that the idea of inheritance furnishes a sure principle of conservation, and a sure principle of transmission; without at all excluding a principle of improvement. It leaves acquisition free; but it secures what it acquires. Whatever advantages are obtained by a state proceeding on these maxims, are locked fast as in a sort of family settlement; grasped as in a kind of mortmain for ever. By a constitutional policy, working after the pattern of nature, we receive, we hold, we transmit our government and our privileges, in the same manner in which we enjoy and transmit our property and our lives. The institutions of policy, the goods of fortune, the gifts of Providence, are handed down, to us and from us, in the same course and order. Our political system is placed in a just correspondence and symmetry with the order of the world, and with the mode of existence decreed to a permanent body composed of transitory parts; wherein, by the disposition of a stupendous wisdom, moulding together the great mysterious incorporation of the human race, the whole, at one time, is never old, or middle-aged, or young, but in a condition of unchangeable constancy, moves on through the varied tenour of perpetual decay, fall, renovation, and progression. Thus, by preserving the method of nature in the conduct of the state, in what we improve we are never wholly new; in what we retain we are never wholly obsolete. By adhering in this manner and on those principles to our forefathers, we are guided not by the superstition of antiquarians, but by the spirit of philosophic analogy, in this choice of inheritance we have given to our frame of polity the image of a relation in blood; binding up the constitution of our country with our dearest domestic ties; adopting our fundamental laws into the bosom of our family affections; keeping inseparable, and cherishing with the warmth of all their combined and mutually reflected charities, our state, our hearths, our sepulchres, and our altars. . . .

France, by the perfidy of her leaders, has utterly disgraced the tone of lenient council in the cabinets of princes, and disarmed it of its most potent topics. She has sanctified the dark suspicious maxims of tyrannous distrust; and taught kings to tremble at (what will hereafter be called) the delusive plausibilities, of moral politicians. Sovereigns will consider those who advise them to place an unlimited confidence in their people, as subverters of their thrones; as traitors who aim at their destruction, by leading their easy good-nature, under specious pretences, to admit combinations of bold and faithless men into a participation of their power. . .

[The French have rebelled] against a mild and lawful monarch, with more fury, outrage, and insult, than ever any people has been known to rise against the most illegal usurper, or the most sanguinary tyrant. Their resistance was made to concession; their revolt was from protection; their blow was aimed at an hand holding out graces, favours, and immunities.

This was unnatural. The rest is in order. They have found their punishment in their success. Laws overturned; tribunals subverted; industry without vigour; commerce expiring; the revenue unpaid, yet the people impoverished; a church pillaged, and a state not relieved; civil and military anarchy made the constitution of the kingdom; every thing human and divine sacrificed to the idol of public credit, and national bankruptcy the consequence; and to crown all, the paper securities of new, precarious, tottering power, the discredited paper securities of impoverished fraud, and beggared rapine, held out as a currency for the support of an empire, in lieu of the two great recognized species that represent the lasting conventional credit of mankind, which disappeared and hid themselves in the earth from whence they came, when the principle of property, whose creatures and representatives they are, was systematically subverted.

Were all these dreadful things necessary? were they the inevitable results of the desperate struggle of determined patriots, compelled to wade through blood and tumult, to the quiet shore of a tranquil and prosperous liberty? No! nothing like it. The fresh ruins of France, which shock our feelings wherever we can turn our eyes, are not the devastation of civil war; they are the sad but instructive monuments of rash and ignorant counsel in time of profound peace. . . .

This unforced choice, this fond election of evil, would appear perfectly unaccountable, if we did not consider the composition of the National Assembly; I do not mean its formal constitution, which, as it now stands, is exceptionable enough, but the materials of which in a great measure it is composed, which is of ten thousand times greater consequence than all the formalities in the world. . . .

After I had read over the list of the persons and descriptions elected into the *Tiers Etat*, nothing which they afterwards did could appear astonishing. Among them, indeed, I saw some of known rank; some of shining talents; but of any practical experience in the state, not one man was to be found. The best were only men of theory. But whatever the distinguished few may have been, it is the substance and mass of the body which constitutes its character, and must finally determine its direction. In all bodies, those who will lead, must also, in a considerable degree, follow. They must conform their propositions to the taste, talent, and disposition of those whom they wish to conduct. . . .

Nothing can secure a steady and moderate conduct in such assemblies, but that the body of them should be respectably composed, in point of condition in life, of permanent property, of education, and of such habits as enlarge and liberalize the understanding.

In the calling of the states general of France, the first thing which struck me, was a great departure from the antient course. I found the representation for the Third Estate composed of six hundred persons. They were equal in number to the representatives of both the other orders. If the orders were to act separately the number would not, beyond the consideration of the expence, be of much moment. But when it became apparent that the three orders were to be melted down into one, the policy and necessary effect of this numerous representation became obvious. A very small desertion from either of the other two orders must throw the power of both into the hands of the third. In fact, the whole power of the state was soon resolved into that body. Its due composition became therefore of infinitely the greater importance.

Judge, Sir, of my surprize, when I found that a very great proportion of the Assembly (a majority, I believe, of the members who attended) was composed of practitioners in the law. It was composed not of distinguished magistrates, who had given pledges to their country of their science, prudence, and integrity; not of leading advocates, the glory of the bar; not of renowned professors in universities; – but for the far greater part, as it must in such a number, of the inferior, unlearned, mechanical, merely instrumental members of the profession. There were distinguished exceptions; but the general composition was of obscure provincial advocates, of stewards of petty local jurisdictions, country attornies, notaries, and the whole train of the ministers of municipal litigation, the fomentors and conductors of the petty war of village vexation. From the moment I read the list I saw distinctly, and very nearly as it has happened, all that was to follow. . . .

Well! but these men were to be tempered and restrained by other descriptions, of more sober minds, and more enlarged understandings. Were they then to be awed by the super-eminent authority and awful dignity of an handful of country clowns who have seats in that Assembly, some of whom are said not to be able to read and write? and by not a greater number of traders, who, though somewhat more instructed, and more conspicuous in the order of society, had never known any thing beyond their counting-house? No! both these descriptions were more formed to be overborne and swayed by the intrigues and artifices of lawyers, than to become their counterpoise. With such a dangerous disproportion, the whole must needs be

governed by them. To the faculty of law was joined a pretty considerable proportion of the faculty of medicine. This faculty had not, any
more than that of the law, possessed in France its just estimation. Its
professors therefore must have the qualities of men not habituated to
sentiments of dignity. But supposing they had ranked as they ought to
do, and as with us they do actually, the sides of sick beds are not the
academies for forming statesmen and legislators. Then came the
dealers in stocks and funds, who must be eager, at any expence, to
change their ideal paper wealth for the more solid substance of land.
To these were joined men of other descriptions, from whom as little
knowledge of or attention to the interests of a great state was to be
expected, and as little regard to the stability of any institution; men
formed to be instruments, not controls. Such in general was the
composition of the *Tiers Etat* in the National Assembly; in which was
scarcely to be perceived the slightest traces of what we call the natural
landed interest of the country.[7]

We know that the British house of commons, without shutting its
doors to any merit in any class, is, by the sure operation of adequate
causes, filled with every thing illustrious in rank, in descent, in
hereditary and in acquired opulence, in cultivated talents, in military,
civil, naval, and politic distinction, that the country can afford. But
supposing, what hardly can be supposed as a case, that the house of
commons should be composed in the same manner with the *Tiers
Etat* in France, would this dominion of chicane be borne with
patience, or even conceived without horror? . . .

> Burke continues with a melodramatic and inaccurate account of the events
> of 5–6 October 1789, when some twenty thousand men of the National
> Guard marched from Paris to Versailles under the hesitant leadership of La
> Fayette, and brought the King and Queen back to Paris. For Burke the
> episode was bloodthirsty and terrifying to the French Royal Family. He
> exaggerated the violence that was used, but undoubtedly from this point the
> King and Queen were virtually prisoners in the Tuileries:

I hear that the august person, who was the principal object of our
preacher's triumph, though he supported himself, felt much on that
shameful occasion. As a man, it became him to feel for his wife and his
children, and the faithful guards of his person, that were massacred in
cold blood about him; as a prince, it became him to feel for the strange
and frightful transformation of his civilized subjects, and to be more
grieved for them, than solicitous for himself. It derogates little from
his fortitude, while it adds infinitely to the honour of his humanity. I
am very sorry to say it, very sorry indeed, that such personages are in a
situation in which it is not unbecoming in us to praise the virtues of
the great.

Edmund Burke (1729–1797)

I hear, and I rejoice to hear, that the great lady, the other object of the triumph, has borne that day (one is interested that beings made for suffering should suffer well) and that she bears all the succeeding days, that she bears the imprisonment of her husband, and her own captivity, and the exile of her friends, and the insulting adulation of addresses, and the whole weight of her accumulated wrongs, with a serene patience, in a manner suited to her rank and race, and becoming the offspring of a sovereign distinguished for her piety and her courage;[8] that like her she has lofty sentiments; that she feels with the dignity of a Roman matron; that in the last extremity she will save herself from the last disgrace, and that if she must fall, she will fall by no ignoble hand.

It is now sixteen or seventeen years since I saw the queen of France, then the dauphiness, at Versailles; and surely never lighted on this orb, which she hardly seemed to touch, a more delightful vision. I saw her just above the horizon, decorating and cheering the elevated sphere she just began to move in – glittering like the morning-star, full of life, and splendor, and joy. Oh! what a revolution! and what an heart must I have, to contemplate without emotion that elevation and that fall! Little did I dream when she added titles of veneration to those of enthusiastic, distant, respectful love, that she should ever be obliged to carry the sharp antidote against disgrace concealed in that bosom; little did I dream that I should have lived to see such disasters fallen upon her in a nation of gallant men, in a nation of men of honour and of cavaliers. I thought ten thousand swords must have leaped from their scabbards to avenge even a look that threatened her with insult. – But the age of chivalry is gone. – That of sophisters, œconomists, and calculators, has succeeded; and the glory of Europe is extinguished for ever. Never, never more, shall we behold that generous loyalty to rank and sex, that proud submission, that dignified obedience, that subordination of the heart, which kept alive, even in servitude itself, the spirit of an exalted freedom. The unbought grace of life, the cheap defence of nations, the nurse of manly sentiment and heroic enterprize is gone! It is gone, that sensibility of principle, that chastity of honour, which felt a stain like a wound, which inspired courage whilst it mitigated ferocity, which ennobled whatever it touched, and under which vice itself lost half its evil, by losing all its grossness.

This mixed system of opinion and sentiment had its origin in the antient chivalry; and the principle, though varied in its appearance by the varying state of human affairs, subsisted and influenced through a long succession of generations, even to the time we live in. If it should ever be totally extinguished, the loss I fear will be great. It is this which has given its character to modern Europe. It is this which has distinguished it under all its forms of government, and distinguished it to its advantage, from the states of Asia, and possibly from those states which flourished in the most brilliant periods of the antique world. It was this, which, without confounding ranks, had produced a noble equality, and handed it down through all the gradations of social life. It was this opinion which mitigated kings into companions, and raised private men to be fellows with kings. Without force, or opposition, it subdued the fierceness of pride and power; it obliged sovereigns to submit to the soft collar of social esteem, compelled stern authority to submit to elegance, and gave a domination vanquisher of laws, to be subdued by manners.

But now all is to be changed. All the pleasing illusions, which made power gentle, and obedience liberal, which harmonized the different shades of life, and which, by a bland assimilation, incorporated into politics the sentiments which beautify and soften private society, are to be dissolved by this new conquering empire of light and reason. All the decent drapery of life is to be rudely torn off. All the superadded ideas, furnished from the wardrobe of a moral imagination, which the heart owns, and the understanding ratifies, as necessary to cover the defects of our naked shivering nature, and to raise it to dignity in our own estimation, are to be exploded as a ridiculous, absurd, and antiquated fashion.

On this scheme of things, a king is but a man; a queen is but a woman; a woman is but an animal; and an animal not of the highest order. All homage paid to the sex in general as such, and without distinct views, is to be regarded as romance and folly. Regicide, and parricide, and sacrilege, are but fictions of superstition, corrupting jurisprudence by destroying its simplicity. The murder of a king, or a queen, or a bishop, or a father, are only common homicide; and if the people are by any chance, or in any way gainers by it, a sort of homicide much the most pardonable, and into which we ought not to make too severe a scrutiny.

On the scheme of this barbarous philosophy, which is the offspring of cold hearts and muddy understandings, and which is as void of solid wisdom, as it is destitute of all taste and elegance, laws are to be supported only by their own terrors, and by the concern, which each individual may find in them, from his own private speculations, or can spare to them from his own private interests. In the groves of *their* academy, at the end of every visto, you see nothing but the gallows.[9] Nothing is left which engages the affections on the part of the commonwealth. On the principles of this mechanic philosophy, our institutions can never be embodied, if I may use the expression, in persons; so as to create in us love, veneration, admiration, or attachment. But that sort of reason which banishes the affections is incapable of filling their place. These public affections, combined with manners, are required sometimes as supplements, sometimes as correctives, always as aids to law. The precept given by a wise man, as well as a great critic, for the construction of poems, is equally true as to states. *Non satis est pulchra esse poemata, dulcia sunto.*[a] There ought to be a system of manners in every nation which a well-formed mind would be disposed to relish. To make us love our country, our country ought to be lovely. . . .

Nothing is more certain, than that our manners, our civilization, and all the good things which are connected with manners, and with civilization, have, in this European world of ours, depended for ages upon two principles; and were indeed the result of both combined; I mean the spirit of a gentleman, and the spirit of religion. The nobility and the clergy, the one by profession, the other by patronage, kept learning in existence, even in the midst of arms and confusions, and whilst governments were rather in their causes than formed. Learning paid back what it received to nobility and to priesthood; and paid it with usury, by enlarging their ideas, and by furnishing their minds. Happy if they had all continued to know their indissoluble union, and their proper place! Happy if learning, not debauched by ambition, had been satisfied to continue the instructor, and not aspired to be the master! Along with its natural protectors and guardians, learning will be cast into the mire, and trodden down under the hoofs of a swinish multitude.[10]

If, as I suspect, modern letters owe more than they are always willing to own to antient manners, so do other interests which we value full as much as they are worth. Even commerce, and trade, and manufacture, the gods of our œconomical politicians, are themselves perhaps but creatures; are themselves but effects, which, as first causes, we choose to worship. They certainly grew under the same shade in which learning flourished. They too may decay with their natural protecting principles. With you, for the present at least, they all threaten to disappear together. Where trade and manufactures are wanting to a people, and the spirit of nobility and religion remains, sentiment supplies, and not always ill supplies their place; but if commerce and the arts should be lost in an experiment to try how well a state may stand without these old fundamental principles, what sort

[a] 'It is not enough for poetry to be beautiful, it must also be comforting' (Horace, *Ars Poetica*, l.99).

46

of a thing must be a nation of gross, stupid, ferocious, and at the same time, poor and sordid barbarians, destitute of religion, honour, or manly pride, possessing nothing at present, and hoping for nothing hereafter? . . .

It is not clear, whether in England we learned those grand and decorous principles, and manners, of which considerable traces yet remain, from you, or whether you took them from us. But to you, I think, we trace them best. You seem to me to be – *gentis incunabula nostræ.*[a] France has always more or less influenced manners in England; and when your fountain is choaked up and polluted, the stream will not run long, or not run clear with us, or perhaps with any nation. This gives all Europe, in my opinion, but too close and connected a concern in what is done in France. Excuse me, therefore, if I have dwelt too long on the atrocious spectacle of the sixth of October 1789, or have given too much scope to the reflections which have arisen in my mind on occasion of the most important of all revolutions, which may be dated from that day, I mean a revolution in sentiments, manners, and moral opinions. As things now stand, with every thing respectable destroyed without us, and an attempt to destroy within us every principle of respect, one is almost forced to apologize for harbouring the common feelings of men.

Why do I feel so differently from the Reverend Dr. Price, and those of his lay flock, who will choose to adopt the sentiments of his discourse? – For this plain reason – because it is *natural* I should; because we are so made as to be affected at such spectacles with melancholy sentiments upon the unstable condition of mortal prosperity, and the tremendous uncertainty of human greatness; because in those natural feelings we learn great lessons; because in events like these our passions instruct our reason; because when kings are hurl'd from their thrones by the Supreme Director of this great drama, and become the objects of insult to the base, and of pity to the good, we behold such disasters in the moral, as we should behold a miracle in the physical order of things. We are alarmed into reflexion; our minds (as it has long since been observed) are purified by terror and pity; our weak unthinking pride is humbled, under the dispensations of a mysterious wisdom. . . .

Society is indeed a contract.[11] Subordinate contracts for objects of mere occasional interest may be dissolved at pleasure – but the state ought not to be considered as nothing better than a partnership agreement in a trade of pepper and coffee, callico or tobacco, or some other such low concern, to be taken up for a little temporary interest,

[a] 'The swaddling-bands of our race'. Cf. Cicero, *De Orat.*, l.23, 'incunabula nostrae doctrinae'.

and to be dissolved by the fancy of the parties. It is to be looked on with other reverence; because it is not a partnership in things subservient only to the gross animal existence of a temporary and perishable nature. It is a partnership in all science; a partnership in all art; a partnership in every virtue, and in all perfection. As the ends of such a partnership cannot be obtained in many generations, it becomes a partnership not only between those who are living, but between those who are living, those who are dead, and those who are to be born. Each contract of each particular state is but a clause in the great primæval contract of eternal society, linking the lower with the higher natures, connecting the visible and invisible world, according to a fixed compact sanctioned by the inviolable oath which holds all physical and all moral natures, each in their appointed place. This law is not subject to the will of those, who by an obligation above them, and infinitely superior, are bound to submit their will to that law. The municipal corporations of that universal kingdom are not morally at liberty at their pleasure, and on their speculations of a contingent improvement, wholly to separate and tear asunder the bands of their subordinate community, and to dissolve it into an unsocial, uncivil, unconnected chaos of elementary principles. It is the first and supreme necessity only, a necessity that is not chosen but chooses, a necessity paramount to deliberation, that admits no discussion, and demands no evidence, which alone can justify a resort to anarchy. This necessity is no exception to the rule; because this necessity itself is a part too of that moral and physical disposition of things to which man must be obedient by consent or force; but if that which is only submission to necessity should be made the object of choice, the law is broken, nature is disobeyed, and the rebellious are outlawed, cast forth, and exiled, from this world of reason, and order, and peace, and virtue, and fruitful penitence, into the antagonist world of madness, discord, vice, confusion, and unavailing sorrow. . . .

I assure you I do not aim at singularity. I give you opinions which have been accepted amongst us, from very early times to this moment, with a continued and general approbation, and which indeed are so worked into my mind, that I am unable to distinguish what I have learned from others from the results of my own meditation.

It is on some such principles that the majority of the people of England, far from thinking a religious, national establishment unlawful, hardly think it lawful to be without one.[12] In France you are wholly mistaken if you do not believe us above all other things attached to it, and beyond all other nations; and when this people has acted unwisely and unjustifiably in its favour (as in some instances they have done most certainly) in their very errors you will at least discover their zeal.

This principle runs through the whole system of their polity. They do not consider their church establishment as convenient, but as essential to their state; not as a thing heterogeneous and separable; something added for accommodation; what they may either keep up or lay aside, according to their temporary ideas of convenience. They consider it as the foundation of their whole constitution, with which, and with every part of which, it holds an indissoluble union. Church and state are ideas inseparable in their minds, and scarcely is the one ever mentioned without mentioning the other.

4. *A Letter to A Noble Lord on the Attacks made upon him and his Pension, in the House of Lords, by the Duke of Bedford and the Earl of Lauderdale, Early in the Present Sessions of Parliament* (1796),

2nd edn (1796), with cuts

A Letter to a Noble Lord, a sixpenny pamphlet published on 24 February, 1796, a year before Burke's death, could be viewed unsympathetically as a blot on his reputation. In it Burke responds with seemingly deranged violence to criticisms of his pension[13] made in the House of Lords on 13 November 1795 by two liberal Whig peers, Bedford and Lauderdale.[14] He seizes the occasion to justify his long career, which – despite the pension – he hints has been inadequately rewarded, since he was never given an important office. One modern scholar has remarked that the *Letter* shows how this great apologist for aristocracy remained himself a 'ranker', sore after a lifetime's service of a caste which included an ultra-liberal mediocrity like the Duke of Bedford.[15] It also reveals his inconsolable grief at the death a year earlier of his only son, and the hysteria always implicit in his response to the French 'regicides', against whom he preached a holy war. This is the Burke whom half the country, his friend Windham once said, considered 'an ingenious madman'. It is also the man who ended his life in 1797 with a millenarian conviction of imminent Doomsday, leaving his doctors at Bath for home at Beaconsfield, 'there to finish my carreer along with that of the civil and moral world'.[16]

A Letter to a Noble Lord is, notwithstanding, a wonderful literary performance. It is far more tightly argued than the *Reflections*, moving logically from the introduction (the Duke's attack on Burke's pension), to Burke's account of the financial reforms he initiated, to his claim that he remains a *preserver* of the state, to his enquiry into the Russell family's services, and thence to the present Duke's relations with the state's enemies. Burke's easy mastery of his argument is an important part of his effect. In contrast to the clumsy young Duke, and the have-not philosophers, he sounds as though he has been at the helm – 'I have lived long and variously in the World' – and as though his claims on his behalf are understatements. He arrives by gentle stages and touches of comedy at his violent vision of the Satanic philosophers, first tormenting, then butchering and carving up the great body of their prey, the Duke. The grotesque vision is wittily lightened because, as in a caricature, Burke's enemies are identified by personal detail – the English chemist Priestley, the French ex-butcher Legendre, and the Duke, who recently appeared in the House of Lords wearing a revolutionary hairstyle (see n. 36). A sustained analysis of the source of revolution underlies Burke's writing of the 1790s, a belief that there has been a subversive combination of a new commercial and intellectual order, organised, self-aware, insufficiently patronised and rewarded by their noble superiors. Casting back to the reign of Henry VIII for their historical precursors is a characteristically complex move, which throws a strange disturbing light on Burke's organic society, the precarious history of the alliance he glorifies between the aristocracy and the Church.

As polemic, *A Letter to a Noble Lord* is even more powerful than the *Reflections*: after this, who would freely own to being a radical philosopher? The pamphlet certainly drew blood: it went into fourteen editions before the end of 1796, and stimulated a wave of anti-intellectualism, illustrated in Canning's *Antijacobin* and Wordsworth's *Borderers* (see p. 216 and p. 253 n. 6). In 1798 its imagery of monstrosity inspired a famous cartoon by Gillray, *The New Morality*, in which the Leviathan Duke of Bedford is led by the nose by a verminous host of writers who include Paine, Godwin, Thelwall, Holcroft, Southey, Coleridge, Lamb, and Lloyd. In Burke's pamphlet, however, the philosophers swell in size in relation to the Duke, and become a monstrous predatory cat, while he dwindles into a mouse.

To be ill spoken of, in whatever language they speak, by the zealots of the new sect in philosophy and politics, of which these noble persons think so charitably, and of which others think so justly, to me, is no matter of uneasiness or surprise. To have incurred the displeasure of the Duke of Orleans[17] or the Duke of Bedford,[18] to fall under the censure of Citizen Brissot[19] or of his friend the Earl of Lauderdale,[20] I ought to consider as proofs, not the least satisfactory, that I have produced some part of the effect I proposed by my endeavours. I have laboured hard to earn, what the noble Lords are generous enough to pay. Personal offence I have given them none. The part they take against me is from zeal to the cause. It is well! It is perfectly well! I have to do homage to their justice. I have to thank the Bedfords and the Lauderdales for having so faithfully and so fully acquitted towards me whatever arrear of debt was left undischarged by the Priestleys and the Paines. . . .

4. *A Letter to a Noble Lord*

It cannot at this time be too often repeated; line upon line; precept upon precept; until it comes into the currency of a proverb, *To innovate is not to reform.* The French revolutionists complained of every thing; they refused to reform any thing; and they left nothing, no nothing at all *unchanged*. The consequences are before us, – not in remote history; not in future prognostication; they are about us; they are upon us. They shake the public security; they menace private enjoyment. They dwarf the growth of the young, they break the quiet of the old. If we travel, they stop our way. They infest us in town: they pursue us to the country. Our business is interrupted; our repose is troubled; our pleasures are saddened; our very studies are poisoned and perverted, and knowledge is rendered worse than ignorance, by the enormous evils of this dreadful innovation. The revolution harpies of France, sprung from night and hell, or from that chaotic anarchy, which generates equivocally, "all monstrous, all prodigious things,"[21] cuckoo-like, adulterously lay their eggs, and brood over and hatch them in the nest of every neighbouring State. . . .

It was then not my love, but my hatred to innovation, that produced my Plan of Reform. Without troubling myself with the exactness of the logical diagram, I considered them as things substantially opposite. It was to prevent that evil, that I proposed the measures, which his Grace is pleased, and I am not sorry he is pleased, to recall to my recollection. I had (what I hope that Noble Duke will remember in all his operations) a State to preserve, as well as a State to reform. I had a People to gratify, but not to inflame, or to mislead. I do not claim half the credit for what I did, as for what I prevented from being done. In that situation of the public mind, I did not undertake, as was then proposed, to new model the House of Commons or the House of Lords; or to change the authority under which any officer of the Crown acted, who was suffered at all to exist. Crown, Lords, Commons, judicial system of administration, existed as they had existed before; and in the mode and manner in which they had always existed. My measures were, what I then truly stated them to the House to be, in their intent, healing, and mediatorial. A complaint was made of too much influence in the House of Commons; I reduced it in both Houses; and I gave my reasons article by article for every reduction, and shewed why I thought it safe for the service of the State. I heaved the lead every inch of way I made. A disposition to expence was complained of; to that I opposed, not mere retrenchment, but a system of œconomy, which would make a random expence without plan or foresight, in future not easily practicable.[22] I proceeded upon principles of research to put me in possession of my matter; on principles of method to regulate it; and on principles in the human mind and in civil affairs to secure and perpetuate the operation. I conceived nothing arbitrarily; nor proposed any thing to be done by the will and pleasure of others, or my own, but by reason, and by reason only. I have ever abhorred, since the first dawn of my understanding to this its obscure twilight, all the operations of opinion, fancy, inclination, and will, in the affairs of Government, where only a sovereign reason, paramount to all forms of legislation and adminstration, should dictate. Government is made for the very purpose of opposing that reason to will and to caprice, in the reformers or in the reformed, in the governors, or in the governed, in Kings, in Senates, or in People. . . .

His Grace may think as meanly as he will of my deserts in the far greater part of my conduct in life. It is free for him to do so. There will always be some difference of opinion in the value of political services. But there is one merit of mine, which he, of all men living, ought to be the last to call in question. I have supported with very great zeal, and I am told with some degree of success, those opinions, or if his Grace likes another expression better, those old prejudices which buoy up the ponderous mass of his nobility, wealth, and titles. I have omitted no exertion to prevent him and them from sinking to that level to which the meretricious French faction, his Grace at least coquets with, omit no exertion to reduce both. I have done all I could to discountenance their enquiries into the fortunes of those, who hold large portions of wealth without any apparent merit of their own. I have strained every nerve to keep the Duke of Bedford in that situation, which alone makes him my superior. Your Lordship has been a witness of the use he makes of that pre-eminence.[23]

But be it, that this is virtue! Be it, that there is virtue in this well selected rigour; yet all virtues are not equally becoming to all men and at all times. . . . What might have been well enough, and have been received with a veneration mixed with awe and terror, from an old, severe crabbed Cato, would have wanted something of propriety in the young Scipios, the ornament of the Roman nobility, in the flower of their life.[24] But the times, the morals, the masters, the scholars, have all undergone a thorough revolution. It is a vile illiberal school, this new French academy of the *sans culottes*. There is nothing in it that is fit for a Gentleman to learn.

Whatever its vogue may be, I still flatter myself, that the parents of the growing generation will be satisfied with what is to be taught to their children in Westminster, in Eton or in Winchester: I still indulge the hope that no *grown* Gentleman or Nobleman of our time will think of finishing at Mr. Thelwall's lecture whatever may have been left incomplete at the old Universities of his country. . . .

I know not how it has happened, but it really seems, that, whilst his Grace was meditating his well considered censure upon me, he fell into a sort of sleep. Homer nods; and the Duke of Bedford may dream; and as dreams (even his golden dreams) are apt to be ill-pieced and incongruously put together, his Grace preserved his idea of reproach to *me*, but took the subject-matter from the Crown grants *to his own family.* This is "the stuff of which his dreams are made." In that way of putting things together, his Grace is perfectly in the right. The grants to the House of Russel were so enormous, as not only to outrage œconomy, but even to stagger credibility. The Duke of Bedford is the Leviathan among all the creatures of the Crown. He tumbles about his unwieldy bulk; he plays and frolics in the ocean of the royal bounty. Huge as he is, and whilst "he lies floating many a rood,"[25] he is still a creature. His ribs, his fins, his whalebone, his blubber, the very spiracles through which he spouts a torrent of brine against his origin, and covers me all over with the spray, – every thing of him and about him is from the Throne. Is it for *him* to question the dispensation of the Royal favour?

I am really at a loss to draw any sort of parallel between the public merits of his Grace, by which he justifies the grants he holds, and these services of mine, on the favourable construction of which I have obtained what his Grace so much disapproves. In private life, I have not at all the honour of acquaintance with the noble Duke. But I ought to presume, and it costs me nothing to do so, that he abundantly deserves the esteem and love of all who live with him. But as to public service, why truly it would not be more ridiculous for me to compare myself in rank, in fortune, in splendid descent, in youth, strength, or figure, with the Duke of Bedford, than to make a parallel between his services, and my attempts to be useful to my country. It would not be gross adulation, but uncivil irony, to say, that he has any public merit of his own to keep alive the idea of the services by which his vast landed Pensions were obtained. My merits, whatever they are, are original and personal; his are derivative. It is his ancestor, the original pensioner, that has laid up this inexhaustible fund of merit, which makes his Grace so very delicate and exceptious about the merit of all other grantees of the Crown. Had he permitted me to remain in quiet, I should have said, 'tis his estate; that's enough. It is his by law; what have I to do with it or its history? He would naturally have said on his side, 'tis this man's fortune. – He is as good now, as my ancestor was two hundred and fifty years ago. I am a young man with very old pensions; he is an old man with very young pensions – that's all.

Why will his Grace, by attacking me, force me reluctantly to compare my little merit with that which obtained from the Crown those prodigies of profuse donation by which he tramples on the mediocrity of humble and laborious individuals?. . .

The first peer of the name, the first purchaser of the grants, was a Mr. Russel, a person of an ancient gentleman's family, raised by being a minion of Henry the Eighth.[26] As there generally is some resemblance of character to create these relations, the favourite was in all likelihood much such another as his master. The first of those immoderate grants was not taken from the ancient demesne of the Crown, but from the recent confiscation of the ancient nobility of the land. The lion having sucked the blood of his prey, threw the offal carcase to the jackal in waiting. Having tasted once the food of confiscation, the favourites became fierce and ravenous. This worthy favourite's first grant was from the lay nobility. The second, infinitely improving on the enormity of the first, was from the plunder of the church. In truth, his Grace is somewhat excusable for his dislike to a grant like mine, not only in its quantity, but in its kind so different from his own.

Mine was from a mild and benevolent sovereign; his from Henry the Eighth.

Mine had not its fund in the murder of any innocent person of illustrious rank,[27] or in the pillage of any body of unoffending men. His grant were from the aggregate and consolidated funds of judgments iniquitously legal, and from possessions voluntarily surrendered by the lawful proprietors with the gibbet at their door. . . .

The merit of the original grantee of his Grace's pensions, was in giving his hand to the work, and partaking the spoil with a Prince, who plundered a part of the national church of his time and country. Mine was in defending the whole of the national church of my own time and my own country, and the whole of the national churches of all countries, from the principles and examples which lead to ecclesiastical pillage, thence to a contempt of *all* prescriptive titles, thence to the pillage of *all* property, and thence to universal desolation. . . .

The political merit of the first pensioner of his Grace's house, was that of being concerned as a counsellor of state in advising, and in his person executing the conditions of a dishonourable peace with France; the surrendering the fortress of Boulogne,[28] then our outguard on the Continent. By that surrender, Calais, the key of France, and the bridle in the mouth of that power, was, not many years afterwards, finally lost. My merit has been in resisting the power and pride of France, under any form of its rule; but in opposing it with the greatest zeal and earnestness, when that rule appeared in the worst form it could assume; the worst indeed which the prime cause and principle of all evil could possibly give it. It was my endeavour by every means to excite a spirit in the house, where I had the honour of a seat, for carrying on with early vigour and decision, the most clearly just and necessary war, that this or any nation ever carried on; in order to save my country from the iron yoke of its power, and from the more dreadful contagion of its principles; to preserve while they can be preserved pure and untainted, the ancient, inbred integrity, piety, good nature, and good humour of the people of England, from the dreadful pestilence which beginning in France, threatens to lay waste the whole moral, and in a great degree the whole physical world, having done both in the focus of its most intense malignity. . . .

Had it pleased God to continue to me the hopes of succession, I should have been, according to my mediocrity, and the mediocrity of the age I live in, a sort of founder of a family; I should have left a son, who in all the points in which personal merit can be viewed, in science, in erudition, in genius, in taste, in honour, in generosity, in humanity, in every liberal sentiment, and every liberal accomplishment, would not have shewn himself inferior to the Duke of Bedford, or to any of those whom he traces in his line.[29] . . .

But a disposer whose power we are little able to resist, and whose wisdom it behoves us not at all to dispute; has ordained it in another manner, and (whatever my querulous weakness might suggest) a far better. The storm has gone over me; and I lie like one of those old oaks which the late hurricane has scattered about me. I am stripped of all my honours; I am torn up by the roots, and lie prostrate on the earth! There, and prostrate there, I most unfeignedly recognize the divine justice, and in some degree submit to it. But whilst I humble myself before God, I do not know that it is forbidden to repel the attacks of unjust and inconsiderate men. The patience of Job is proverbial. After some of the convulsive struggles of our irritable nature, he submitted himself, and repented in dust and ashes. But even so, I do not find him blamed for reprehending, and with a considerable degree of verbal asperity, those ill-natured neighbours of his, who visited his dunghill to read moral, political, and œconomical lectures on his misery. I am alone. I have none to meet my enemies in the gate. . . . But we are all of us made to shun disgrace, as we are made to shrink from pain, and poverty, and disease. It is an instinct; and under the direction of reason; instinct is always in the right. . . .

Edmund Burke (1729–1797)

The Crown has considered me after long service: the Crown has paid the Duke of Bedford by advance. He has had a long credit for any service which he may perform hereafter. He is secure, and long may he be secure, in his advance, whether he performs any services or not. But let him take care how he endangers the safety of the Constitution which secures his own utility or his own insignificance; or how he discourages those, who take up, even puny arms, to defend an order of things, which, like the Sun of Heaven, shines alike on the useful and the worthless. His grants are engrafted on the public law of Europe, covered with the awful hoar of innumerable ages. . . . The Duke of Bedford will stand as long as prescriptive law endures; as long as the great stable laws of property, common to us with all civilized nations, are kept in their integrity, and without the smallest intermixture of the laws, maxims, principles, or precedents, of the Grand Revolution. . . .

But if the rude inroad of the Gallic tumult, with its sophistical Rights of Man, to falsify the account, and its sword as a make-weight to throw into the scale, shall be introduced into our city by a misguided populace, set on by proud great men, themselves blinded and intoxicated by a frantic ambition, we shall, all of us, perish and be overwhelmed in a common ruin. If a great storm blow on our coast, it will cast the whales on the strand as well as the periwinkles. His grace will not survive the poor grantee he despises, no not for a twelvemonth. If the great look for safety in the services they render to this Gallic cause, it is to be foolish, even above the weight of privilege allowed to wealth. If his Grace be one of these whom they endeavour to proselytize, he ought to be aware of the character of the sect, whose doctrines he is invited to embrace. With them, insurrection is the most sacred of revolutionary duties to the state. Ingratitude to benefactors is the first of revolutionary virtues. . . .

Am I to blame, if I attempt to pay his Grace's hostile reproaches to me with a friendly admonition to himself? Can I be blamed to point out to him in what manner he is like to be affected, if the sect of the cannibal philosophers of France should proselytize any considerable part of this people, and, by their joint proselytizing arms, should conquer that Government, to which his Grace does not seem to me to give all the support his own security demands? Surely it is proper, that he, and that others like him, should know the true genius of this sect, what their opinions are; what they have done: and to whom, and what (if a prognostic is to be formed from the dispositions and actions of men) it is certain they will do hereafter. He ought to know, that they have sworn assistance, the only engagement they ever will keep, to all in this country, who bear a resemblance to themselves, and who think as such, that *The whole duty of man*[30] consists in destruction. They are a misallied and disparaged branch of the house of Nimrod.[31] They are the Duke of Bedford's natural hunters; and he is their natural game. Because he is not very profoundly reflecting, he sleeps in profound security; they on the contrary, are always vigilant, active, enterprizing, and though far removed from any knowledge, which makes men estimable or useful, in all the instruments and resources of evil, their leaders are not meanly instructed, or insufficiently furnished. In the French Revolution, every thing is new; and, from want of preparation to meet so unlooked for an evil, every thing is dangerous. Never, before this time, was a set of literary men converted into a gang of robbers and assassins. Never before, did a den of bravoes and banditti, assume the garb and tone of an academy of philosophers. . . .

These philosophers are fanatics; independent of any interest, which if it operated alone would make them much more tractable, they are carried with such an headlong rage towards every desperate trial, that they would sacrifice the whole human race to the slightest of their experiments. I am better able to enter into the character of this description of men than the noble Duke can be. I have lived long and variously in the World. Without any considerable pretensions to literature in myself, I have aspired to the love of letters. I have lived for a great many years in habitudes with those who professed them. I can form a tolerable estimate of what is likely to happen from a character, chiefly dependent for fame and fortune, on knowledge and talent, as well in its morbid and perverted state, as in that which is sound and natural. Naturally, men so formed and finished, are the first gifts of Providence to the World. But when they have once thrown off the fear of God, which was in all ages too often the case, and the fear of man, which is now the case, and when in that state they come to understand one another, and to act in corps, a more dreadful calamity cannot arise out of Hell to scourge mankind. Nothing can be conceived more hard than the heart of a thorough bred metaphysician. It comes nearer to the cold malignity of a wicked spirit than to the frailty and passion of a man. It is like that of the principle of Evil himself, incorporeal, pure, and unmixed, dephlegmated, defecated evil. It is no easy operation to eradicate humanity from the human breast. What Shakspeare calls "the compunctious visitings of nature,"[32] will sometimes knock at their hearts, and protest against their murderous speculations. But they have a means of compounding with their nature. Their humanity is not dissolved. They only give

57

it a long prorogation. They are ready to declare, that they do not think two thousand years too long a period for the good that they pursue. It is remarkable, that they never see any way to their projected good, but by the road of some evil. Their imagination is not fatigued, with the contemplation of human suffering through the wild waste of centuries added to centuries, of misery and desolation. Their humanity is at their horizon – and, like the horizon, it always flies before them. The geometricians, and the chymists bring, the one from the dry bones of their diagrams, and the other from the foot of their furnaces, dispositions that make them worse than indifferent about those feelings and habitudes, which are the supports of the moral world. Ambition is come upon them suddenly; they are intoxicated with it, and it has rendered them fearless of the danger, which may from thence arise to others or to themselves. These philosophers, consider men in their experiments, no more regard than they do mice in an air pump, or in a recipient of mephitic gas.[33] Whatever his Grace may think of himself, they look upon him, and every thing that belongs to him, with no more regard than they do upon the whiskers of that little long tailed-animal, that has been long the game of the grave, demure, insidious, spring-nailed, velvet-awed, green-eyed philosophers, whether going upon two legs, or upon four. . . .

Is the Genius of Philosophy not yet known? You may as well think the Garden of the Tuilleries was well protected with the cords of ribbon insultingly stretched by the National Assembly to keep the sovereign canaille from intruding on the retirement of the poor King of the French, as that such flimsy cobwebs will stand between the savages of the Revolution and their natural prey. Deep philosophers are no triflers; brave Sans-culottes are no formalists. They will no more regard a Marquis of Tavistock than an Abbot of Tavistock; the Lord of Wooburn will not be more respectable in their eyes than the Prior of Wooburn; they will make no difference between a Superior of a Covent Garden of nuns and of a Covent Garden of another description.[34] They will not care a rush whether his coat is long or short; whether the colour be purple or blue and buff.[35] They will not trouble *their* heads, with what part of *his* head, his hair is cut from; and they will look with equal respect on a tonsor and a crop.[36] Their only question will be that of their *Legendre*,[37] or some other of their legislative butchers, How he cuts up? how he tallows in the cawl or on the kidneys?

Is it not a singular phænomenon, that whilst the Sans culotte Carcase Butchers, and the Philosophers of the shambles, are pricking their dotted lines upon his hide, and like the print of the poor ox that we see in the shop windows at Charing Cross, alive as he is, and thinking no harm in the world, he is divided into rumps, and sirloins, and briskets, and into all sorts of pieces for roasting, boiling, and stewing, that all the while they are measuring *him*, his Grace is measuring *me*; is invidiously comparing the bounty of the Crown with the deserts of the defender of his order, and in the same moment fawning on those who have the knife half out of the sheath – poor innocent!

> Pleas'd to the last, he crops the flowr'y food
> And licks the hand just rais'd to shed his blood.[38]

No man lives too long, who lives to do with spirit, and suffer with resignation, what Providence pleases to command or inflict: but indeed they are sharp incommodities which beset old age. It was but the other day, that on putting in order some things which had been brought here on my taking leave of London for ever, I looked over a number of fine portraits, most of them of persons now dead, but whose society, in my better days, made this a proud and happy place. Amongst these was the picture of Lord Keppel.[39]

Here Burke inserts an emotional recollection of his friend Admiral Keppel (1725–1786), a popular naval hero against the French during the American war, and the Duke of Bedford's uncle. Keppel was associated politically with Burke's party, the Rockingham Whigs, and was highly critical of the ministry in power, with the result that politically inspired charges were brought against him in 1779. Burke assisted his friend's defence, and the court martial ended in a triumphant acquittal. Burke's use of Keppel's memory here thus has a complex effect: he was both a seasoned patriot who fought against the French, and like Burke, a notable critic of that earlier war. Burke's pamphlet ends:

What would he [Lord Keppel] have said, if he had heard it made a matter of accusation against me, by his nephew the Duke of Bedford, that I was the author of the war? Had I a mind to keep that high distinction to myself, as from pride I might, but from justice I dare not, he would have snatched his share of it from my hand, and held it with the grasp of a dying convulsion to his end.

It would be a most arrogant presumption in me to assume to myself the glory of what belongs to his Majesty, and to his Ministers, and to his Parliament, and to the far greater majority of his faithful people. But had I stood alone to counsel, and that all were determined to be guided by my advice, and to follow it implicitly – then I should have been the sole author of a war. But it should have been a war on my ideas and my principles. Whatever his Grace may think of my demerits with regard to the war with Regicide, he will find my guilt confined to that alone. He never shall, with the smallest colour of reason, accuse me of being the author of a peace with Regicide. But that is high matter; and ought not be mixed with any thing of so little moment, as what may belong to me, or even to the Duke of Bedford.

5. *Thoughts and Details on Scarcity*, Originally Presented to the Right Hon. William Pitt, in the month of November, 1795 (1800),

pp. 1–20, 24–30, 45–8

Frost early in 1795 led to a very bad harvest, followed by high prices for wheat and bread; this meant a sudden worsening of the lot of the poor, though in the long run the country, with its rising urban population, was ceasing anyway to be self-sufficient in wheat. Especially in the low-wage southern counties, magistrates were faced with the possibility of civil disorder and actual starvation. In Devon they issued a list of minimum wages; at the Oxford Quarter Sessions in January 1795 they gave poor relief to supplement low wages, the amount calculated according to the price of bread, and the system, taking its name arbitrarily from the Berkshire Hundred of Speenhamland, became common in most counties in southern England. Meanwhile the newly formed Board of Agriculture under Arthur Young (see below, pp. 96–106), together with concerned members of Parliament,[40] vigorously solicited information from the counties, and suggested measures, such as better cottages for farm labourers, and small plots of land so that those deprived of common grazing rights by enclosure could nevertheless keep hens and pigs and grow vegetables. There were economic objections to such palliatives, as there were to the Speenhamland system: they allowed farmers to keep wages low, pauperised the rural population, and deprived them of the incentive to move elsewhere in search of work.

It is as a student of economic theory that Burke opposes state intervention and systematic charity, in characteristically principled 'philosophic' terms. He argues that the interests of the employer and employee are not at variance. The system works by a relatively simple mechanism – an employment of wage-labour by capital so as to yield a profit to the capitalist, whose interests are served by healthy workers. Burke concedes that the old and sick may present problems, but these should be solved by Christian charity. In terms of the public discussion in November and December 1795 – let alone Paine's welfare proposals three years earlier in *The Rights of Man* (see pp. 118ff.) – Burke's tone is 'hard', in contrast with the 'soft' line of Young, Samuel Whitbread, and a Mr William Malcolm, who, on reporting on Surrey and Bucks (Burke's own county) to the Board of Agriculture, suggested that opulent farmers were keeping back corn in order to maintain prices.[41]

Burke's *Thoughts on Scarcity* is the product of his characteristically Whig-

5. *Thoughts and Details on Scarcity*

gish interest in political economy, which evolved even before the publication of Adam Smith's classic *Wealth of Nations* (1776). This is not the imaginative, if ominous, vision of Thomas Malthus, a more genuinely original and speculative economist than Burke, whose *Essay on the Principle of Population* (1798) is virtually contemporaneous. Burke writes like a working politician, and he addresses himself to his natural constituency, the landed gentry, but not in any crude appeal to their self–interest; if the *Thoughts on Scarcity* is compared with Arthur Young's *France, a Warning* (see pp. 102ff), which is for the same readership on a similar topic, the refinement of Burke's argument becomes plain. Burke, always in his last years mindful of the French Revolution, keeps France in view in order to show that it is only England which has a system naturally capable of maintaining the prosperity of all its inhabitants. In this system, farmers, merchants, and middlemen play the key part, that of the capitalist, which is also the gentry's part – 'The landed gentleman is never to forget, that the farmer is his representative' (p. 67). Burke thus encourages the gentleman to pursue efficiency, and reassures him that efficiency is benevolence. In a period when the gentry were becoming entrepreneurial, this was not so much to persuade them to act differently as to give them a purposive, idealised view of what they were doing already; clarification, rather than leadership, is what ideas are for in politics. *Thoughts on Scarcity* makes an uplifting and unifying appeal to all the propertied, minimising snobbish hierarchical differences, and stressing a unity of interest within an economy dominated by the landed classes in their revised managerial role. Here, compared with the *Reflections*, religion, tradition, and law are underplayed, and the discourse sounds modern because it is that of the marketplace. It is a tone which has much in common with the rhetoric of twentieth-century British conservatism, yet it is also classic eighteenth-century Scottish political economy, subtly modified in the defence of threatened aristocracy.

Of all things, an indiscreet tampering with the trade of provisions is the most dangerous, and it is always worst in the time when men are most disposed to it: – that is, in the time of scarcity. Because there is nothing on which the passions of men are so violent, and their judgment so weak, and on which there exists such a multitude of ill-founded popular prejudices.

The great use of Government is as a restraint; and there is no restraint which it ought to put upon others, and upon itself too, rather than on the fury of speculating under circumstances of irritation. . . .

To provide for us in our necessities is not in the power of Government. It would be a vain presumption in statesmen to think they can do it. The people maintain them, and not they the people. It is in the power of Government to prevent much evil; it can do very little positive good in this, or perhaps in any thing else. It is not only so of the state and statesman, but of all the classes and descriptions of

61

the Rich – they are the pensioners of the poor, and are maintained by their superfluity. They are under an absolute, hereditary, and indefeasible dependence on those who labour, and are miscalled the Poor.

The labouring people are only poor, because they are numerous. Numbers in their nature imply poverty. In a fair distribution among a vast multitude, none can have much. That class of dependent pensioners called the rich, is so extremely small, that if all their throats were cut, and a distribution made of all they consume in a year, it would not give a bit of bread and cheese for one night's supper to those who labour, and who in reality feed both the pensioners and themselves.

But the throats of the rich ought not to be cut, nor their magazines plundered; because, in their persons they are trustees for those who labour, and their hoards are the banking-houses of these latter. Whether they mean it or not, they do, in effect, execute their trust – some with more, some with less fidelity and judgment. But, on the whole, the duty is performed, and everything returns, deducting some very trifling commission and discount, to the place from when it arose. When the poor rise to destroy the rich, they act as wisely for their own purposes as when they burn mills, and throw corn into the river, to make bread cheap. . . .

I further assert, that even under all the hardships of the last year, the labouring people did, either out of their direct gains, or from charity, (which it seems is now an insult to them) in fact, fare better than they did in seasons of common plenty, 50 or 60 years ago; or even at the period of my English observation, which is about 44 years. I even assert, that full as many in that class, as ever were known to do it before, continued to save money; and this I can prove, so far as my own information and experience extend.

It is not true that the rate of wages has not increased with the nominal price of provisions. I allow it has not fluctuated with that price, nor ought it; and the Squires of Norfolk had dined, when they gave it as their opinion, that it might or ought to rise and fall with the market of provisions.[42] The rate of wages in truth has no *direct* relation to that price. Labour is a commodity like every other, and rises or falls according to the demand. This is in the nature of things; however, the nature of things has provided for their necessities. Wages have been twice raised in my time, and they bear a full proportion, or even a greater than formerly, to the medium of provision during the last bad cycle of twenty years. They bear a full proportion to the result of their labour. If we were wildly to attempt to force them beyond it, the stone which we had forced up the hill would only fall back upon them in a diminished demand, or, what indeed is the far lesser evil, an aggravated price of all the provisions, which are the result of their manual toil.

There is an implied contract, much stronger than any instrument or article of agreement between the labourer in any occupation and his employer – that the labour, so far as that labour is concerned, shall be sufficient to pay to the employer a profit on his capital, and a compensation for his risk; in a word, that the labour shall produce an advantage equal to the payment. Whatever is above that, is a direct *tax*; and if the amount of that tax be left to the will and pleasure of another, it is an *arbitrary tax*.

If I understand it rightly, the tax proposed on the farming interest of this kingdom is to be levied at what is called the discretion of justices of peace.[43]

The questions arising on this scheme of arbitrary taxation are these – Whether it is better to leave all dealing, in which there is no force or fraud, collusion or combination, entirely to the persons mutually concerned in the matter contracted for; or to put the contract in the hands of those, who can have none, or a very remote interest in it, and little or no knowledge of the subject.

It might be imagined that there would be very little difficulty in solving this question; for what man, of any degree of reflection, can think, that a want of interest in any subject closely connected with a want of skill in it, qualifies a person to intermeddle in any the least affair; much less in affairs that vitally concern the agriculture of the kingdom, the first of all its concerns, and the foundation of all its prosperity in every other matter, by which that prosperity is produced?

The vulgar error on this subject arises from a total confusion in the very idea of things widely different in themselves; – those of convention, and those of judicature. When a contract is making, it is a matter of discretion and of interest between the parties. In that intercourse, and in what is to arise from it, the parties are the masters. If they are not completely so, they are not free, and therefore their contracts are void. . . .

What is doing, supposes or pretends that the farmer and the labourer have opposite interests; – that the farmer oppresses the labourer; and that a gentleman, called a justice of peace, is the protector of the latter, and a control and restraint on the former; and this is a point I wish to examine in a manner a good deal different from that in which gentlemen proceed, who confide more in their abilities than is fit, and suppose them capable of more than any natural abilities, fed with no other than the provender furnished by their own private speculations, can accomplish. Legislative acts, attempting to regulate this part of œconomy, do, at least as much as any other, require the exactest detail of circumstances, guided by the surest general principles that are necessary to direct experiment and inquiry, in order again from those details to elicit principles, firm and luminous general principles, to direct a practical legislative proceeding.

First, then, I deny that it is in this case, as in any other of necessary implication, that contracting parties should originally have had different interests. By accident it may be so undoubtedly at the outset; but then the contract is of the nature of a compromise; and compromise is founded on circumstances that suppose it the interests of the parties to be reconciled in some medium. The principle of compromise adopted, of consequence the interests cease to be different.

But in the case of the farmer and the labourer, their interests are always the same, and it is absolutely impossible that their free contracts can be onerous to either party. It is the interest of the farmer, that his work should be done with effect and celerity: and that cannot be, unless the labourer is well fed, and otherwise found with such necessaries of animal life, according to his habitudes, as may keep the body in full force, and the mind gay and cheerful. . . . In all things whatever, the mind is the most valuable and the most important; and in this scale the whole of agriculture is in a natural and just order; the beast is as an informing principle to the plough and cart; the labourer is as reason to the beast; and the farmer is as thinking and presiding principle to the labourer. An attempt to break this chain of subordination in any part is equally absurd, but the absurdity is the most mischievous in practical operation, where it is the most easy, that is, where it is the most subject to an erroneous judgment.

It is plainly more the farmer's interest that his men should thrive, than that his horses should be well fed, sleek, plump, and fit for use, or than that his waggon and ploughs should be strong, in good repair, and fit for service.

On the other hand, if the farmer ceases to profit of the labourer, and that his capital is not continually manured and fructified, it is impossible that he should continue that abundant nutriment, and clothing, and lodging, proper for the protection of the instruments he employs.

It is therefore the first and fundamental interest of the labourer, that the farmer should have a full incoming profit on the product of his labour. The proposition is self-evident, and nothing but the malignity, perverseness, and ill governed passions of mankind, and particularly the envy they bear to each other's prosperity, could prevent their seeing and acknowledging it, with thankfulness to the benign and wise disposer of all things, who obliges men, whether they will or not, in pursuing their own selfish interests, to connect the general good with their own individual success.

But who are to judge what the profit and advantage ought to be? certainly no authority on earth. It is a matter of convention dictated by the reciprocal conveniences of the parties, and indeed by their reciprocal necessities. – But, if the farmer is excessively avaricious? – why so much the better – the more he desires to increase his gains, the more interested is he in the good condition of those, upon whose labour his gains must principally depend.

I shall be told by the zealots of the sect of regulation, that this may be true, and may be safely committed to the convention of the farmer and the labourer, when the latter is in the prime of his youth, and at the time of his health and vigour, and in ordinary times of abundance. But in calamitous seasons, under accidental illness, in declining life, and with the pressure of a numerous offspring, the future nourishers of the community but the present drains and blood-suckers of those who produce them, what is to be done? When a man cannot live and maintain his family by the natural hire of his labour, ought it not to be raised by authority? On this head I must be allowed to submit, what my opinions have ever been; and somewhat at large.

And, first, I premise that labour is, as I have already intimated, a commodity, and as such, an article of trade. If I am right in this notion, then labour must be subject to all the laws and principles of trade, and not to regulations foreign to them, and that may be totally inconsistent with those principles and those laws. When any commodity is carried to market, it is not the necessity of the vender, but the necessity of the purchaser that raises the price. The extreme want of the seller has rather (by the nature of things with which we shall in vain contend) the direct contrary operation. If the goods at market are beyond the demand, they fall in their value; if below it, they rise. The impossibility of the subsistence of a man, who carries his labour to a market, is totally beside the question in this way of viewing it. The only question is, what is it worth to the buyer?

But if authority comes in and forces the buyer to a price, what is this in the case (say) of a farmer, who buys the labour of ten or twelve labouring men, and three or four handy-crafts, what is it, but to make an arbitrary division of his property among them?

The whole of his gains, I say it with the most certain conviction, never do amount any thing like in value to what he pays to his labourers and artificers; so that a very small advance upon what *one* man pays to *many*, may absorb the whole of what he possesses, and amount to an actual partition of all his substance among them. A perfect equality will indeed be produced; – that is to say, equal want, equal wretchedness, equal beggary, and on the part of the petitioners, a woeful, helpless, and desperate disappointment. Such is the event of all compulsory equalizations. They pull down what is above. They never raise what is below: and they depress high and low together beneath the level of what was originally the lowest.

If a commodity is raised by authority above what it will yield with a profit to the buyer, that commodity will be the less dealt in. If a second blundering interposition be used to correct the blunder of the first, and an attempt is made to force the purchase of the commodity (of labour for instance), the one of these two things must happen, either that the forced buyer is ruined, or the price of the product of the labour, in that proportion, is raised. Then the wheel turns round, and the evil complained of falls with aggravated weight on the complainant. The price of corn, which is the result of the expence of all the operations of husbandry, taken together, and for some time continued, will rise on the labourer, considered as a consumer. The very best will be, that he remains where he was. But if the price of the corn should not compensate the price of labour, what is far more to be feared, the most serious evil, the very destruction of agriculture itself, is to be apprehended. . . .

But what if the rate of hire to the labourer comes far short of his necessary subsistence, and the calamity of the time is so great as to threaten actual famine? Is the poor labourer to be abandoned to the flinty heart and griping hand of base self-interest, supported by the sword of law, especially when there is reason to suppose that the very avarice of farmers themselves has concurred with the errors of Government to bring famine on the land[?]

In that case, my opinion is this. Whenever it happens that a man can claim nothing according to the rules of commerce, and the principles of justice, he passes out of that department, and comes within the jurisdiction of mercy. In that province the magistrate has nothing at all to do: his interference is a violation of the property which it is his office to protect. Without all doubt, charity to the poor is a direct and obligatory duty upon all Christians, next in order after the payment of debts, full as strong, and by nature made infinitely more delightful to us. . . . The manner, mode, time, choice of objects, and proportion, are left to private discretion; and perhaps, for that very reason it is performed with the greater satisfaction, because the discharge of it has been more the appearance of freedom; recommending us besides very specially to the divine favour, as the exercise of a virtue most suitable to a being sensible of its own infirmity.

5. *Thoughts and Details on Scarcity*

The cry of the people in cities and towns, though unfortunately (from a fear of their multitude and combination) the most regarded, ought, in *fact*, to be the *least* attended to upon this subject; for citizens are in a state of utter ignorance of the means by which they are to be fed, and they contribute little or nothing, except in an infinitely circuitous manner, to their own maintenance. They are truly,*"Fruges consumere nati."*[a] They are to be heard with great respect and attention upon matters within their province, that is, on trades and manufactures; but on any thing that relates to agriculture, they are to be listened to with the same *reverence* which we pay to the dogmas of other ignorant and presumptuous men. . . .

A greater and more ruinous mistake cannot be fallen into, than that the trades of agriculture and grazing can be conducted upon any other than the common principles of commerce; namely, that the producer should be permitted, and even expected, to look to all possible profit, which, without fraud or violence, he can make; to turn plenty or scarcity to the best advantage he can; to keep back or to bring forward his commodities at his pleasure; to account to no one for his stock or for his gain. On any other terms he is the slave of the consumer; and that he should be so is of no benefit to the consumer. No slave was ever so beneficial to the master, as a freeman that deals with him on an equal footing by convention, formed on the rules and principles of contending interests and compromised advantages. The consumer, if he were suffered, would, in the end always be the dupe of his own tyranny and injustice. The landed gentleman is never to forget, that the farmer is his representative. . . .

What is true of the farmer is equally true of the middle man; whether the middle man acts as factor, jobber, salesman, or speculator, in the markets of grain. These traders are to be left to their free course; and the more they make, and the richer they are, and the more largely they deal, the better both for the farmer and consumer, between whom they form a natural and most useful link of connection; though, by the machinations of the old evil counsellor, *Envy*, they are hated and maligned by both parties.

I hear that middle men are accused of monopoly. Without question, the monopoly of authority is, in every instance and in every degree, an evil; but the monopoly of capital is the contrary. It is a great benefit, and a benefit particularly to the poor. A tradesman who has but an hundred pounds capital, which (say) he can turn but once a year, cannot live upon a *profit* of 10 *per cent* because he cannot live upon ten pounds a year; but a man of ten thousand pounds capital can

---

[a] 'Men born [only] to eat the fruit of the land' (Horace, *Epistles*, 1.2.27).

live and thrive upon 5 *per cent* profit in the year, because he has five hundred pounds a year. The same proportion holds in turning it twice or thrice. These principles are plain and simple; and it is not our ignorance, so much as the levity, the envy, and the malignity, of our nature, that hinders us from perceiving and yielding to them: but we are not to suffer our vices to usurp the place of our judgment.

The balance between consumption and production makes price. The market settles, and alone can settle, that price. Market is the meeting and conference of the *consumer* and *producer*, when they mutually discover each other's wants. Nobody, I believe, has observed with any reflection what market is, without being astonished at the truth, the correctness, the celerity, the general equity, with which the balance of wants is settled. They, who wish the destruction of that balance, and would fain by arbitrary regulation decree, that defective production should not be compensated by increased price, directly lay their *axe* to the root of production itself.

They may, even in one year of such false policy, do mischiefs incalculable; because the trade of a farmer is, as I have before explained, one of the most precarious in its advantages, the most liable to losses, and the least profitable of any that is carried on. It requires ten times more of labour, of vigilance, of attention, of skill, and, let me add, of good fortune also, to carry on the business of a farmer with success, than what belongs to any other trade. Seeing things in this light, I am far from presuming to censure the late circular instruction of Council to Lord Lieutenants – but I confess I do not clearly discern its object.[44] I am greatly afraid that the enquiry will raise some alarm as a measure, leading to the French system of putting corn into requisition. For that was preceded by an inquisition somewhat similar in its principle, though, according to their mode, their principles are full of that violence, *which here* is not much to be feared. It goes on a principle directly opposite to mine; it presumes, that the market is no fair *test* of plenty or scarcity. It raises a suspicion, which may affect the tranquillity of the public mind, "that the farmer keeps back, and takes unfair advantages by delay"; on the part of the dealer, it gives rise obviously to a thousand nefarious speculations.

In case the return should on the whole prove favourable, is it meant to ground a measure for encouraging exportation and checking the import of corn? If it is not, what end can it answer? And, I believe, it is not.

This opinion may be fortified by a report gone abroad, that intentions are entertained of erecting public granaries, and that this enquiry is to give Government an advantage in its purchases.[45]

5. *Thoughts and Details on Scarcity*

I hear that such a measure has been proposed, and is under deliberation; that is, for Government to set up a granary in every market town, at the expence of the state, in order to extinguish the dealer, and to subject the farmer to the consumer, by securing corn to the latter at a certain and steady price.

If such a scheme is adopted, I should not like to answer for the safety of the granary, of the agents, or of the town itself, in which the granary was erected – the first storm of popular phrenzy would fall upon that granary.

So far in a political light.

In an economical light, I must observe, that the construction of such granaries throughout the kingdom, would be at an expence beyond all calculation. The keeping them up would be at a great charge. The management and attendance would require an army of agents, store-keepers, clerks, and servants. The capital to be employed in the purchase of grain would be enormous. The waste, decay, and corruption, would be a dreadful drawback on the whole dealing; and the dissatisfaction of the people, at having decayed, tainted, or corrupted corn sold to them, as must be the case, would be serious. . . .

But if the object of this scheme should be, what I suspect it is, to destroy the dealer, commonly called the middle man, and by incurring a voluntary loss to carry the baker to deal with Government, I am to tell them that they must set up another trade, that of a miller or a mealman, attended with a new train of expences and risks. If in both these trades they should succeed, so as to exclude those who trade on natural and private capitals, then they will have a monopoly in their hands, which, under the appearance of a monopoly of capital, will, in reality, be a monopoly of authority, and will ruin whatever it touches. The agriculture of the kingdom cannot stand before it. . . .

After all, have we not reason to be thankful to the Giver of all good? . . . Never since I have known England, have I known more than a comparative scarcity. The price of wheat, taking a number of years together, has had no very considerable fluctuation, nor has it risen exceedingly until within this twelvemonth. Even now, I do not know of one man, woman, or child, that has perished from famine; fewer, if any, I believe, than in years of plenty, when such a thing may happen by accident. This is owing to a care and superintendence of the poor, far greater than any I remember.

The consideration of this ought to bind us all, rich and poor together, against those wicked writers of the newspapers, who would inflame the poor against their friends, guardians, patrons, and protectors. Not only very few (I have observed, that I know of none, though I live in a place as poor as most) have actually died of want, but we have seen no traces of those dreadful exterminating epidemics, which, in consequence of scanty and unwholesome food, in former times, not unfrequently wasted whole nations. Let us be saved from too much wisdom of our own, and we shall do tolerably well.

It is one of the finest problems in legislation, and what has often engaged my thoughts whilst I followed that profession, "What the State ought to take upon itself to direct by the public wisdom, and what it ought to leave, with as little interference as possible, to individual discretion." Nothing, certainly, can be laid down on the subject that will not admit of exceptions, many permanent, some occasional. But the clearest line of distinction which I could draw, whilst I had my chalk to draw any line, was this; that the State ought to confine itself to what regards the State, or the creatures of the State, namely the exterior establishment of its religion; its magistracy; its revenue; its military force by sea and land; the corporations that owe their existence to its fiat; in a word, to every thing that is *truly and properly* public, to the public peace, to the public safety, to the public order, to the public prosperity. In its preventive police it ought to be sparing of its efforts, and to employ means, rather few, unfrequent, and strong, than many, and frequent, and, of course, as they multiply their puny politic race, and dwindle, small and feeble. Statesmen who know themselves will, with the dignity which belongs to wisdom, proceed only in this the superior orb and first mover of their duty steadily, vigilantly, severely, courageously: whatever remains will, in a manner, provide for itself. But as they descend from the state to a province, from a province to a parish, and from a parish to a private house, they go on accelerated in their fall. They *cannot* do the lower duty; and, in proportion as they try it, they will certainly fail in the higher. They ought to know the different departments of things; what belongs to laws, and what manners alone can regulate. To these, great politicians may give a leaning, but they cannot give a law.

Our Legislature has fallen into this fault as well as other governments; all have fallen into it more or less. The once mighty State, which was nearest to us locally, nearest to us in every way, and whose ruins threaten to fall upon our heads, is a strong instance of this error. I can never quote France without a foreboding sigh. . . . That state has fallen by the hands of the parricides of their country, called the Revolutionists, and Constitutionalists, of France. . . . My dear departed friend,[46] whose loss is even greater to the public than to me, had often remarked, that the leading vice of the French monarchy (which he had well studied) was in good intention ill-directed, and a restless desire of governing too much. The hand of authority was seen in every thing, and in every place. All, therefore, that happened amiss in the course even of domestic affairs, was attributed to the Government. . . .

Tyranny and cruelty may make men justly wish the downfall of abused powers, but I believe that no government ever yet perished from any other direct cause than its own weakness. My opinion is against an over-doing of any sort of administration, and more especially against this most momentous of all meddling on the part of authority; the meddling with the subsistence of the people.

Mary Wollstonecraft

(1729–1797)

6. A Vindication of the Rights of Men, in a Letter to the Right Hon. Edmund Burke; occasioned by his Reflections on the Revolution in France (1790),

2nd edn, pp. 9–13, 22–7

Mary Wollstonecraft was christened in the Church of England, but she got her intellectual and political education from Dr Richard Price and other rational Dissenters in the London suburb of Newington Green, where she kept a school in the 1780s.[1] She was already an educationalist (*Thoughts on the Education of Daughters*, 1787), a novelist (*Mary, a Fiction*, 1788), a writer for children (*Original Stories from Real Life*, 1788), and a reviewer for Joseph Johnson's *Analytical Review* when Burke's *Reflections* appeared on 1 November 1790. Her speedy reply to Burke – she published the first edition anonymously on 29 November, the second, slightly enlarged and corrected, with her name on the title-page, on 18 December – probably reflects the views of her Dissenter friends and of the Johnson circle,[2] but it is also characteristic of Wollstonecraft herself. Though she accuses Burke of emotionalism rather than rationality, her own manner (in her words) glows with indignation. She does not construct an argument, or use freshly coined words or images (the 'torpedo' on p. 73 is a cliché), although, as James Boulton fairly observes, it may well be that her spontaneity and strong feelings, or 'eager warmth and positiveness' (*Monthly Review*) were good tactics in a quick reply.[3] The range of her ideas, as illustrated here, already has a genuine radical force. She sees Burke as the defender of hierarchy in all its forms, the spokesman for a society founded on systematic oppression, in which heavy taxes, press-ganging and the game laws are characteristic impositions of the powerful upon the weak.

I glow with indignation when I attempt, methodically, to unravel your slavish paradoxes, in which I can find no fixed first principle to refute; I shall not, therefore, condescend to shew where you affirm in one page what you deny in another; and how frequently you draw conclusions without any previous premises: – it would be something like cowardice to fight with a man who had never exercised the weapons with which his opponent chose to combat, and irksome to refute sentence after sentence in which the latent spirit of tyranny appeared.

I perceive, from the whole tenor of your Reflections, that you have a mortal antipathy to reason; but, if there is any thing like argument, or first principles, in your wild declamation, behold the result: – that we are to reverence the rust of antiquity, and term the unnatural customs, which ignorance and mistaken self-interest have consolidated, the sage fruit of experience: nay, that, if we do discover some errors, our *feelings* should lead us to excuse, with blind love, or unprincipled filial affection, the venerable vestiges of ancient days. These are gothic notions of beauty – the ivy is beautiful, but, when it insidiously destroys the trunk from which it receives support, who would not grub it up?

Further, that we ought cautiously to remain for ever in frozen inactivity, because a thaw, whilst it nourishes the soil, spreads a temporary inundation; and the fear of risking any personal present convenience should prevent a struggle for the most estimable advantages. This is sound reasoning, I grant, in the mouth of the rich and short-sighted. . . .

The civilization which has taken place in Europe has been very partial, and, like every custom that an arbitrary point of honour has established, refines the manners at the expence of morals, by making sentiments and opinions current in conversation that have no root in the heart, or weight in the cooler resolves of the mind. – And what has stopped its progress? – hereditary property – hereditary honours. The man has been changed into an artificial monster by the station in which he was born, and the consequent homage that benumbed his faculties like the torpedo's touch; – or a being, with a capacity of reasoning, would not have failed to discover, as his faculties unfolded, that true happiness arose from the friendship and intimacy which can only be enjoyed by equals; and that charity is not a condescending distribution of alms, but an intercourse of good offices and mutual benefits, founded on respect for justice and humanity. . . .

It is necessary emphatically to repeat, that there are rights which men inherit at their birth, as rational creatures, who were raised above the brute creation by their improvable faculties; and that, in receiving these, not from their forefathers but, from God, prescription can never undermine natural rights.

A father may dissipate his property without his child having any right to complain; – but should he attempt to sell him for a slave, or fetter him with laws contrary to reason; nature, in enabling him to discern good from evil, teaches him to break the ignoble chain, and not to believe that bread becomes flesh, and wine blood, because his parents swallowed the Eucharist with this blind persuasion.

There is no end to this implicit submission to authority – some where it must stop, or we return to barbarism. . . .

Our penal laws punish with death the thief who steals a few pounds; but to take by violence, or trepan, a man, is no such heinous offence.[4] – For who shall dare to complain of the venerable vestige of the law that rendered the life of a deer more sacred than that of a man? But it was the poor man with only his native dignity who was thus oppressed – and only metaphysical sophists and cold mathematicians can discern this insubstantial form; it is a work of abstraction – and a *gentleman* of lively imagination must borrow some drapery from fancy before he can love or pity a *man*. – Misery, to reach your heart, I perceive, must have its cap and bells; your tears are reserved, very *naturally* considering your character, for the declamation of the theatre, or for the downfall of queens, whose rank alters the nature of folly, and throws a graceful veil over vices that degrade humanity; whilst the distress of many industrious mothers, whose *helpmates* have been torn from them, and the hungry cry of helpless babes, were vulgar sorrows that could not move your commiseration, though they might extort an alms.

7. *A Vindication of the Rights of Woman, with Strictures on Political and Moral Subjects* (1792),

2nd corr. edn, pp. 36–8, 44–5, 50–3, 58–9, 67–9, 72–4; from ch. 2, 'The Prevailing Opinion of a Sexual Character Discussed'

Wollstonecraft's book is not always seen as strictly a part of the Revolution controversy, yet its arguments clearly relate to the egalitarian and radical case she had already advanced against Burke. *Rights of Woman* illustrates the strengths and weaknesses of the radical intellectuals. It applies to the subject of women the favourite Dissenter precepts of equality and natural rights, with the kind of conviction that arises from membership of an intellectual group which sustains rather than challenges its own opinions. In other senses, too, the book seems indifferent to, or myopic about, the effect it might have on readers outside London intellectual circles. Wollstonecraft scorns romantic love (then as now an important ideal for women, even if vulnerable to criticism), and rather too emphatically concedes the present inferiority of most women. Her approach is both tactless, and untactical: she does not put forward a platform of actual measures which could be campaigned for, such as changes to marriage and divorce laws, child benefits, schools, a new curriculum, job training, equal pay, public office, even the vote. Her radicalism, like that of her future husband William Godwin, thus has its impractical aspect – though the title and timing of *Rights of Woman*, issued as the campaign against Paine's *Rights of Man* built up, also conveys the author's flair.

Egalitarian arguments on women's behalf, as well as complaints at their legal, economic, and educational disabilities, were reasonably familiar in late-eighteenth-century England, as in France. Rousseau's proposition that women should be brought up to be passive had only one important English radical advocate, Thomas Day. Otherwise the dominant intellectual role of Protestantism within English radicalism is very apparent in the treatment of feminist topics: Wollstonecraft is in harmony with the ethos of Dissent when she stresses the equality before God of the souls of men and women, and represents sexuality as at best a weakness. In English liberal circles it had become usual to argue that girls and boys should all learn to reason, and to know the principles of science and mathematics in preference to fashionable 'accomplishments'. The Edgeworths' *Practical Education* (1798), which derives from the same tradition as the educational writing of the Dissenters Joseph Priestley[5] and Anna Laetitia Barbauld,[6] supposes that girls and boys in a family will be taught intellectual self-reliance together; the point is amplified in Maria Edgeworth's series of educational stories, *The Parent's Assistant* (from 1796) and *Early Lessons* (from 1801), and in her novels for adults, beginning with *Belinda* (1801).[7]

Mary Wollstonecraft's writings became notorious when her personal history was fully revealed in Godwin's *Memoirs of Mary Wollstonecraft* – a frank and moving book, and an injudicious one in the anti-radical persecution of 1798. Political capital could be made of her attempts at suicide, her liaisons outside marriage, and her illegitimate child, all of which were embarrassments to those subscribing to her own arguments for rationality, and against romantic love and sexuality. When *Rights of Woman* was first published, it could be praised temperately by moderates, and some of its propositions developed. The Norwich journal *The Cabinet*, which is made up of anonymous contributions, carries two articles in 1795 'On the Rights of Woman', which describe Mary Wollstonecraft, on the evidence of *Rights of Woman*, as 'a woman of strong understanding and good heart',[8] and pursue further her 'hint' that women ought to be represented in Parliament.

In treating . . . of the manners of women, let us, disregarding sensual arguments, trace what we should endeavour to make them in order to co-operate, if the expression be not too bold, with the supreme Being.

By individual education, I mean, for the sense of the word is not precisely defined, such an attention to a child as will slowly sharpen the senses, form the temper, regulate the passions, as they begin to ferment, and set the understanding to work before the body arrives at maturity; so that the man may only have to proceed, not to begin, the important task of learning to think and reason.

To prevent any misconstruction, I must add, that I do not believe that a private education can work the wonders which some sanguine writers have attributed to it. Men and women must be educated, in a great degree, by the opinions and manners of the society they live in. In every age there has been a stream of popular opinion that has carried all before it, and given a family character, as it were, to the century. It may then fairly be inferred, that, till society be differently constituted, much cannot be expected from education. . . .

Consequently the most perfect education, in my opinion, is such an exercise of the understanding as is best calculated to strengthen the body and form the heart. Or, in other words, to enable the individual to attain such habits of virtue as will render it independent. In fact, it is a farce to call any being virtuous whose virtues do not result from the exercise of its own reason. This was Rousseau's opinion respecting men: I extend it to women, and confidently assert that they have been drawn out of their sphere by false refinement, and not by an endeavour to acquire masculine qualities. Still the regal homage which they receive is so intoxicating, that till the manners of the times are changed, and formed on more reasonable principles, it may be impossible to convince them that the illegitimate power, which they obtain, by degrading themselves, is a curse, and that they must return to nature and equality, if they wish to secure the placid satisfaction that unsophisticated affections impart. But for this epoch we must wait – wait, perhaps, till kings and nobles, enlightened by reason, and preferring the real dignity of man to childish state, throw off their gaudy hereditary trappings: and if then women do not resign the arbitrary power of beauty – they will prove that they have *less* mind than man.

I may be accused of arrogance; still I must declare what I firmly believe, that all the writers who have written on the subject of female education and manners, from Rousseau to Dr. Gregory, have contributed to render women more artificial, weak characters, than they would otherwise have been; and, consequently, more useless members of society. . . .

Riches and hereditary honours have made cyphers of women to give consequence to the numerical figure; and idleness has produced a mixture of gallantry and despotism into society, which leads the very men who are the slaves of their mistresses to tyrannize over their sisters, wives, and daughters. This is only keeping them in rank and file, it is true. Strengthen the female mind by enlarging it, and there will be an end to blind obedience; but, as blind obedience is ever sought for by power, tyrants and sensualists are in the right when they endeavour to keep women in the dark, because the former only want slaves, and the latter a play-thing. The sensualist, indeed, has been the most dangerous of tyrants, and women have been duped by their lovers, as princes by their ministers, whilst dreaming that they reigned over them.

I now principally allude to Rousseau,[9] for his character of Sophia is, undoubtedly, a captivating one, though it appears to me grossly unnatural; however, it is not the superstructure, but the foundation of her character, the principles on which her education was built, that I mean to attack; nay, warmly as I admire the genius of that able writer, whose opinions I shall often have occasion to cite, indignation always takes place of admiration, and the rigid frown of insulted virtue effaces the smile of complacency, which his eloquent periods are wont to raise, when I read his voluptuous reveries. Is this the man, who, in his ardour for virtue, would banish all the soft arts of peace, and almost carry us back to Spartan discipline? . . .

To speak disrespectfully of love is, I know, high treason against sentiment and fine feelings; but I wish to speak the simple language of truth, and rather to address the head than the heart. To endeavour to reason love out of the world, would be to out Quixote Cervantes, and equally offend against common sense; but an endeavour to restrain this tumultuous passion, and to prove that it should not be allowed to dethrone superior powers, or to usurp the sceptre which the under-standing should ever coolly wield, appears less wild.

Youth is the season for love in both sexes; but in those days of thoughtless enjoyment provision should be made for the more important years of life, when reflection takes place of sensation. But Rousseau, and most of the male writers who have followed his steps, have warmly inculcated that the whole tendency of female education ought to be directed to one point: – to render them pleasing.

Let me reason with the supporters of this opinion who have any knowledge of human nature, do they imagine that marriage can eradicate the habitude of life? The woman who has only been taught to please will soon find that her charms are oblique sunbeams, and that they cannot have much effect on her husband's heart when they are seen every day, when the summer is passed and gone. Will she then have sufficient native energy to look into herself for comfort, and cultivate her dormant faculties? . . .

The worthy Dr. Gregory fell into a similar error. I respect his heart; but entirely disapprove of his celebrated Legacy to his Daughters.[10]

He advises them to cultivate a fondness for dress, because a fondness for dress, he asserts, is natural to them. I am unable to comprehend what either he or Rousseau mean, when they frequently use this indefinite term. If they told us that in a pre-existent state the soul was fond of dress, and brought this inclination with it into a new body, I should listen to them with a half smile, as I often do when I hear a rant about innate elegance. – But if he only meant to say that the exercise of the faculties will produce this fondness – I deny it. – It is not natural; but arises, like false ambition in men, from a love of power. . . .

In order to fulfil the duties of life, and to be able to pursue with vigour the various employments which form the moral character, a master and mistress of a family ought not to continue to love each other with passion. I mean to say, that they ought not to indulge those emotions which disturb the order of society, and engross the thoughts that should be otherwise employed. The mind that has never been engrossed by one object wants vigour – if it can long be so, it is weak.

A mistaken education, a narrow, uncultivated mind, and many sexual prejudices, tend to make women more constant than men; but, for the present, I shall not touch on this branch of the subject. I will go still further, and advance, without dreaming of a paradox, that an unhappy marriage is often very advantageous to a family, and that the neglected wife is, in general, the best mother.[11] And this would almost always be the consequence if the female mind were more enlarged: for, it seems to be the common dispensation of Providence, that what we gain in present enjoyment should be deducted from the treasure of life, experience; and that when we are gathering the flowers of the day and revelling in pleasure, the solid fruit of toil and wisdom should not be caught at the same time. . . .

As a philosopher, I read with indignation the plausible epithets which men use to soften their insults; and, as a moralist, I ask what is meant by such heterogeneous associations, as fair defects, amiable weaknesses, &c.? If there is but one criterion of morals, but one archetype for man, women appear to be suspended by destiny, according to the vulgar tale of Mahomet's coffin; they have neither the unerring instinct of brutes, nor are allowed to fix the eye of reason on a perfect model. They were made to be loved, and must not aim at respect, lest they should be hunted out of society as masculine. . . .

Avoiding, as I have hitherto done, any direct comparison of the two sexes collectively, or frankly acknowledging the inferiority of woman, according to the present appearance of things, I shall only insist that men have increased that inferiority till women are almost sunk below the standard of rational creatures. Let their faculties have room to unfold, and their virtues to gain strength, and then determine where the whole sex must stand in the intellectual scale. . . .

I love man as my fellow; but his scepter, real or usurped, extends not to me, unless the reason of an individual demands my homage; and even then the submission is to reason, and not to man. In fact, the conduct of an accountable being must be regulated by the operations of its own reason; or on what foundation rests the throne of God? . . .

As to the argument respecting the subjection in which the sex has ever been held, it retorts on man. The many have always been enthralled by the few; and monsters, who scarcely have shewn any discernment of human excellence, have tyrannized over thousands of their fellow creatures. Why have men of superiour endowments submitted to such degradation? For, is it not universally acknowledged that kings, viewed collectively, have ever been inferior, in abilities and virtue, to the same number of men taken from the common mass of mankind – yet, have they not, and are they not still treated with a degree of reverence that is an insult to reason? China is not the only country where a living man has been made a God. *Men* have submitted to superiour strength to enjoy with impunity the pleasure of the moment – *women* have only done the same, and therefore till it is proved that the courtier, who servilely resigns the birthright of a man, is not a moral agent, it cannot be demonstrated that woman is essentially inferior to man because she has always been subjugated.

Brutal force has hitherto governed the world, and that the science of politics is in its infancy, is evident from philosophers scrupling to give the knowledge most useful to man that determinate distinction.

I shall not pursue this argument any further than to establish an obvious inference, that as sound politics diffuse liberty, mankind, including woman, will become more wise and virtuous.

Helen Maria Williams

(?1762–1827)

8. *Letters from France*, vol. I (1790),

pp. 5–14, 21, 123–4, 146–53, 192–6

As a minor poet in London in the 1780s, Helen Maria Williams was the protégée of a family friend, the leading Dissenter Dr Andrew Kippis, through whom she gained access to the literary circles grouped around the London booksellers. Her early poetry takes up themes attractive to a liberal readership, such as abolition of the slave trade and, after the Fall of the Bastille, the cause of liberty in France. She first visited France at the invitation of Augustin François Thomas du Fossé, a member of a Norman noble family, whose father had disapproved of his marriage to a bourgeoise and had used that notorious feature of the *ancien régime*, a *lettre de cachet*, to have his son confined for two years from 17 July 1778 in a convent at St Yon, near Rouen. Williams arrived in Paris in July 1790, on the eve of the first anniversary of the Fall of the Bastille, which she saw commemorated in a festival called the Fédération. Returning to England, she published an enthusiastic account of the Fédération and of the du Fossés in the first of her three series of *Letters from France*.

The following year Williams returned to France, where she lived for the rest of her life. Her Parisian salon became a meeting place for members of the Girondin party, like Madame Roland, and for the British radicals who flocked to Paris. With one of the latter, John Hurford Stone, she cohabited until his death in 1818. In 1793, when the Girondins were finally defeated by the Jacobins, many of Williams's closest associates were thrown into prison; some were executed. She herself was imprisoned with her family in the Luxembourg in October 1793 in a round-up of British subjects in Paris. In spite of all vicissitudes, she retained her faith in the Revolution, though she became an outspoken critic of Robespierre, the Directory, and Napoleon.

Williams's most influential volume of *Letters from France* was the first, from which the following extract is taken. Virtually coinciding with Burke's *Reflections* upon the same event, her relatively artless report has the advantage of being first-hand. Her attitudes are the naive ones of literary sentimentalism at its most simple and popular: she sets out to enlist the reader's sympathy with victimised individuals, whom she tends to represent as virtuous and childlike. The liberal circles which shared her ideals and tastes read her, and remembered her portraits and anecdotes: Wordsworth, already the author of a youthful sonnet (1787) addressed to her, drew in his poem *Vaudracour and*

80

8. *Letters from France*

Julia on her story of the du Fossés, which he initially made part of his account of the French Revolution in *The Prelude* (Book IX, but 1805 version only: the story is omitted, except for a brief summary, in the first published edition of 1850).

Letter II

I promised to send you a description of the Federation; but it is not to be described! One must have been present, to form any judgment of a scene, the sublimity of which depended much less on its external magnificence than on the effect it produced on the minds of the spectators. "The people, sure, the people were the sight!" I may tell you of pavilions, of triumphal arches, of altars on which incense was burnt, of two hundred thousand men walking in procession; but how am I to give you an adequate idea of the behaviour of the spectators? How am I to paint the impetuous feelings of that immense, that exulting multitude? Half a million of people assembled at a spectacle, which furnished every image that can elevate the mind of man; which connected the enthusiasm of moral sentiment with the solemn pomp of religious ceremonies; which addressed itself at once to the imagination, the understanding, and the heart.

The Champ de Mars was formed into an immense amphitheatre; round which were erected forty rows of seats, raised one above another with earth, on which wooden forms were placed. Twenty days labour, animated by the enthusiasm of the people, accomplished what seemed to require the toil of years. Already in the Champ de Mars the distinctions of rank were forgotten; and, inspired by the same spirit, the highest and lowest orders of citizens gloried in taking up the spade, and assisting the persons employed in a work on which the common welfare of the State depended. Ladies took the instruments of labour in their hands, and removed a little of the earth, that they might be able to boast that they also had assisted in the preparations at the Champ de Mars; and a number of old soldiers were seen voluntarily bestowing on their country the last remains of their strength. A young Abbé of my acquaintance told me, that the people beat a drum at the door of the convent where he lived, and obliged the Superior to let all the Monks come out, and work in the Champ de Mars. The Superior with great reluctance acquiesced: "Quant à moi," said the young Abbé, "je ne demandois pas mieux."[1]

At the upper end of the amphitheatre a pavilion was built for the reception of the King, the Queen, their attendants, and the National Assembly, covered with striped tent-cloth of the national colours, and decorated with streamers of the same beloved tints, and fleurs de lys. The white flag was displayed above the spot where the king was seated. In the middle of the Champ de Mars *l'Autel de la Patrie* was placed, on which incense was burnt by priests dressed in long white robes, with sashes of national ribbon. Several inscriptions were written on the altar; but the words visible at the greatest distance were, "La Nation, la Loi, & le Roi."

At the lower end of the amphitheatre, opposite to the pavilion, three triumphal arches were erected, adorned with emblems and allegorical figures. . . .

In the streets, at the windows, and on the roofs of the houses, the people, transported with joy, shouted and wept as the procession passed. Old men were seen kneeling in the streets, blessing God that they had lived to witness that happy moment. The people ran to the doors of their houses, loaded with refreshments, which they offered to the troops; and crouds of women surrounded the soldiers, and holding up their infants in their arms, and melting into tears, promised to make their children imbibe, from their earliest age, an inviolable attachment to the principles of the new constitution. . . .

But the spectacle of all others the most interesting to my feelings, was the rejoicings at the Bastille. The ruins of that execrable fortress were suddenly transformed, as if with the wand of necromancy, into a scene of beauty and of pleasure. The ground was covered with fresh clods of grass, upon which young trees were placed in rows, and illuminated with a blaze of light. Here the minds of the people took a higher tone of exultation than in the other scenes of festivity. Their mutual congratulations, their reflections on the horror of the past, their sense of present felicity, their cries of "Vive la Nation," still ring in my ear! I too, though but a sojourner in their land, rejoiced in their happiness, joined the universal voice, and repeated with all my heart and soul, "Vive la nation!". . .

Joseph Priestley

(1733–1804)

9. Letters to the Right Hon. Edmund Burke, Occasioned by his Reflections on the Revolution in France (Birmingham, 1791),

2nd corr. edn, 1791, pp. 49–53, 58–64, 143–7

By 1790 Priestley was easily the most formidable of Dissenting controversialists. His ascendancy depended upon his intellectual eminence: though primarily distinguished as a chemist, and one of the leading scientists of his day, he was also prolific and influential when writing on education and theology. It is not surprising that, as a clever Cambridge undergraduate of the 1790s, Coleridge followed Priestley into unitarianism and psychology.[1]

Priestley's diverse interests brought him into contact with many of the most vigorous elements in English intellectual life. He contributed to the politicised debate on language his *Rudiments of Grammar* (1761) and *Lectures on the Theory of Language and Universal Grammar* (1762). He helped to form the curriculum of the Dissenting Academy at Warrington (see below, p. 83), at a time when Warrington, Hackney, and Hoxton figured as frequently and significantly in the education of intellectuals as Oxford and Cambridge. He was a member of the Lunar Society of Birmingham, which has been described as an informal research institute and the powerhouse of the Industrial Revolution, along with Wedgwood, Boulton, Watt, Erasmus Darwin, and R. L. Edgeworth. He corresponded with academies of science in Paris, St Petersburg, Turin, Haarlem, and Philadelphia. In 1780, Priestley was elected minister at the New Meeting, Birmingham. The West Midlands and North West, the large region with Birmingham as its natural centre, was now taking off into industrial revolution. Dissenters, who were dominant among the entrepreneurs, had come to play an increasingly important part in the civic and intellectual life of the cities, co-operating with or challenging the leadership of the neighbouring landed gentry. Priestley's move to Birmingham looked advantageous for the intellectual life of the Midlands, but not, as it turned out, for the public peace.

Priestley has the personality of a stirrer, not of a research scientist or sage. His *History of the Corruptions of Christianity* (1782) and *History of Early Opinions Concerning Jesus Christ* (1786) immediately became notorious as assaults upon received religion. Though written as works of theology, they have an intellectual appeal outside the sects, since their admiration for the simplicity of the early Christian churches chimes in with fashionable primitivism, with its broad political connotations. Bishop Samuel Horsley led a counter-attack on Priestley, and the controversy between the two lasted from 1783 to 1790. But Priestley became even more celebrated when Fox brought his motion for repeal of the Test Acts before the Commons on 2 March 1790, since opponents of the motion circulated an unwary phrase in one of Priestley's pamphlets, in which he described his writings as 'grains of gunpowder' for which his opponents were 'providing the match'. This, together with the *Letters to Burke*, which were published on 1 January 1791, and ran into three editions, gave him an extraordinary notoriety among the Tories of Birmingham.

On 14 July 1791, a reform society met in Birmingham to mark the second anniversary of Bastille Day, and a mob assembled to demonstrate against them. In the four days of rioting which followed, Priestley's meeting house and home at Fairhill, with its laboratory, were burnt to the ground, along with the homes of other leading Dissenters. There is little doubt that Priestley and his friends were correct in their surmise that the local Tory gentry, their political opponents in the city, commissioned the attack.[2] After a night spent in walking about in the lanes watching the fires, Priestley escaped to London, where he worked for three years as Richard Price's successor, preaching at Hackney, before he finally emigrated to America. Birmingham lost its most energetic and able citizens in 1791, and the Midlands Dissenting network its nerve-centre. The sudden break-up of a stable, confident intellectual circle prefigures the slower disintegration of the Dissenting intellectual community in the capital.

As a writer, Priestley relies upon his personal authority. He uses a commanding tone even for an opponent like Burke. His credentials are clearly stated on the title-page, beginning with L.L.D. and F.R.S., and going on to his membership of foreign societies. He is clear and epigrammatic, and his almost schoolmasterley vein of sarcasm suggests a practised pedagogue. This is an unconcessive approach, not likely to win new friends, but confirming Priestley's authority among the converted for whom he is writing. As usual, he is not merely sectarian: his quarrel with Burke becomes a clash between the Catholic and Protestant mentality, not a personal or temporary difference. Priestley does not expect Eden or Utopia, but he believes that a more open, egalitarian, humane, and prosperous England is attainable, on the American model; a middle-class state which would dispense with aristocratic policies such as war and colonialism.

Letter VI

Of the Interference of the State in Matters of Religion in general

DEAR SIR,

It was the devout wish of Job, who, with exemplary patience, had borne much calumny, as well as sufferings of other kinds, that his *adversary had written a book.*[3] The favour which this good man could not obtain, the despised and oppressed Dissenters have at length been indulged with from you, at least so far as relates to the cause of your strong attachment to the established church of this country, which, no doubt, induced you to enter so warmly as you did into the opposition to our late claims in the House of Commons.[4]. . .

I rather wonder, however, at this conduct in *you*, when I find you lamenting, p. 136, that "it has been our misfortune, and not, as these gentlemen think it" (meaning, no doubt, myself as well as others) "the glory, of this age, that every thing is to be *discussed*." For certainly such a publication as this of yours, you could not but think, must lead to much discussion. If, therefore, you thought this to be a dangerous process, with respect either to *Church* or *State*, you certainly ought not to have entered upon it, by publishing any thing on the subject;[5] unless, indeed, you had thought (which perhaps may have been the case) that your publication would effectually deter all opponents; your reasoning being so forcible as to preclude, and be an effectual bar to, all farther discussion on the subject. . . .

"Our church establishment," you say, p. 136, "is the first of our prejudices. It is,", you say again, "the first, the last, and the midst in our minds," that is, it occupies the whole capacity of them, so that they cannot admit any thing else, at least any thing of an opposite nature. Of course, the maxims on which you proceed must to *you* appear incontrovertible. You, therefore, very naturally add, "it is not a prejudice destitute of reason, but involving in it profound and extensive wisdom." For such is the opinion that we all entertain of prejudices deeply rooted in our own minds; though it is no uncommon thing for what appears to be *profound and extensive wisdom* to one man, to appear the extreme of *folly* to another; and unfortunately (owing perhaps to the difference of our educations, and early habits) this is precisely the difference between you and me. What you admire I despise, and what you think highly useful, I am persuaded is very mischievous.

However, notwithstanding the great difference in our *conclusions*, we have, I perceive, some great and leading *common principles*; so that it may not be difficult to discover which of us has departed the farthest from them. I shall endeavour to shew our readers, that with these common principles, your conclusions are wholly discordant; and I flatter myself that, differently as we think on a variety of subjects, we have more common principles than you have given sufficient attention to, and more than you really act upon. You cannot, for example, have that dislike to *discussion* which you profess, because, in this and in other publications, as well as in your speeches in the House of Commons, you have entered largely into many discussions; and you must also agree with me in thinking that the more important any subject is, or the more interesting it is to men, either as individuals, or members of society, the greater call there is for an accurate discussion of every thing relating to it; because, in things of this nature, mistakes are the most dangerous, and you are far from supposing *religion* to be a matter of indifference, either to individuals, or to society. And how can we guard against, or indeed be apprized of, any mistakes, without due examination, or *discussion*?

That our readers may see at one view what it is that you maintain with respect to civil establishments of religion, I shall, before I enter upon the discussion of them, give our readers a summary view of all your positions. Confounding, as you evidently do, the idea of *religion* itself, with that of the *civil establishment* of it, you say, "It is the basis of civil society, and essential to every state," insomuch that you even question whether it be *lawful* to be without one. So far, you think, is the church from having any dependence upon the state, that the state has not even "the property, or dominion," of any thing belonging to the church, being only the "guardian" of the revenues of the church, and holding them in trust for its use. You, therefore, hold that the property of the church is unalienable, and not to be touched in any emergency of state whatever. Religion, you maintain, derives its *estimation* and *effect*, from the riches and magnificence of its establishment; that such establishment is calculated for *the multitude*, that it is peculiarly useful both to the poor and the rich, and, though necessary to all states, is more proper for a *democratical*, than any other form of government.

Now, Sir, strange as it may appear to you, my ideas, in all these respects, are the very reverse of yours. Religion I consider as a thing that requires no civil establishment whatever, and that its beneficial operation is injured by such establishment, and the more in proportion to its riches. I am satisfied that such an establishment, instead of being any advantage, is a great incumbrance to a state, and in general highly unfavourable to its liberties. Civil establishments of christianity were altogether unknown in the early ages, and gained ground by very slow degrees, as other corruptions and abuses in the system did. I am clearly of opinion, that the state has a right to dispose of *all* property within itself; that of the church, as well as of every thing else of a public nature; and that religion has naturally nothing at all to do with any particular form of civil government; being useful indeed to all persons, the rich as well as the poor, but only as individuals. . . .

Your mind has been so dazzled with the fascinating idea of the *majesty of the church* (a phrase, I believe peculiar to yourself) that you have not been able to see any thing distinctly on the subject. . . . You have not even been able to distinguish, whether it was St. Paul's at London, St. Peter's at Rome, or the church of Sancta Sophia at Constantinople. For your description applies equally to them all. It seems to have been sufficient for you that it was not a *conventicle*.

As to every thing under *this* denomination, it has been your maxim, without any examination, to turn your back upon it. You would, no doubt, have done the same with respect to any place, in which Peter, or Paul, was permitted to preach; the christian religion being in their time, unfortunately, nothing more than a *sect*, taught in *conventicles*, and no where *authorised by law*. Had you lived at that time, you would, according to your general maxim, have "cherished your old" heathen "prejudices, because they were old," and have lived and died a humble worshipper of the Gods, and especially the *Goddesses*, of ancient Greece and Rome.[6]

I the less wonder at this power of imagination, and prejudice, and this stupefaction of all your rational faculties in matters of *religion*, as it is apparent that you have been under a similar suspension of your *reason*, and equally under the power of *imagination*, in your views of the principles of *civil government*. Such, Sir, is "your proud submission, and the subordination of your very heart," to *princes*, and *nobles*; such your devotion to *rank* and *sex*, in conjunction with your *religious enthusiasm*, that one might suspect that your book was composed after some solemn vigil, such as watching your arms at the shrine of the blessed virgin; after which you issued forth the champion, in form, of religion, of monarchy, and of the immaculate virtue of all handsome queens.[7] . . .

Letter XIV
Of the Prospect of the general Enlargement of Liberty, civil and religious, opened by the Revolution in France.

DEAR SIR,

I cannot conclude these *Letters*, without congratulating, not *you*, Sir, or the many admirers of your performance, who have no feeling of *joy* on the occasion, but the French nation, and the world, I mean the liberal, the rational, and the virtuous part of the world, on the great revolution that has taken place in France, as well as on that which some time ago took place in America. Such events as these teach the doctrine of *liberty, civil* and *religious*, with infinitely greater clearness and force, than a thousand treatises on the subject. They speak a language intelligible to all the world, and preach a doctrine congenial to every human heart. . . .

The generality of governments have hitherto been little more than a combination of *the few*, against *the many*; and to the mean passions and low cunning of these few, have the great interests of mankind been too long sacrificed. Whole nations have been deluged with blood, and every source of future prosperity has been drained, to gratify the caprices of some of the most despicable, or the most execrable, of the human species. For what else have been the generality of kings, their ministers of state, or their mistresses, to whose wills whole kingdoms have been subject? . . .

Hitherto, also, infinite have been the mischiefs in which all nations have been involved, on account of *religion*, with which, as it concerns only God and men's own consciences, civil government, as such, has nothing to do. Statesmen, misled by ignorant or interested priests, have taken upon them to prescribe what men should believe and practice, in order to get to heaven, when they themselves have often neither believed, nor practised, any thing under that description. . . . By this means have mankind been kept for ages in a state of bondage worse than Egyptian, the bondage of the mind.[8]

How glorious, then, is the prospect, the reverse of all the past, which is now opening upon us, and upon the world. Government, we may now expect to see, not only in theory, and in books, but in actual practice, calculated for the general good, and taking no more upon it than the general good requires; leaving all men the enjoyment of as many of their *natural rights* as possible, and no more interfering with matters of religion, with men's notions concerning God, and a future state, than with philosophy, or medicine.

After the noble example of America, we may expect, in due time, to see the governing powers of all nations confining their attention to the *civil* concerns of them, and consulting their welfare in the present state only;[9] in consequence of which they may all be flourishing and happy. . . .

Together with the general prevalence of the true principles of civil government, we may expect to see the extinction of all *national prejudice* and enmity, and the establishment of *universal peace* and good will among all nations. When the affairs of the various societies of mankind shall be conducted by those who shall truly represent them, who shall feel as they feel, and think as they think; who shall really understand, and consult their interests, they will no more engage in those mutually offensive *wars*, which the experience of many centuries has shown to be constantly expensive and ruinous. They will no longer covet what belongs to others, and which they have found to be of no real service to them, but will content themselves with making the most of their own.

The very idea of *distant possessions* will be even ridiculed. The East and the West Indies, and every thing *without ourselves* will be disregarded, and wholly excluded from all European systems; and only those divisions of men, and of territory, will take place, which the common convenience requires, and not such as the mad and insatiable ambition of princes demands. No part of America, Africa, or Asia, will be held in subjection to any part of Europe, and all the intercourse that will be kept up among them, will be for their mutual advantage.

James Mackintosh

(1765–1832)

10. *Vindiciae Gallicae. Defence of the French Revolution and its English Admirers, against the Accusations of the Right Hon. Edmund Burke* (1791),

3rd edn, with Additions (1791), pp. iv–xiii, 114–18, 121–5

James Mackintosh's *Vindiciae Gallicae*, which first appeared on 7 May 1791, was one of the most widely admired replies to Burke. Mackintosh was a clever, impecunious young Scotsman, the son of an old family with a small estate near Inverness. He trained first in Scotland as a doctor, afterwards (from 1790) in London as a lawyer. When he moved south in 1788 he was already an admirer of Priestley; in 1789 he married the sister of Daniel Stuart, afterwards editor successively of the anti-government *Courier* and *Morning Post*, and in 1790 he joined the Society for Constitutional Information and supported Tooke's radical candidature in the Westminster by-election. But Mackintosh is always more a liberal Whig than a radical, and the enormous success of his reply to Burke rests on its Whiggish moderation and respectability. He writes, as James Boulton says, 'for the intelligent middle and upper classes – Burke's own audience – to whom Paine's matter and manner were repellent'.[1] The success of the *Vindiciae* brought him into the Whiggish society, the Friends of the People, and by 1796 he became a firm admirer of Burke. Mackintosh gave a successful, fashionable series of lectures in early 1799 on 'The Law of Nature and of Nations', designed to emphasise his conversion; only the *Introductory Discourse* (1798) was published, but this attacked Godwin, a friend of Mackintosh's, with some sharpness. His later career is that of a lawyer (Recorder of Bombay, 1804–11), a liberal Whig M.P. (from 1813), a student of German philosophy, and a just if cautious reviewer for the *Edinburgh Review*.

Mackintosh's style is over-elaborate for modern tastes: the laborious sentence-structure and the constant play of literary allusion have dated, though at the time they made the useful point that he was Burke's social equal. But his argument remains accessible, because he writes for individuals rather than a sect, and because he conveys a flattering image of his notional reader: a principled liberal and humanitarian, neither prejudiced nor already committed, but open to persuasion by reasoned argument and by accurate evidence about events in France. Mackintosh conveys his own idealism, but he controls it because he wants to be seen as more analytical, methodical, and reliable than Burke. Above all, he works to get the reader to reject Burke's call to irrational, intuitive loyalty, his 'abject distrust of our powers' (p. 93). Mackintosh discovers in both Burke and Calonne a hysterical reaction to events, born of fear – a growing force in European politics which can already be identified by the word 'counter-revolution' (p. 92).

[The *Reflections*] is certainly in every respect a performance, of which to form a correct estimate, would prove one of the most arduous efforts of critical skill. "We scarcely can praise it, or blame it too much." Argument every where dextrous and specious, sometimes grave and profound, cloathed in the most rich and various imagery, and aided by the most pathetic and picturesque description, speaks the opulence and the powers of that mind, of which age has neither dimmed the discernment nor enfeebled the fancy, neither repressed the ardor, nor narrowed the range. . . .

Of the Senate and people of France, his language is such as might have been expected to a country which his fancy has peopled only with plots, assassinations, and massacres, and all the brood of dire chimeras which are the offspring of a prolific imagination, goaded by an ardent and deluded sensibility. The glimpses of benevolence, which irradiate this gloom of invective, arise only from generous illusion, from misguided and misplaced compassion – his eloquence is not at leisure to deplore the fate of beggared artizans, and famished peasants, the victims of suspended industry, and languishing commerce. The sensibility which seems scared by the homely miseries of the vulgar, is attracted only by the splendid sorrows of royalty, and agonizes at the slenderest pang that assails the heart of sottishness or prostitution, if they are placed by fortune on a throne.[2]

To the English friends of French freedom, his language is contemptuous, illiberal, and scurrilous. In one of the ebbings of his fever he is disposed not to dispute "their good intentions." But he abounds in intemperate sallies, in ungenerous insinuations, which wisdom ought to have checked, as ebullitions of passion, which genius ought to have disdained, as weapons of controversy.

The arrangement of his work is as singular as the matter. Availing himself of all the privileges of epistolary effusion, in their utmost latitude and laxity, he interrupts, dismisses, and resumes argument at pleasure. His subject is as extensive as political science – his allusions and excursions reach almost every region of human knowledge. It must be confessed that in this miscellaneous and desultory warfare, the superiority of a man of genius over common men is infinite. He can cover the most ignominious retreat by a brilliant allusion. He can parade his arguments with masterly generalship, where they are strong. He can escape from an untenable position into a splendid declamation. He can sap the most impregnable conviction by pathos, and put to flight a host of syllogisms with a sneer. Absolved from the laws of vulgar method, he can advance a groupe of magnificent horrors to make a breach in our hearts, through which the most undisciplined rabble of arguments may enter in triumph.

Analysis and method, like the discipline and armour of modern nations, correct in some measure the inequalities of controversial dexterity, and level on the intellectual field the giant and the dwarf. Let us then analyse the production of Mr. Burke, and dismissing what is extraneous and ornamental, we shall discover certain leading questions, of which the decision is indispensible to the point at issue. . . .

With this reply to Mr. Burke will be mingled some strictures on the late publication of M. Calonne.[3] That minister, who has for some time exhibited to the eyes of indignant Europe the spectacle of an exiled robber living in the most splended impunity, has, with an effrontery that beggars invective, assumed in his work the tone of afflicted patriotism, and delivers his polluted Philippics as the oracles of persecuted virtue.

His work is more methodical than that of his coadjutor, Mr. Burke. . . . The only part of his production that here demands reply, is that which relates to general political questions. Remarks on what he has offered concerning them will naturally find a place under the corresponding sections of the Reply to Mr. Burke. Its most important view is neither literary nor argumentative. It appeals to judgments more decisive than those of criticism, and aims at wielding weapons more formidable than those of logic.

It is the manifesto of a Counter Revolution, and its obvious object is to inflame every passion and interest, real or supposed, that has received any shock in the establishment of freedom. He probes the bleeding wounds of the princes, the nobility, the priesthood, and the great judicial aristocracy. He adjures one body by its dignity degraded, another by its inheritance plundered, and a third by its authority destroyed, to repair to the holy banner of his philanthropic crusade. Confident in the protection of all the monarchs of Europe, whom he alarms for the security of their thrones, and having insured the moderation of a fanatical rabble, by giving out among them the savage *war-whoop* of atheism, he already fancies himself in full march to Paris, not to re-instate the deposed despotism (for he disclaims the purpose, and who would not trust such virtuous disavowals!!) but at the head of this army of priests, mercenaries and fanatics, to dictate as the tutelar genius of France, the establishment of a just and temperate freedom, obtained without commotion and without carnage, and equally hostile to the interested ambition of demagogues and the lawless authority of kings.

Crusades were an effervescence of chivalry, and the modern St. Francis has a knight for the conduct of these crusaders, who will convince Mr. Burke, that the age of chivalry is not past, nor the glory of Europe gone for ever. The Comte d'Artois,[4] that scyon worthy of Henry the Great, the rival of the Bayards and Sidneys, the new model of French Knighthood, is to issue from Turin with ten thousand cavaliers to deliver the peerless and immaculate Antonietta of Austria from the durance vile in which she has so long been immured in the Thuilleries, from the swords of the discourteous knights of Paris, and the spells of the sable wizards of democracy. . . .

Legislators are under no obligation to retain a constitution, because it has been found "*tolerably* to answer the common purposes of Government." It is absurd to *expect*, but it is not absurd to *pursue* perfection. It is absurd to acquiesce in evils, of which the remedy is obvious, because they are less grievous than those which are endured by others. To suppose the social order is not capable of improvement from the progress of the human understanding, is to betray the inconsistent absurdity of an arrogant confidence in our attainments, and an abject distrust of our powers. If indeed the sum of evil produced by political institutions, even in the least imperfect Governments, were small, there might be some pretence for this dread of innovations, this horror at remedy, which has raised such a clamour over Europe: But, on the contrary, in an estimate of the sources of human misery, after granting that one portion is to be attributed to disease, and another to private vices, it might perhaps be found that a *third equal* part arose from the oppressions and corruptions of Government, disguised under various forms. All the Governments that now exist in the world (except the United States of America) have been fortuitously formed. They are the produce of change, not the work of art. They have been altered, impaired, improved and destroyed by accidental circumstances, beyond the foresight or controul of wisdom. Their parts thrown up against present emergencies formed no systematic whole. It was certainly not to have been presumed, that these *fortuitous Governments* should have surpassed the works of intellect, and precluded all nearer approaches to perfection. Their origin without doubt furnishes a strong presumption of an opposite nature. It might teach us to expect in them many discordant principles, many jarring forms, much unmixed evil, and much imperfect good, many institutions which had long survived their motive, and many of which reason had never been the author, nor utility the object. Experience, *even in the best of these Governments*, accords with such expectations.

A Government of *art*, the work of legislative intellect, reared on the immutable basis of natural right and general happiness, which should combine the excellencies, and exclude the defects of the various constitutions which change had scattered over the world, instead of being precluded by the perfection of any of those forms, was loudly demanded by the injustice and absurdity of them all. It was time that men should learn to tolerate nothing ancient that reason does not respect, and to shrink from no novelty to which reason may conduct. It was time that the human powers, so long occupied by subordinate objects, and inferior arts, should mark the commencement of a new æra in history, by giving birth to the art of improving government, and increasing the civil happiness of man. It was time, as it has been wisely and eloquently said, that Legislators, instead of that narrow and dastardly *coasting* which never ventures to lose sight of usage and precedent, should, guided by the *polarity* of reason, hazard a bolder navigation, and discover, in unexplored regions, the treasure of public felicity.

The talk of the French Legislators was, however, less hazardous. The philosophers of Europe had for a century discussed all objects of public œconomy. The conviction of a great majority of enlightened men had, after many controversies, become on most questions of general politics, uniform. A degree of certainty, perhaps nearly equal to that which such topics will admit, had been attained. The National Assembly were therefore not called on to make discoveries. It was sufficient if they were not uninfluenced by the opinions, nor exempt from the spirit of their age. They were fortunate enough to live in a period when it was only necessary to affix the stamp of laws to what had been prepared by the research of philosophy. They will here, however, be attacked by a futile common-place. The most specious *theory*, it will be said, is often impracticable, and any attempt to transfer speculative doctrines into the practice of States is chimerical and frantic. If by theory be understood vague conjecture, the objection is not worth discussion; but if by theory be meant inference from the moral nature and political state of man, then I assert, that whatever such theory pronounces to be true, must be practicable, and that whatever on the subject is impracticable, must be false. . . .

All the great questions of general politics had, as we have remarked, been nearly decided and almost all the decisions had been hostile to established institutions – yet these institutions, still flourished in all their vigour. The same man who cultivated liberal science in his cabinet was compelled to administer a barbarous jurisprudence on the bench. The same MONTESQUIEU, who at Paris reasoned as a philosopher of the eighteenth, was compelled to decide at Bourdeaux as a magistrate of the fourteenth century.[5] The apostles of toleration and the ministers of the Inquisition were cotemporaries.[6] The torture continued to be practised in the age of Beccaria.[7] The Bastile devoured its victims in the country of Turgot.[8] The criminal code, even of nations in which it was the mildest, was oppressive and savage. The laws respecting religious opinion, even where there was a *pretended* toleration, outraged the most evident deductions of reason. The true principles of commercial policy, though they had been reduced to demonstration, influenced the councils of no State. Such was the fantastic spectacle presented by the European nations, who, philosophers in theory, and barbarous in practice, exhibited to the observing eye two opposite and inconsistent aspects of manners and opinions. But such a State carried in itself the seeds of its own destruction. Men will not long dwell in hovels, with the model of a palace before their eyes.

A State approaching to it in some measure existed indeed in the ancient world. But the art of Printing had not then provided a channel by which the opinions of the learned pass insensibly into the popular mind. A bulwark then existed between the body of mankind and the reflecting few. They were distinct nations, inhabiting the same country, and the opinions of the one (I speak *comparatively* with modern times) had little influence on the other. But that bulwark is now levelled with the ground. – The convictions of philosophy insinuate themselves by a slow, but certain progress, into popular sentiment. It is vain for the arrogance of learning to condemn the people to ignorance by reprobating superficial knowledge – The people cannot be profound, but the truths which regulate the moral and political relations of man, are at no great distance from the surface. The great works in which discoveries are contained cannot be read by the people; but their substance passes through a variety of minute and circuitous channels to the shop and the hamlet. The conversion of these works of unproductive splendor into latent use and unobserved activity, resembles the process of nature in the external world. The expanse of a noble lake, the course of a majestic river, imposes on the imagination by every impression of dignity and sublimity. But it is the moisture that insensibly arises from them, which, gradually mingling with the soil, nourishes all the luxuriancy of vegetation, fructifies and adorns the surface of the earth.[9]

Arthur Young

(1741–1820)

11. *Travels in France during the years 1787, 1788 and 1789* (1792),

2nd corr. edn, London, 1794, vol. I, pp. 148–57

Young was the most celebrated British agriculturalist of his day. Already well known and admired among the scientific and progressive gentry and middle classes, he made an authoritative contribution to the Revolution debate with his first-hand report on the mismanagement and hardship which precipitated the upheaval of 1789. The *Travels* came out not as a pamphlet but as an opulent book, with its author's learned credentials following his name: the third edition consists, for example, of two handsome quarto volumes. The rapid succession of expensive editions testifies to the book's prestige with affluent readers.

Young is writing a documentary. He proceeds day by day, with no artfully sustained linking narratives, or themes. A marked personality emerges, of a man with strong, even testy responses (like his annoyance at Metz, on 13 July 1789, to discover that the only British agriculturalist the local academy has heard of is one Dom Cowley, of London). Young remains resolutely an Englishman abroad, unseduced by the quaintess of foreign customs (traditional hairstyles in Alsace must make a haven for parasites), and indifferent to the French language, in which his spelling is careless. His refusal to idealise the French, in years when admirers of the Revolution regularly did so, marvellously establishes his credentials. Young is an ideal journalistic guide precisely because he appears to have little interest in philosophical generalisation, and no strong axe to grind. His encounter with the careworn peasant woman on 12 July is all the more powerful: this entry is one of the compelling passages of English writing on the Revolution, a vignette far more plausible than Helen Maria Williams on the Fédération, of a kind with Wordsworth's 'hunger-bitten girl' in the *Prelude* – ' 'Tis against *that*/That we are fighting' (Bk IX, ll. 517–18).

In the later nineteenth century, an age when travels were more appreciated than polemics, John Morley calls Young's book 'the substantial and decisive reply to Burke . . . worth a hundred times more than Burke, Mackintosh and Paine all put together', because 'the writer plainly enumerates without trope or invective the intolerable burdens under which the great mass of the French people had for long years been groaning'.[1] In its own day, the *Travels* impressed an educated, politically moderate readership: it speaks to, and represents, the rational optimism about the Revolution that was common among educated British people before the middle of 1792.

[July] 12th [1789]. Walking up a long hill, to ease my mare, I was joined by a poor woman, who complained of the times, and that it was a sad country; on my demanding her reasons, she said her husband had but a morsel of land, one cow, and a poor little horse, yet he had a *franchar* (42 *lb.*) of wheat, and three chickens, to pay as a quit-rent to one Seigneur; and four *franchar* of oats, one chicken and 1 *sou* to pay to another, beside very heavy tailles and other taxes. She had seven children, and the cow's milk helped to make the soup. But why, instead of a horse, do not you keep another cow? Oh, her husband could not carry his produce so well without a horse; and asses are little used in the country. It was said, at present, that *something was to be done by some great folks for such poor ones, but she did not know who nor how, but God send us better, car les tailles et les droits nous écrasent*. This woman, at no great distance, might have been taken for sixty or seventy, her figure was so bent, and her face so furrowed and hardened by labour, – but she said she was only twenty-eight. An Englishman, who has not travelled, cannot imagine the figure made by infinitely the greater part of the countrywomen in France; it speaks, at the first sight, hard and severe labour: I am inclined to think, that they work harder than the men, and this, united with the more miserable labour of bringing a new race of slaves into the world, destroys absolutely all symmetry of person and every feminine appearance. To what are we to attribute this difference in the manners of the lower people in the two kingdoms? To GOVERNMENT. – 23 miles.

[July] 13th. Leave Mar-le-Tour at four in the morning: the village herdsman was sounding his horn; and it was droll to see every door vomiting out its hogs or sheep, and some a few goats, the flock collecting as it advances. Very poor sheep, and the pigs with mathematical backs, large segments of small circles. They must have abundance of commons here, but, if I may judge by the report of the animals' carcases, dreadfully overstocked. To Metz, one of the strongest places in France; pass three draw-bridges, but the command of water must give a strength equal to its works. The common garrison is 10,000 men, but there are fewer at present. Waited on M. de Payen, secretary of the Academy of Sciences; he asked my plan, which I explained; he appointed me at four in the afternoon at the academy, as there would be a *séance* held; and he promised to introduce me to some persons who could answer my enquiries. I attended accordingly, when I found the academy assembled at one of their weekly meetings. . . . In the *Almanach des Trois Évêchés*,[2] 1789, this academy is said to have been instituted particularly for agriculture; I turned to the list of their honorary members to see what attention they have paid to the men who, in the present age, have advanced that art. I found an Englishman, Dom Cowley, of London. Who is Dom Cowley? – Dined at the *table d'hôte*, with seven officers, out of whose mouths, at this important moment, in which conversation is as free as the press, not one word issued for which I would give a straw, nor a subject touched on of more importance than a coat, or a puppy dog. At *table d'hôtes* of officers, you have a voluble garniture of bawdry or nonsense; at those of merchants, a mournful and stupid silence. Take the mass of mankind, and you have more good sense in half-an-hour in England than in half a year in France. – Government! Again: – all – all – is government. – 15 miles.

[July] 14th. They have a *cabinet litéraire* at Metz, something like that I described at Nantes, but not on so great a plan; and they admit any person to read or go in and out for a day, on paying 4 *sous*. To this I eagerly resorted, and the news from Paris, both in the public prints, and by the information of a gentleman, I found to be interesting. Versailles and Paris are surrounded by troops; 35,000 men are assembled, and 20,000 more on the road, large trains of artillery collected, and all the preparations of war. The assembling of such a number of troops has added to the scarcity of bread; and the magazines that have been made for their support are not easily by the people distinguished from those they suspect of being collected by monopolists. This has aggravated their evils almost to madness; so that the confusion and tumult of the capital are extreme. A gentleman of an excellent understanding, and apparently of consideration, from the attention paid him, with whom I had some conversation on the subject, lamented, in the most pathetic terms, the situation of his country; he considers a civil war as impossible to be avoided. There is not, he added, a doubt but the court, finding it impossible to bring the National Assembly to terms, will get rid of them; a bankruptcy at the same moment is inevitable; the union of such confusion must be a civil war; and it is now only by torrents of blood that we have any hope of establishing a freer constitution: yet it must be established; for the old government is riveted to abuses that are insupportable. He agreed with me entirely, that the propositions of the *séance royale*,[3] though certainly not sufficiently satisfactory, yet were the ground for a negotiation that would have secured by degrees *all even that the sword can give us, let it be as successful as it will. The purse – the power of the purse is everything; skilfully managed, with so necessitous a government as ours, it would, one after another, have gained all we wished. As to a war, Heaven knows the event; and if we have success, success itself may ruin us; France may have a Cromwell in its bosom, as well as England. . . .*

[July] 15th. I went to Nancy, with great expectation, having heard it represented as the prettiest town in France. I think, on the whole, it is not undeserving the character in point of building, direction, and breadth of streets. – Bourdeaux is far more magnificent; Bayonne and Nantes are more lively; but there is more equality in Nancy; it is almost all good; and the public buildings are numerous. The *Place Royale* and the adjoining area are superb. Letters from Paris! all confusion! the ministry removed; Mons. Necker ordered to quit the kingdom without noise. The effect on the people of Nancy was considerable. I was with Mons. Willemet[4] when his letters arrived, and for some time his house was full of enquirers; all agreed, that it was fatal news, and that it would occasion great commotions. *What will be the result at Nancy?* The answer was in effect the same from all I put this question to: – *We are a provincial town, we must wait to see what is done at Paris; but everything is to be feared from the people, because bread is so dear, they are half-starved, and are consequently ready for commotion.* This is the general feeling; they are as nearly concerned as Paris; but they dare not stir; they dare not even have an opinion of their own till they know what Paris thinks; so that if a starving populace were not in question, no one would dream of moving. This confirms what I have often heard remarked, that the *déficit* would not have produced the revolution but in concurrence with the price of bread. Does not this show the infinite consequence of great cities to the liberty of mankind? Without Paris, I question whether the present revolution, which is fast working in France, could possibly have had an origin. It is not in the villages of Syria or Diarbekir[5] that the Grand Signor meets with a murmur against his will; it is at Constantinople that he is obliged to manage and mix caution even with despotism. . . .

[July] 20th. To Strasbourg, through one of the richest scenes of soil and cultivation to be met with in France, and exceeded by Flanders only. I arrived at Strasbourg at a critical moment, which I thought would have broken my neck; a detachment of horse, with their trumpets on one side, a party of infantry, with their drums beating on the other, and a great mob hallooing, frightened my French mare; and I could scarcely keep her from trampling on Messrs. the *tiers état*. On arriving at the inn, hear the interesting news of the revolt of Paris. The

Arthur Young (1741–1820)

Gardes Françaises joining the people; the little dependence on the rest of the troops; the taking the Bastile; and the institution of the *milice bourgeoise*; in a word, of the absolute overthrow of the old government. Everything being now decided, and the kingdom in the hands of the Assembly, they have the power to make a new constitution, such as they think proper; and it will be a great spectacle for the world to view, in this enlightened age, the representatives of twenty-five millions of people sitting on the construction of a new and better order and fabric of liberty, than Europe has yet offered. It will now be seen, whether they will copy the constitution of England, freed from its faults, or attempt, from theory, to frame something absolutely speculative: in the former case, they will prove a blessing to their country; in the latter they will probably involve it in inextricable confusions and civil wars, perhaps not in the present period, but certainly at some future one. I hear not of their removing from Versailles; if they stay there under the control of an armed mob, they must make a government that will please the mob; but they will, I suppose, be wise enough to move to some central town, Tours, Blois, or Orléans, where their deliberations may be free. But the Parisian spirit of commotion spreads quickly; it is here; the troops, that were near breaking my neck, are employed to keep an eye on the people who show signs of an intended revolt. They have broken the windows of some magistrates that are no favourites; and a great mob of them is at this moment assembled demanding clamorously to have meat at 5 *sous* a pound. They have a cry among them that will conduct them to good lengths: – *Point d'impôt et vivent les états.* . . .

[July] 21st. I have spent some time this morning at the *cabinet littéraire*, reading the gazettes and journals that give an account of the transactions at Paris; and I have had some conversation with several sensible and intelligent men on the present revolution. The spirit of revolt is gone forth into various parts of the kingdom; the price of bread has prepared the populace everywhere for all sorts of violence; at Lyons there have been commotions as furious as at Paris, and the same at a great many other places: Dauphiné is in arms; and Bretagne in absolute rebellion. The idea is, that the people will, from hunger, be driven to revolt; and when once they find any other means of subsistence than that of honest labour, everything will be to be feared. Of such consequence it is to a country, and indeed to every country, to have a good police of corn; a police that shall by securing a high price to the farmer, encourage his culture enough to secure the people at the same time from famine. . . .

Night– I have been witness to a scene curious to a foreigner; but dreadful to Frenchmen that are considerate. Passing through the square of the *Hôtel de Ville*, the mob were breaking the windows with stones, notwithstanding an officer and a detachment of horse was in the square. Perceiving that their numbers not only increased, but that they grew bolder and bolder every moment, I thought it worth staying to see what it would end in, and clambered on to the roof of a row of low stalls opposite the building against which their malice was directed. Here I beheld the whole commodiously. Finding that the troops would not attack them, except in words and menaces, they grew more violent, and furiously attempted to beat the doors in pieces with iron crows; placing ladders to the windows. In about a quarter of an hour, which gave time for the assembled magistrates to escape by a back door, they burst all open, and entered like a torrent with a universal shout of the spectators. From that minute a shower of casements, sashes, shutters, chairs, tables, sophas, books, papers, pictures, etc., rained incessantly from all the windows of the house, which is 70 or 80 feet long, and which was then succeeded by tiles, skirting boards, bannisters, framework, and every part of the building that force could detach. The troops, both horse and foot, were quiet spectators. They were at first too few to interpose, and, when they became more numerous, the mischief was too far advanced to admit of any other conduct than guarding every avenue around, permitting none to go to the scene of action, but letting everyone that pleased retire with his plunder; guards being at the same time placed at the doors of the churches, and all public buildings. I was for two hours a spectator at different places of the scene, secure myself from the falling furniture, but near enough to see a fine lad of about fourteen crushed to death by something as he was handing plunder to a woman, I suppose his mother, from the horror that was pictured in her countenance. I remarked several common soldiers, with their white cockades, among the plunderers, and instigating the mob even in sight of the officers of the detachment. There were amongst them people so decently dressed, that I regarded them with no small surprise: – they destroyed all the public archives; the streets for some way around strewed with papers. This has been a wanton mischief, for it will be the ruin of many families unconnected with the magistrates.

[July] 22nd. To Schelestadt. At Strasbourg, and the country I passed, the lower ranks of women wear their hair in a *toupée* in front, and behind braided into a circular plait, three inches thick, and most curiously contrived to convince one that they rarely pass a comb through it. I could not but picture them as the *nidus* of living colonies, that never approached me (they are not burdened with too much beauty,) but I scratched my head from sensations of imaginary itching. The moment you are out of a great town all in this country is German;[6] the inns have one common large room, many tables and cloths ready spread, where every company dines; gentry at some, and the poor at others. Cookery also German; *Schnitz* is a dish of bacon and fried pears; has the appearance of an infamous mess;[7] but I was surprised, on tasting, to find it better than passable. . . .

[July] 24th. To Isenheim, by Colmar. . . . The news at the *table d'hôte* at Colmar curious, that the Queen had a plot,[8] nearly on the point of execution, to blow up the National Assembly by a mine, and to march the army instantly to massacre all Paris. A French officer present presumed but to doubt of the truth of it, and was immediately overpowered with numbers of tongues. A deputy had written the news: they had seen the letter, and not a hesitation could be admitted: I strenuously contended, that it was folly and nonsense, a mere invention to render persons odious who, for what I knew, might deserve to be so, but certainly not by such means; if the angel Gabriel had descended and taken a chair at table to convince them, it would not have shaken their faith. Thus it is in revolutions, one rascal writes, and an hundred thousand fools believe – 25 miles.

12. *The Example of France, A Warning to Britain* (1793),

pp. 2–4, 26–34

France, A Warning made almost as strong an impression when it appeared on 26 February 1793 as Young's *Travels* had made the previous year, for in his new pamphlet Young powerfully demonstrated that the Revolution had gone too far for middle-class English liberals to support it. He places himself firmly in the position of the landowner and farmer, and shows that in the second half of 1792 the interests of this class in France were subordinated to the interests of the peasants and of the Parisian artisans, or *sans-culottes*. Burke wrote to congratulate him on the pamphlet;[9] his enthusiasm was justified, for Young's argument and manner were well calculated to rally the propertied classes in the first month of the war with France, after an autumn in which Paine seemed to have democratised politics in England. Shortly after the appearance of *France, A Warning*, Pitt created a Board of Agriculture and appointed Young secretary at £400 a year. Accusations were made, predictably, that Young had been suborned, or at least rewarded. But surely *France, A Warning* shows Young speaking sincerely for his kind, who on the whole ceased to view the new French government benevolently once its activities threatened property.

Having resided a good deal in France during the progress of the Revolution, to which I was, for some time, a warm friend; having passed through every province of the kingdom; examined all her principal manufactures; gained much instruction relative to the state of her commerce, and attended minutely to the situation of her people, it was natural on my return to England to consult with attention the legislative acts of the new government, and to procure by correspondence and conversation, with persons on whom I could depend, such intelligence as was necessary to enable me to satisfy my curiosity concerning the result of the most singular Revolution recorded in the annals of mankind. . . .

But in attempting to give expressions inadequate to the indignation every one must feel at the horrible events now passing in France, I am sensible that I may be reproached with changing my politics, my "principles," as it has been expressed. – My principles I certainly have not changed, because if there is one principle more predominant than another in my politics, it is the *principle of change*. I have been too long a farmer to be governed by anything but events; I have a constitutional abhorrence of theory, of all trust in abstract reasoning; and consequently a reliance merely on experience, in other words, on events, the only principle worthy of an experimenter. Thus founded on sure ground, it shall be my business in the ensuing pages, to bring to the reader's notice some facts proper to explain.

FIRST, the real state of France: and

SECOND, the causes of her evils; and I shall then apply her example to the landed, monied, commercial, and labouring interests of these kingdoms. . . .

It can hardly be doubted but that robbery, even of land itself, must spread [to] all the kingdom when the committee of general security could thus report to the Convention: – *The national resources may be augmented by imposing contributions upon persons of fortune*, personnes aisees *and the obstinate who wait tranquilly at home the event of the Revolution.*[10] Contributions imposed on persons for two reasons; first, for the crime of being men of fortune; and, secondly, for remaining in tranquillity! With such a legislation can property be respected?

With such a principle, recognized in the Convention, we need not ask how taxes are levied. The poor and small proprietors of a few acres, who every where form the majority of each municipality, escape all taxation, but are vigilant in forcing those of more considerable property to pay to the last farthing; and as all taxes are assessed and levied by the parochial vote, at assemblies, to which *all* resort, the men without property order everything at will, and have various ways, much more effective, for the division of property than a direct agrarian would be.

Let the farmers of this kingdom represent to themselves a picture of what their situation would be, if their labourers, their servants, and the paupers whom they support by poors-rates, were all armed, and, in some measure, regimented, and in possession of the vestry, voting not only the money to be raised by rates, but the division of it among themselves; decreeing what the price of all the farmer's products should be; what wages should be paid to servants, and what pay to labourers. Under such a system of government I beg to ask, what security would remain for a single shilling in the pockets of those who are at present in a state of ease and affluence? . . .

Before we quit this subject of the security of property at present in France, let us examine shortly the case of that most interesting portion of property, the crop in the hands of the farmer: we know well in England, from the conviction of long experience, that if this species of property is not sacred, all the classes of the society instantly suffer; it is a vital wound that affects the whole system.

The late crop in that kingdom is said to be plentiful; but natural plenty, under a government of anarchy, avails little; the mob prohibiting the free transport of corn, the immediate consequence was so high a price in many districts, that the people found it more convenient to *seize* the corn than to *pay* for it: this, of course, added every where to the mischief; for the farmers were not ready to carry their products into the jaws of plunder. These distractions – these blessings of a government that had the power of converting even good crops into the means of famine, drew from the minister of the home department threats even of violence; he wrote to a variety of cities, from all which papers it would be too tedious to give extracts. He thus expresses himself to Tours: "The municipalities ought to use all possible means of persuasion with the farmers, for engaging them to supply the markets; for I must tell you, that if the possessors of corn resist these *paternal* invitations, MEANS OF EXTREMITY must be used against them: *on sera bien contraint d'employer envers eux les moyens extremes.*"[11] It is worth the attention of English farmers, to reflect well on the nature of this case: their brethren in France, content with a moderate and fair price for their corn, carry it freely to market; the operations of the people raise this price; and then, to revenge the result of their own violence, they plunder. Such a conduct is sure to create, at least, apprehensions of famine; and to obviate it, the minister does not threaten the mob, from whom all the mischief arises, but the FARMERS; he threatens them with EXTREMITIES, as a punishment for having been plundered by the rabble – by the *nation*. . . .

The same minister writes to the Convention, Oct. 15. – "I am informed that the overseers of the military subsistences do not cease to fly through the country, and to force, with arms in their hands, the farmers to furnish their commodities. Such practices destroy every measure of order, and infinitely impede the free circulation of corn. I cannot dissemble with the Convention, that this conduct of the military contractors tends to spread disorder every where, and that if they continue to take by force, or at their own price, provision from the farmers, it will be impossible to insure the supply of Paris."[12]

Now this, if possible, exceeds every thing the Jacobin administration, acting on the ideas of Jacobin liberty, could devise to shew their perfect contempt of the whole farming race. He states the glaring magnitude of the evil to the Convention; and what is his conclusion? Why he tells them, that if such things are allowed, it will *be impossible to supply Paris!!* . . .

In all these and a thousand and other instances, we see the living and effective consequences of Paine's doctrines; he expatiated on the luxury of great estates, and recommended their seizure; French practice realized the doctrine, and doubtless there were French farmers, who rejoiced at the spectacle of all the great properties of the kingdom being levelled by the nation; they did not however foresee, that it would be their own turn next; that the principle of equality being once abroad, would infallibly level ALL property; and would give to the beggar, without a loaf, but with a pike on his shoulder, the means of levelling the enormous inequality between his own wallet without a kernel, and the well-stored grainery of a warm farmer. Let ours, therefore, never forget, that the same principle which attacks a property of 40,000 l. a year, because it is too large relatively to other properties, attacks also a farm of 200 l. a year, for the same reason; nay, of 50 l. a year, because that also is large, when compared with the property of those who have little. And let us all be well persuaded, that the fearful events at present passing in France, with a celerity of mischief that surpasses equally all that history has to offer, or fancy to conceive, afford a spectacle interesting to every man who possesses PROPERTY; and to none more than to farmers. The quarrel now raging in that once flourishing kingdom, is not between liberty and tyranny, or between protecting and oppressive systems of government; it is, on the contrary, collected to a single point, – it is alone a question of property; it is a trial at arms, whether those who have *nothing* shall not seize and possess the property of those who have *something*.

Tom Paine

(1737–1809)

13. *The Rights of Man,*
Part I (Feb. 1791), Part II (Feb. 1792),

from Part II, chs. 3 and 5, pp. 19–22, 36–9, 89–92, 100–11, 122–30

Born at Thetford, Norfolk, the son of a Quaker staymaker and small farmer, Paine worked in his youth as a staymaker, privateer, and exciseman. Dismissed from the latter occupation after he had drawn up an account of excisemen's grievances, he sailed for America in 1774. His career has much in common with that of Cobbett, the other great democratic polemicist of the period. Both men rose from the ranks and served their literary apprenticeship in America. There Noah Webster, compiler of the first American dictionary, was arriving at a simpler system of spelling, and formulating a critique of English grammarians like Johnson, with their literariness and classicism, their contempt for usage and the spoken tongue.[1] Americans in effect needed a discourse free of the hierarchical assumptions built into English educational tradition, with its respect for authority and for expensively acquired qualities like stylishness and correctness. Paine, who rose to fame during the American Revolution with his pamphlet *Common Sense* (1776), was the first major prose writer to make practical use of his age's critique of linguistic élitism.

Like Godwin, his only real rival as an antagonist of Burke, Paine responds intuitively to the primitive appeal of the *Reflections*, the level at which Burke's book turns inarticulate fears and insecurities into a case for tradition, authority, the divine right of Louis XVI and Marie Antoinette. Paine reacts by emphasising the healthy individual's independence. His own personality, apparently naively presented in his work, is that of a superior journeyman, confident in his own skill and effectiveness, impatient with others less useful than himself. He sees himself as a successful man, but self-employed, in a smaller way of business than that of the entrepreneurs whose case was made in Smith's *Wealth of Nations*. Instead of singing the praises of unfettered competition, he sees the benefit for ordinary people of a spirit of co-operation, and of state intervention on behalf of the weak, the sick, the very old or very young. Paine outstrips Burke's appeal to the feelings with a more practical appeal of his own, when he proposes the redistribution of the national income from taxation in favour of the poor, and thus anticipates the benevolent social democracy of the twentieth century.

Paine's tactics with the traditionalist case are to give it short shrift. He depicts the ruling orders without reverence, as incompetents, parasites, pilferers, and confidence tricksters. 'What is called monarchy, always appears to me a silly, contemptible thing' (see p. 110). Burke's pompous accounts of the past are frauds; but there is no need to reply with a rigmarole (as the Dissenters were wont to do) about rights, contracts and Revolution settlements. Paine scoffs at the sacred topics of conservatism – monarchy, aristocracy, church, constitution – much as Godwin was about to do, but less theoretically, indeed with brutal directness. For Paine, the questions to ask of kings and aristocracies are: What use are they? Do their typical actions (like warmongering) help me or only help them?

The tone conveys the message even in Part I, but it is only in Part II that the vision of what an egalitarian society might be like is worked out in telling detail. Part I, priced three shillings, sold fifty thousand copies in 1791, already considerably more than the sales of Burke's *Reflections*. Part I was reprinted when Part II was published in 1792, both selling at six pence.[2] E. P. Thompson believes that Parts I and II together must have sold two hundred thousand copies between 1791 and 1793. Altick considers this figure too high, but agrees that Part II sold more than Part I, which certainly puts the joint sale above one hundred thousand.[3] Paine himself estimated something far more ambitious – in 1809, the year of his death, he believed that his sales had reached one and a half million, which, even if an exaggeration, gives some notion of its penetrative power. The biographies and autobiographies of early-nineteenth-century radicals, including Cobbett and Richard Carlile, indicate how many working men must have come to political consciousness by reading Paine.[4] The fears of the Attorney-General at his trial, of members of the Administration and of the upper orders throughout the 1790s, were not in this sense without foundation.

In spite of the undeniable historical importance of Paine, he has only recently been taken seriously as a master of prose.[5] He combines, to a fascinating degree, a plainness of diction appropriate to his attack on mystique, with the symmetry and balance of the rhythms of earlier eighteenth-century verse and prose. A paragraph on kingship illustrates this range, and his evident control over it:

> When extraordinary power and extraordinary pay are allotted to any individual in a government, he becomes the center round which every kind of corruption generates and forms. Give to any man a million a year, and add thereto the power of creating and disposing of places, at the expence of a country, and the liberties of that country are no longer secure. What is called the splendor of a throne is no other than the corruption of the state. It is made up of a band of parasites, living in luxurious indolence, out of the public taxes.[6]

The first three sentences use antithesis, tersely compressed in the third into epigram. The effect is dignified, and it makes the slangy informality of the next sentence – 'a band of parasites' – doubly startling by contrast.

At other points, Paine can seem wholly anti-literary and functional, with his abrupt changes, and his borrowed tables of figures. Yet even his loose ends and brevities (some of which would not be noted in a book being read aloud) should be considered as legitimate features of a style designed to hold the attention, and secure the trust, of an audience which was accustomed to being governed but not to being written for.

Chapter 3
Of the Old and New Systems of Government

Nothing can appear more contradictory than the principles on which the old governments began, and the condition to which society, civilization, and commerce, are capable of carrying mankind. Government on the old system, is an assumption of power, for the aggrandisement of itself; on the new, a delegation of power, for the common benefit of society. The former supports itself by keeping up a system of war; the latter promotes a system of peace, as the true means of enriching a nation. The one encourages national prejudices; the other promotes universal society, as the means of universal commerce. The one measures its prosperity, by the quantity of revenue it extorts; the other proves its excellence, by the small quantity of taxes it requires.

Mr Burke has talked of old and new whigs. If he can amuse himself with childish names and distinctions, I shall not interupt his pleasure. It is not to him, but to the Abbé Sieyès,[7] that I address this chapter. I am already engaged to the latter gentleman, to discuss the subject of monarchical government; and as it naturally occurs in comparing the old and new systems, I make this the opportunity of presenting to him my observations. I shall occasionally take Mr Burke in my way.

Though it might be proved that the system of government now called the NEW, is the most ancient in principle of all that have existed, being founded on the original inherent Rights of Man: yet, as tyranny and the sword have suspended the exercise of those rights for many centuries past, it serves better the purpose of distinction to call it the *new*, than to claim the right of calling it the old.

The first general distinction between those two systems, is, that the one now called the old is *hereditary*, either in whole or in part; and the new is entirely *representative*. It rejects all hereditary government:

First, As being an imposition on mankind.

Secondly, As inadequate to the purposes for which government is necessary.

With respect to the first of these heads – It cannot be proved by what right hereditary government could begin: neither does there exist within the compass of mortal power, a right to establish it. Man has no authority over posterity in matters of personal right; and therefore, no man, or body of men, had, or can have, a right to set up hereditary government. Were even ourselves to come again into existence, instead of being succeeded by posterity, we have not now the right of taking from ourselves the rights which would then be ours. On what ground, then, do we pretend to take them from others?

All hereditary government is in its nature tyranny. An heritable crown, or an heritable throne, or by what other fanciful name such things may be called, have no other significant explanation than that mankind are heritable property. To inherit a government, is to inherit the people, as if they were flocks and herds.

With respect to the second head, that of being inadequate to the purposes for which government is necessary, we have only to consider what government essentially is, and compare it with the circumstances to which hereditary succession is subject.

Government ought to be a thing always in full maturity. It ought to be so constructed as to be superior to all the accidents to which individual man is subject; and therefore, hereditary succession, by being *subject to them all*, is the most irregular and imperfect of all the systems of government.

We have heard the *Rights of Man* called a *levelling* system; but the only system to which the word *levelling* is truly applicable is the hereditary monarchical system. It is a system of *mental levelling*. . . . Kings succeed each other, not as rationals, but as animals. It signifies not what their mental or moral characters are. . . .

Whether I have too little sense to see, or too much to be imposed upon; whether I have too much or too little pride, or of anything else, I leave out of the question; but certain it is, that what is called monarchy, always appears to me a silly, contemptible thing. I compare it to something kept behind a curtain, about which there is a great deal of bustle and fuss, and a wonderful air of seeming solemnity; but when, by any accident, the curtain happens to be open, and the company see what it is, they burst into laughter.

In the representative system of government, nothing of this can happen. Like the nation itself, it possesses a perpetual stamina, as well of body as of mind, and presents itself on the open theatre of the world in a fair and manly manner. Whatever are its excellences or its defects, they are visible to all. It exists not by fraud and mystery; it deals not in cant and sophistry; but inspires a language, that, passing from heart to heart, is felt and understood.

We must shut our eyes against reason, we must basely degrade our understanding, not to see the folly of what is called monarchy. Nature is orderly in all her works; but this is a mode of government that counteracts nature. It turns the progress of the human faculties upside down. It subjects age to be governed by children, and wisdom by folly.

On the contrary, the representative system is always parallel with the order and immutable laws of nature, and meets the reason of man in every part. For example:

In the American federal government, more power is delegated to the President of the United States, than to any other individual member of congress.[8] He cannot, therefore, be elected to this office under the age of thirty-five years. By this time the judgement of man becomes matured, and he has lived long enough to be acquainted with men and things, and the country with him. . . .

That monarchy is all a bubble, a mere court artifice to procure money, is evident, (at least to me), in every character in which it can be viewed. It would be impossible, on the rational system of representative government, to make out a bill of expenses to such an enormous amount as this deception admits. Government is not of itself a very chargeable institution. The whole expense of the federal government of America, founded, as I have already said, on the system of representation, and extending over a country nearly ten times as large as England, is but six hundred thousand dollars, or one hundred and thirty-five thousand pounds sterling.

I presume, that no man in his sober senses, will compare the character of any of the kings of Europe with that of General Washington. Yet, in France, and also in England, the expence of the civil list only, for the support of one man, is eight times greater than the whole expence of the federal government in America. To assign a reason for this, appears almost impossible. The generality of people in America, especially the poor, are more able to pay taxes, than the generality of people either in France or England.

But the case is, that the representative system diffuses such a body of knowledge throughout a nation, on the subject of government, as to explode ignorance and preclude imposition. The craft of courts cannot be acted on that ground. There is no place for mystery; nowhere for it to begin. Those who are not in the representation, know as much of the nature of business as those who are. An affectation of mysterious importance would there be scouted. Nations can have no secrets; and the secrets of courts, like those of individuals, are always their defects.

In the representative system, the reason for everything must publicly appear. Every man is a proprietor in government, and considers it a necessary part of his business to understand. It concerns his interest,

~~because it affects~~ his property. He examines the cost, and compares it with the advantages; and above all, he does not adopt the slavish custom of following what in other governments are called LEADERS.

It can only be by blinding the understanding of man, and making him believe that government is some wonderful mysterious thing, that excessive revenues are obtained. Monarchy is well calculated to ensure this end. It is the popery of government; a thing kept up to amuse the ignorant, and quiet them into taxes.

The government of a free country, properly speaking, is not in the persons, but in the laws. The enacting of those requires no great expence; and when they are administered, the whole of civil government is performed – the rest is all court contrivance.

Chapter 5
WAYS and MEANS of improving the condition of Europe, interspersed with Miscellaneous Observations.

. . . . No question has arisen within the records of history that pressed with the importance of the present. It is not whether this or that party shall be in or not, or whig or tory, or high or low shall prevail; but whether man shall inherit his rights, and universal civilization take place? Whether the fruits of his labours shall be enjoyed by himself, or consumed by the profligacy of governments? Whether robbery shall be banished from courts, and wretchedness from countries?

When, in countries that are called civilized, we see age going to the workhouse and youth to the gallows, something must be wrong in the system of government. . . .

Civil government does not consist in executions; but in making that provision for the instruction of youth, and the support of age, as to exclude, as much as possible, profligacy from the one, and despair from the other. Instead of this, the resources of a country are lavished upon kings, upon courts, upon hirelings, impostors, and prostitutes; and even the poor themselves, with all their wants upon them, are compelled to support the fraud that oppresses them.

Why is it, that scarcely any are executed but the poor? The fact is a proof, among other things, of a wretchedness in their condition. Bred up without morals, and cast upon the world without a prospect, they are the exposed sacrifice of vice and legal barbarity. The millions that are superfluously wasted upon governments, are more than sufficient to reform those evils, and to benefit the condition of every man in a nation, not included within the purlieus of a court. This I hope to make appear in the progress of this work.

13. *The Rights of Man*

It is the nature of compassion to associate with misfortune. In taking up this subject I seek no recompence – I fear no consequence. Fortified with that proud integrity, that disdains to triumph or to yield, I will advocate the Rights of Man.

It is to my advantage that I have served an apprenticeship to life. I know the value of moral instruction, and I have seen the danger of the contrary.

At an early period, little more than sixteen years of age, raw and adventurous, and heated with the false heroism of a master[9] who had served in a man of war, I began the carver of my own fortune, and entered on board the Terrible privateer, Capt. Death. From this adventure I was happily prevented by the affectionate and moral remonstrance of a good father, who, from his own habits of life, being of the Quaker profession, must begin to look upon me as lost. But the impression, much as it effected at the time, began to wear away, and I entered afterwards in the King of Prussia privateer, Capt. Mendez, and went with her to sea. Yet, from such a beginning, and with all the inconvenience of early life against me, I am proud to say, that with a perseverence undismayed by difficulties, a disinterestedness that compelled respect, I have not only contributed to raise a new empire in the world, founded on a new system of government, but I have arrived at an eminence in political literature, the most difficult of all lines to succeed and excel in, which aristocracy, with all its aids, has not been able to reach or to rival.

Knowing my own heart, and feeling myself, as I now do, superior to all the skirmish of party, the inveteracy of interested or mistaken opponents, I answer not to falsehood or abuse, but proceed to the defects of the English government.[10] . . .

What is called the House of Peers, is constituted on a ground very similar to that, against which there is a law in other cases. It amounts to a combination of persons in one common interest. No reason can be given, why an house of legislation should be composed entirely of men whose occupation consists in letting landed property, than why it should be composed of those who hire, or of brewers, or bakers, or any other separate class of men.

Mr Burke calls this house, '*the great ground and pillar of security to the landed interest*.' Let us examine this idea.

What pillar of security does the landed interest require more than any other interest in the state, or what right has it to a distinct and separate representation from the general interest of a nation? The only use to be made of this power, (and which it has always made,) is to ward off taxes from itself, and throw the burden upon such articles of consumption by which itself would be least affected.

That this has been the consequence, (and will always be the consequence of constructing governments on combinations,) is evident with respect to England, from the history of its taxes.

Notwithstanding taxes have encreased and multiplied upon every article of common consumption, the land-tax, which more particularly affects this 'pillar,' has diminished. In 1788, the amount of the land-tax was £1,950,000, which is half a million less than it produced almost a hundred years ago,[11] notwithstanding the rentals are in many instances doubled since that period.

Before the coming of the Hanoverians, the taxes were divided in nearly equal portions between the land and articles of consumption, the land bearing rather the largest share: but since that æra, nearly thirteen millions annually of new taxes have been thrown upon consumption. The consequence of which has been a constant encrease in the number and wretchedness of the poor, and in the amount of the poor-rates.

This is one of the consequences resulting from an house of legislation, composed on the ground of a combination of common interest; for whatever their separate politics as to parties may be, in this they are united. Whether a combination acts to raise the price of any article for sale, or the rate of wages; or whether it acts to throw taxes from itself upon another class of the community, the principle and the effect are the same; and if the one be illegal, it will be difficult to show that the other ought to exist.

It is no use to say that taxes are first proposed in the house of commons; for as the other house has always a negative, it can always defend itself; and it would be ridiculous to suppose that its acquiescence in the measures to be proposed were not understood beforehand. Besides which, it has obtained so much influence by borough-traffic, and so many of its relations and connexions are distributed on both sides of the commons, as to give it, besides an absolute negative in one house, a preponderancy in the other, in all matters of common concern.

It is difficult to discover what is meant by the *landed interest*, if it does not mean a combination of aristocratical land-holders, opposing their own pecuniary interest to that of the farmer, and every branch of trade, commerce, and manufacture. In all other respects it is the only interest that needs no partial protection. It enjoys the general protection of the world. Every individual, high or low, is interested in the fruits of the earth; men, women, and children, of all ages and degrees, will turn out to assist the farmer, rather than a harvest should not be got in; and they will not act thus by any other property. It is the only one for which the common prayer of mankind is put up, and the only one that can never fail from the want of means. It is the interest, not of the policy, but of the existence of man, and when it ceases, he must cease to be.

No other interest in a nation stands on the same united support. Commerce, manufactures, arts, sciences, and everything else, compared with this, are supported but in parts. Their prosperity or their decay has not the same universal influence. When the valleys laugh and sing, it is not the farmer only, but all creation that rejoice. It is a prosperity that excludes all envy; and this cannot be said of anything else.

Why then does Mr Burke talk of his house of peers, as the pillar of the landed interest? Were that pillar to sink into the earth, the same landed property would continue, and the same ploughing, sowing, and reaping would go on. The aristocracy are not the farmers who work the land, and raise the produce, but are the mere consumers of the rent; and when compared with the active world are the drones, a seraglio of males, who neither collect the honey nor form the hive, but exist only for lazy enjoyment. . . .

These are but a part of the mischiefs flowing from the wretched scheme of an house of peers.

As a combination, it can always throw a considerable portion of taxes from itself; and as an hereditary house, accountable to nobody, it resembles a rotten borough, whose consent is to be courted by interest. There are but few of its members who are not in some mode or other participators, or disposers of the public money. One turns a candle-holder, or a lord in waiting; another a lord of the bed-chamber, a groom of the stole, or any insignificant nominal office, to which a salary is annexed, paid out of the public taxes, and which avoids the direct appearance of corruption. Such situations are derogatory to the character of man; and where they can be submitted to, honour cannot reside.

To all these are to be added the numerous dependants, the long list of younger branches and distant relations, who are to be provided for at the public expence: in short, were an estimation to be made of the charge of aristocracy to a nation, it will be found nearly equal to that of supporting the poor. The Duke of Richmond alone (and there are cases similar to his) takes away as much for himself as would maintain two thousand poor and aged persons. Is it, then, any wonder, that under such a system of government, taxes and rates have multiplied to their present extent? . . .

Mr Burke, in speaking of the aristocratical law of primogeniture, says, 'it is the standing law of our landed inheritance; and which, without question, has a tendency, and I think,' continues he, 'a happy tendency, to preserve a character of weight and consequence.'

Mr Burke may call this law what he pleases, but humanity and impartial reflection will denounce it a law of brutal injustice. . . . It is an attaint upon character; a sort of privateering of family property. . . . Speaking for myself, my parents were not able to give me a shilling, beyond what they gave me in education; and to do this they distressed themselves: yet, I possess more of what is called consequence in the world, than anyone in Mr Burke's catalogue of aristocrats.

Having thus glanced at some of the defects of the two houses of parliament, I proceed to what is called the crown upon which I shall be very concise.

It signifies a nominal office of a million sterling a year, the business of which consists in receiving the money. Whether the person be wise or foolish, sane or insane, a native or a foreigner, matters not. Every ministry acts upon the same idea that Mr Burke writes, namely, that the people must be hood-winked, and held in superstitious ignorance by some bugbear or other; and what is called the crown answers this purpose, and therefore it answers all the purposes to be expected from it. This is more than can be said of the other two branches.

The hazard to which this office is exposed in all countries, is not from anything that can happen to the man, but from what may happen to the nation – the danger of its coming to its senses.[12]

It has been customary to call the crown the executive power, and the custom is continued, though the reason has ceased.

It was called the *executive*, because the person whom it signified used, formerly, to sit in the character of a judge, in administering or executing the laws. The tribunals were then a part of the court. The power, therefore, which is now called the judicial, is what was called the executive; and, consequently, one or other of the terms is redundant, and one of the offices useless. When we speak of the crown now, it means nothing; it signifies neither a judge nor a general: besides which it is the laws that govern, and not the man. The old terms are kept up, to give an appearance of consequence to empty forms; and the only effect they have is that of encreasing expenses.

Before I proceed to the means of rendering governments more conducive to the general happiness of mankind than they are at present, it will not be improper to take a review of the progress of taxation in England.

It is a general idea, that when taxes are once laid on, they are never taken off. However true this may have been of late, it was not always so. Either, therefore, the people of former times were more watchful over government than those of the present, or government was administered with less extravagance.

It is now seven hundred years since the Norman conquest, and the establishment of what is called the crown. Taking this portion of time in seven separate periods of one hundred years each, the amount of the annual taxes, at each period, will be as follows: –

Annual amount of taxes levied by William the Conqueror,
   beginning in the year 1066   —   £400,000
Annual amount of taxes at one hundred years from the
   conquest, (1166)   —   200,000
Annual amount of taxes at two hundred years from the
   conquest, (1266)   —   150,000
Annual amount of taxes at three hundred years from the
   conquest, (1366)   —   130,000
Annual amount of taxes at four hundred years from the
   conquest, (1466)   —   100,000

These statements, and those which follow, are taken from Sir John Sinclair's History of the Revenue; by which it appears, that taxes continued decreasing for four hundred years, at the expiration of which time they were reduced three-fourths, viz. from four hundred thousand pounds to one hundred thousand. The people of England of the present day, have a traditionary and historical idea of the bravery of their ancestors; but whatever their virtues or their vices might have been, they certainly were a people who would not be imposed upon, and who kept government in awe as to taxation, if not as to principle. Though they were not able to expel the monarchical usurpation, they restricted it to a republican oeconomy of taxes.

Let us now review the remaining three hundred years.

Annual amount of taxes at five hundred years from the
   conquest, (1566)   —   £500,000
Annual amount of taxes at six hundred years from the
   conquest, (1666)   —   1,800,000
Annual amount of taxes at the present time, (1791)   —   17,000,000

The difference between the first four hundred years and the last three, is so astonishing, as to warrant an opinion, that the national character of the English has changed. It would have been impossible to have dragooned the former English, into the excess of taxation that now exists; and when it is considered that the pay of the army, the navy, and of all the revenue officers, is the same now as it was above a hundred years ago, when the taxes were not above a tenth part of what they are at present, it appears impossible to account for the enormous encrease in expenditure, on any other ground, than extravagance, corruption, and intrigue.[13] . . .

Taking, therefore, one million and an half as a sufficient peace establishment for all the honest purposes of government, which is three hundred thousand pounds more than the peace establishment in the profligate and prodigal times of Charles the Second, (notwithstanding, as has been already observed, the pay and salaries of the army, navy, and revenue officers, continue the same as at that period), there will remain a surplus of upwards of six millions out of the present current expences. The question then will be, how to dispose of this surplus. . . .

In the first place, then, the poor-rates are a direct tax which every housekeeper feels, and who knows also, to a farthing, the sum which he pays. The national amount of the whole of the poor-rates is not positively known, but can be procured. Sir John Sinclair, in his History of the Revenue, has stated it at £2,100,587. A considerable part of which is expended in litigations, in which the poor, instead of being relieved, are tormented. The expence, however, is the same to the parish from whatever cause it arises.

In Birmingham, the amount of the poor-rates is fourteen thousand pounds a year. This, though a large sum, is moderate, compared with the population. Birmingham is said to contain seventy thousand souls, and on a proportion of seventy thousand to fourteen thousand pounds poor-rates, the national amount of poor rates, taking the population of England at seven millions, would be but one million four hundred thousand pounds. It is, therefore, most probable, that the population of Birmingham is over-rated. Fourteen thousand pounds is the proportion upon fifty thousand souls, taking two millions of poor-rates as the national amount.

Be it, however, what it may, it is no other than the consequence of the excessive burden of taxes, for, at the time when the taxes were very low, the poor were able to maintain themselves; and there were no poor-rates.[14] In the present state of things, a labouring man, with a wife and two or three children, does not pay less than between seven and eight pounds a year in taxes. He is not sensible of this, because it is disguised to him in the articles which he buys, and he thinks only of their dearness; but as the taxes take from him, at least, a fourth part of his yearly earnings, he is consequently disabled from providing for a family, especially if himself, or any of them, are afflicted with sickness.

The first step, therefore, of practical relief, would be to abolish the poor rates entirely, and in lieu thereof, to make a remission of taxes to the poor of double the amount of the present poor-rates, viz. four millions annually out of the surplus taxes. By this measure, the poor will be benefited two millions, and the housekeepers two millions. This alone would be equal to a reduction of one hundred and twenty millions of the national debt, and consequently equal to the whole expence of the American war.

It will then remain to be considered, which is the most effectual mode of distributing this remission of four millions.

It is easily seen, that the poor are generally composed of large families of children, and old people past their labour. If these two classes are provided for, the remedy will so far reach to the full extent of the case, that what remains will be incidental and, in a great measure, fall within the compass of benefit clubs, which, though of humble invention, merit to be ranked among the best of modern institutions.

Admitting England to contain seven millions of souls; if one-fifth thereof are of that class of poor which need support, the number will be one million four hundred thousand. Of this number, one hundred and forty thousand will be aged poor, as will be hereafter shown, and for which a distinct provision will be proposed.

There will then remain one million two hundred and sixty thousand, which, at five souls to each family, amount to two hundred and fifty-two thousand families, rendered poor from the expence of children and the weight of taxes. . . .

Allowing five children (under fourteen years) to every two families,

The number of children will be —	630,000
The number of parents were they all living, would be —	504,000

It is certain, that if the children are provided for, the parents are relieved of consequence, because it is from the expence of bringing up children that their poverty arises.

Having thus ascertained the greatest number that can be supposed to need support on account of young families, I proceed to the mode of relief or distribution, which is,

To pay as a remission of taxes to every poor family, out of the surplus taxes, and in room of poor-rates, four pounds a year for every child under fourteen years of age; enjoining the parents of such children to send them to school, to learn reading, writing, and common arithmetic; the ministers of every parish, of every denomination, to certify jointly to an office, for that purpose, that this duty is performed.

The amount of this expence will be,
For six hundred and thirty thousand children,
at four pounds *per ann.* each,   — £2,520,000

By adopting this method, not only the poverty of the parents will be relieved, but ignorance will be banished from the rising generation, and the number of poor will hereafter become less, because their abilities, by the aid of education, will be greater. Many a youth, with good natural genius, who is apprenticed to a mechanical trade, such as a carpenter, joiner, millwright, shipwright, blacksmith, &c. is prevented getting forward the whole of his life, from the want of a little common education when a boy.

I now proceed to the case of the aged.

I divide age into two classes. First, the approach of age beginning at fifty. Secondly, old age commencing at sixty.

At fifty, though the mental faculties of man are in full vigour, and his judgement better than at any preceding date, the bodily powers for laborious life are on the decline. He cannot bear the same quantity of fatigue as at an earlier period. He begins to earn less, and is less capable of enduring wind and weather; and in those more retired employments where much sight is required, he fails apace, and sees himself, like an old horse, beginning to be turned adrift.

At sixty his labour ought to be over, at least from direct necessity. It is painful to see old age working itself to death, in what are called civilized countries, for daily bread.

To form some judgement of the number of those above fifty years of age, I have several times counted the persons I met in the streets of London, men, women, and children, and have generally found that the average is about one in sixteen or seventeen. If it be said that aged persons do not come much in the streets, so neither do infants; and a great proportion of grown children are in school, and in work-shops as apprentices. Taking then sixteen for a divisor, the whole number of persons in England, of fifty years and upwards of both sexes, rich and poor, will be four hundred and twenty thousand.

The persons to be provided for out of this gross number will be, husbandmen, common labourers, journeymen of every trade and their wives, sailors, and disbanded soldiers, worn out servants of both sexes, and poor widows.

There will be also a considerable number of middling tradesmen, who having lived decently in the former part of life, begin, as age approaches, to lose their business, and at last fall to decay.

Besides these, there will be constantly thrown off from the revolutions of that wheel, which no man can stop, nor regulate, a number from every class of life connected with commerce and adventure. . . .

Having thus ascertained the probable proportion of the number of aged persons, I proceed to the mode of rendering their condition comfortable, which is,

To pay to every such person of the age of fifty years, and until he shall arrive at the age of sixty, the sum of six pounds *per ann.* out of the surplus taxes; and ten pounds *per ann.* during life after the age of sixty. The expence of which will be,

Seventy thousand persons at £6 *per ann.*		420,000
Seventy thousand ditto at £10 *per ann.*		700,000
		£1,120,000

This support, as already remarked, is not of the nature of a charity, but of a right. Every person in England, male and female, pays on an average in taxes, two pounds eight shillings and sixpence *per ann.* from the day of his (or her) birth; and, if the expence of collection be added, he pays two pounds eleven shillings and sixpence; consequently, at the end of fifty years he has paid one hundred and twenty-eight pounds fifteen shillings; and at sixty, one hundred and fifty-four pounds ten shillings. Converting, therefore, his (or her) individual tax into a tontine,[a] the money he shall receive after fifty years, is but little more than the legal interest of the net money he has paid; the rest is made up from those whose circumstances do not require them to draw such support, and the capital in both cases defrays the expences of government. It is on this ground that I have extended the probable claims to one third of the number of aged persons in the nation. – Is it then better that the lives of one hundred and forty thousand aged persons be rendered comfortable, or that a million a year of public money be expended on any one individual, and him often of the most worthless or insignificant character? Let reason and justice, let honour and humanity, let even hypocrisy, sycophancy and Mr Burke, let George, let Louis, Leopold, Frederic, Catharine, Cornwallis, or Tippoo Saib, answer the question.[15]

---

[a] A financial scheme whereby the subscribers to a common fund receive an annuity during their lives, which increases as their number is diminished by death.

14. *The Age of Reason; being an Investigation of True and Fabulous Theology,* Part I (Paris, 1794),

pp. 1–7

Paine's assault upon religion, though perhaps less original than his *Rights of Man*, has the same rhetorical power. Organised Christianity was a prime target of iconoclasts in the France of Voltaire and the *philosophes*. The classic performance on the subject in English was David Hume's essay, 'Of Miracles', with its urbane modern-minded request to see the evidence; and Paine seems to get some of his points, perhaps even his prevailing tone, from Hume. He brings his argument up to date by putting much more stress upon comparative religion, that often partisan interest in the 'heathen mythology' so characteristic of the late eighteenth century. The greatest English scholar in the field was the avowedly liberal but not polemical Sir William Jones (1746–94). Paine more closely echoes the impudent tone of the wealthy connoisseurs Sir William Hamilton and Richard Payne Knight, who privately circulated among fellow-members of the Society of Dilettanti a 'Discourse on the Worship of Priapus' (1786) which states firmly what Paine here insinuates, that Roman Catholic Christianity has descended from priapic paganism (see pp. 12 and 234 n. 18). But much the most popular book yet to appear in France or England on this topic, and the one to which Paine's most clearly relates, is Volney's *Ruins of Empires*.[16] Paine follows Volney in perceiving the interconnections of various religions not so much in terms of organic growths, but as evidence of a sinister conspiracy by a ruling caste which, in all ages and in all civilisations, cynically uses the mystifications of religion as instruments of policy. 'The Christian theory is little else than the idolatry of the ancient mythologists, accommodated to the purposes of power and revenue; and it yet remains to reason and philosophy to abolish the amphibious fraud' (p. 126). Paine's opening, with its plain and impressive declaration of faith in the one God and in the immortality of the soul, sounds as if it might have been written by the unitarian Priestley, a man of God devoutly committed to that separation of Church and State for which Jefferson stood in America.[17] But Paine's book quickly becomes too outspoken, impudent, and destructive to be endured by Dissenters, however rational. Among the forty or more who published pamphlets against *The Age of Reason* are Priestley, Wakefield, and Watson (the 'Dissenters' bishop': see pp. 145, 196). Coleridge's letters and notebooks reveal how shocked he was in 1795–6 by the atheistic tone now prevalent among leading English radicals such as Paine, Thelwall, Godwin, and Darwin. Throughout the nineteenth century, secularism was to be an important strand in British radicalism, but a divisive one, which helped to deter liberals whose motives were, like Coleridge's, humane and ethical in a Protestant Christian tradition.

The title-page of the first edition of *The Age of Reason*, Part I, states that it was printed in Paris by Barrois and sold in London by D. I. Eaton at the Cock and Swine, 74 Newgate Street, for one shilling and sixpence. Part II appeared in London in 1795, Part III in New York in 1807 and London in 1811. The controversy and the prosecutions of booksellers that accompanied the book's complicated progress make too long a story to be told, for they continue with the reissue of Paine's *Political Works* by Richard Carlile in 1817.[18] The French circumstances in which Part I was written were even more oppressive, as Paine describes in his Preface of 1795 to Part II:

The intolerant spirit of religious persecution had transferred itself into politics; the tribunals, styled Revolutionary, supplied the place of the Inquisition; and the Guillotine of the State out did the Fire and Faggot of the Church. I saw many of my most intimate friends destroyed;[19] others daily carried to prison; and I had reason to believe, and had also intimations given me, that the same danger was approaching myself.

Under these disadvantages, I began the former part of the Age of Reason; I had, besides, neither Bible nor Testament to refer to, though I was writing against both; nor could I procure any; notwithstanding which, I have produced a work that no Bible Believer, though writing at his ease, and with a Library of Church Books about him, can refute. Towards the latter end of December of that year, a motion was made and carried, to exclude foreigners from the Convention. . . .

Conceiving, after this, that I had but a few days of liberty, I sat down, and brought the work to a close as speedily as possible; and I had not finished it more than six hours, in the state it has since appeared, before a guard came, about three in the morning, with an order, signed by the two Committees of Public Safety and Surety General, for putting me in arrestation as a foreigner, and conveying me to the prison of the Luxembourg.[20] I contrived, in my way there, to call on Joel Barlow,[21] and I put the Manuscript of the work into his hands, as more safe than in my possession in prison: and not knowing what might be the fate in France, either of the writer or the work, I addressed it to the protection of the citizens of the United States.

The opening passage of Part I:

It has been my intention, for several years past, to publish my thoughts upon religion. . . . The circumstance that has now taken place in France of the total abolition of the whole national order of priesthood, and of every thing appertaining to compulsive systems of religion, and compulsive articles of faith, has not only precipitated my intention, but rendered a work of this kind exceedingly necessary; lest, in the general wreck of superstition, of false systems of government, and false theology, we lose sight of morality, of humanity, and of the theology that is true.

As several of my colleagues, and others of my fellow-citizens of France, have given me the example of making their voluntary and individual profession of faith, I also will make mine; and I do this with all that sincerity and frankness with which the mind of man communicates with itself.

I believe in one God, and no more; and I hope for happiness beyond this life.

I believe the equality of man, and I believe that religious duties consist in doing justice, loving mercy, and endeavouring to make our fellow-creatures happy.

Tom Paine (1737–1809)

But lest it should be supposed that I believe many other things in addition to these, I shall, in the progress of this work, declare the things I do not believe, and my reasons for not believing them.

I do not believe in the creed professed by the Jewish church, by the Roman church, by the Greek church, by the Turkish church, by the Protestant church, nor by any church that I know of. My own mind is my own church.

All national institutions of churches, whether Jewish, Christian or Turkish, appear to me no other than human inventions set up to terrify and enslave mankind, and monopolize power and profit.

I do not mean by this declaration to condemn those who believe otherwise. They have the same right to their belief as I have to mine. But it is necessary to the happiness of man, that he be mentally faithful to himself. Infidelity does not consist in believing, or in disbelieving: it consists in professing to believe what he does not believe. . . .

Soon after I had published the pamphlet, COMMON SENSE, in America, I saw the exceeding probability that a revolution in the System of Government would be followed by a revolution in the System of Religion. The adulterous connection of church and state, wherever it had taken place, whether Jewish, Christian, or Turkish, had so effectually prohibited, by pains and penalties, every discussion upon established creeds, and upon first principles of religion, that until the system of government should be changed, those subjects could not be brought fairly and openly before the world: but that whenever this should be done, a revolution in the system of religion would follow. Human inventions and priest-craft would be detected: and man would return to the pure, unmixed, and unadulterated belief of one God, and no more.

Every national church or religion has established itself by pretending some special mission from God communicated to certain individuals. The Jews have their Moses; the Christians their Jesus Christ, their apostles and saints; and the Turks their Mahomet; as if the way to God was not open to every man alike.

Each of those churches show certain books which they call *revelation*, or the word of God. The Jews say, that their word of God was given by God to Moses face to face; the Christians say, that their word of God came by divine inspiration; and the Turks say, that their word of God (the Koran) was brought by an angel from Heaven. Each of those churches accuses the other of unbelief; and, for my own part, I disbelieve them all.

As it is necessary to affix right ideas to words, I will, before I proceed further into the subject, offer some observations on the word *revelation*. Revelation, when applied to religion, means something communicated *immediately* from God to man.

No one will deny or dispute the power of the Almighty to make such a communication if he pleases. But admitting, for the sake of a case, that something has been revealed to a certain person, and not revealed to any other person, it is revelation to that person only. When he tells it to a second person, a second to a third, a third to a fourth, and so on, it ceases to be a revelation to all those persons. It is revelation to the first person only, and *hearsay* to every other; and consequently, they are not obliged to believe it.

It is a contradiction in terms and ideas to call any thing a revelation that comes to us at second hand, either verbally or in writing. Revelation is necessarily limited to the first communication. After this, it is only an account of something which that person says was a revelation made to him; and though he may find himself obliged to believe it, it cannot be incumbent on me to believe it in the same manner, for it was not a revelation made to *me*, and I have only his word for it that it was made to *him*.

When Moses told the children of Israel that he received the two tables of the commandments from the hand of God, they were not obliged to believe him, because they had no other authority for it than his telling them so; and I have no other authority for it than some historian telling me so. The commandments carrying no internal evidence of divinity with them. They contain some good moral precepts, such as any man qualified to be a law-giver or a legislator could produce himself, without having recourse to supernatural intervention.[22]

When I am told that the Koran was written in Heaven, and brought to Mahomet by an angel, the account comes to near the same kind of hearsay evidence, and second hand authority, as the former. I did not see the angel myself, and therefore I have a right not to believe it.

When also I am told that a woman, called the Virgin Mary, said, or gave out, that she was with child without any cohabitation with a man, and that her betrothed husband, Joseph, said, that an angel told him so, I have a right to believe them or not: such a circumstance required a much stronger evidence than their bare word for it: but we have not even this: for neither Joseph nor Mary wrote any such matter themselves. It is only reported by others that *they said so*. It is hearsay upon hearsay, and I do not chuse to rest my belief upon such evidence.

It is, however, not difficult to account for the credit that was given to the story of Jesus Christ being the Son of God. He was born when the Heathen mythology had still some fashion and repute in the world, and that mythology had prepared the people for the belief of such a story. Almost all the extraordinary men that lived under the Heathen mythology were reputed to be the sons of some of their gods. It was not a new thing at that time to believe a man to have been celestially begotten: the intercourse of gods with women was then a matter of familiar opinion. Their Jupiter, according to their accounts, had cohabited with hundreds: the story, therefore, had nothing in it either new, wonderful, or obscene: it was conformable to the opinions that then prevailed among the people called Gentiles, or mythologists, and it was those people only that believed it. The Jews who had kept strictly to the belief of one God, and no more, and who had always rejected the Heathen mythology, never credited the story.

It is curious to observe how the theory of what is called the Christian church, sprung out of the tail of the Heathen mythology. A direct incorporation took place in the first instance, by making the reputed founder to be celestially begotten. The trinity of gods that then followed was no other than a reduction of the former plurality, which was about twenty or thirty thousand. The statue of Mary succeeded the statue of Diana of Ephesus. The deification of heroes, changed into the canonization of saints.[23] The mythologists had gods for every thing; the Christian mythologists had saints for every thing. The church became as crouded with the one, as the pantheon had been with the other; and Rome was the place of both. The Christian theory is little else than the idolatry of the ancient mythologists, accommodated to the purposes of power and revenue; and it yet remains to reason and philosophy to abolish the amphibious fraud.

Nothing that is here said can apply, even with the most distant disrespect, to the *real* character of Jesus Christ. He was a virtuous and an amiable man. The morality that he preached and practised was of the most benevolent kind; and though similar systems of morality had been preached by Confucius, and by some of the Greek philosophers, many years before; by the Quakers since; and by many good men in all ages; it has not been exceeded by any.

Jesus Christ wrote no account of himself, of his birth, parentage, or any thing else. Not a line of what is called the New Testament is of his own writing. The history of him is altogether the work of other people; and as to the account given of his resurrection and ascension, it was the necessary counterpart to the story of his birth. His historians, having brought him into the world in a supernatural manner, were obliged to take him out again in the same manner, or the first part of the story must have fallen to the ground.

14. *The Age of Reason*

But the resurrection of a dead person from the grave, and his ascension through the air, is a thing very different as to the evidence it admits of, to the invisible conception of a child in the womb. The resurrection and ascension, supposing them to have taken place, admitted of public and occular demonstration, like that of the ascension of a balloon, or the sun at noon day, to all Jerusalem at least. A thing which every body is required to believe, requires that the proof and evidence of it should be equal to all and universal; and as the public visibility of this last related act was the only evidence that could give sanction to the former part, the whole of it falls to the ground, because that evidence never was given. Instead of this, a small number of persons, not more than eight or nine, are introduced as proxies for the whole world, to say, they *saw it*, and all the rest of the world are called upon to believe it. But it appears that Thomas did not believe the resurrection; and, as they say, would not believe, without having occular and manual demonstration himself. *So neither will I*; and the reason is equally as good for me and every other person, as for Thomas.

It is in vain to attempt to palliate or disguise this matter. The story, so far as relates to the supernatural part has every mark of fraud and imposition stamped upon the face of it. Who were the authors of it is as impossible for us now to know, as it is for us to be assured, that the books in which the account is related, were written by the persons whose names they bear. The best surviving evidence we now have respecting this affair is the Jews. They are regularly descended from the people who lived in the times this resurrection and ascension is said to have happened, and they say, *it is not true.* . . .

That such a person as Jesus Christ existed, and that he was crucified, which was the mode of execution at that day, are historical relations strictly within the limits of probability. He preached most excellent morality, and the equality of man; but he preached also against the corruptions and avarice of the Jewish priests, and this brought upon him the hatred and vengeance of the whole order of priesthood. The accusation which those priests brought against him, was that of sedition and conspiracy against the Roman government, to which the Jews were then subject and tributary; and it is not improbable that the Roman government might have some secret apprehension of the effects of his doctrine as well as the Jewish priests; neither is it improbable that Jesus Christ had in contemplation the delivery of the Jewish nation from the bondage of the Romans. Between the two, however, this virtuous reformer and revolutionist lost his life.

It is upon this plain narrative of facts, together with another case I

am going to mention, that the Christian mythologists, calling themselves the Christian Church, have erected their fable, which for
absurdity and extravagance is not exceeded by any thing that is to be
found in the mythology of the ancients.

William Cobbett

(1762–1835)

15. The Soldier's Friend: or, Considerations on the Late Pretended Augmentation of the Subsistence of the Private Soldiers (1792),

pp. 1–15, complete but for brief cuts

The self-educated son of a tavern-keeper from Farnham, Surrey, Cobbett began life as a labourer and enlisted in 1784 in a regiment of foot, with which he served on the Canadian–American border for seven years. After rising to the rank of Sergeant-Major and making himself indispensable in his regiment as an amanuensis and administrator (admittedly, by his own account), he returned to England late in 1791 bent on exposing the corruptions and other malpractices of most of the officers, by which the private soldier was regularly defrauded of a considerable proportion of his pay. Cobbett's intrepid attempt to bring four officers of his regiment to trial was beset with official procrastination and double-dealing, and ended in March 1792 in a conspiracy to frame him. Cobbett, who had just read Paine's *Rights of Man*, wrote a pamphlet to expose the abuse, *The Soldier's Friend*, which appeared anonymously, price sixpence, at some time between February and June 1792. A new edition in 1793 sold at two pence, or ten shillings and sixpence per 100; it was reissued at the time of the naval mutiny at the Nore in 1797 (see p. 219).

Together with Paine, Cobbett is the writer who achieves most with the new popular egalitarian rhetoric. Sometimes he seems to echo Paine's manner closely, as in his peroration (on p. 136); sometimes the resemblances seem more general, perhaps because their careers were so oddly similar – both spent their early manhood in America, and both came to political conscious- ness through a grievance over pay. Cobbett was not yet a radical ideologue, or indeed a radical at all. He fled to France in 1792 to escape arrest over the case he had instigated, and thence to America, where he established himself during the 1790s as a matchless journalist under the pen-name Peter Porcupine. A sturdy Englishman, despite his treatment at home, Cobbett attacked the pro-French Republican party of Jefferson, and broadly supported the pro- English Democrats, led by Washington. This made him a conservative in domestic American terms, and it was as a conservative, pro-Government propagandist that he returned to England in 1800. But as *The Soldier's Friend* demonstrates, Cobbett is a born populist, a writer who speaks to the underdog masses. After 1804, his *Political Register* became a radical journal.

William Cobbett (1762–1835)

In the revival of unrest and radicalism that followed the ending of the Napoleonic Wars, he played the part pioneered by Paine in 1792: he printed a large number of the editorials of the *Political Register*, and sold them as broadsheets for two pence. Once again it was not the seditious content that alarmed propertied opinion, ministers, and the conservative press, but the danger that a rhetorician of genius would politicise the masses. *Habeas Corpus* was suspended, as it had been on several occasions in the 1790s, and Cobbett left for America in March 1817 just in time to escape arrest. Appropriately, when he returned in 1819 he was bringing back Paine's bones, over which he hoped to raise a suitable monument in his native land.[1]

Cobbett quickly achieved a power comparable with Paine's. The impact of the brief *Soldier's Friend* could hardly be greater. Its egalitarian message breathes through its simple vocabulary and idiomatic phrasing. Cobbett is writing about more than soldier's pay, about more even than the exploitation of one class by another; he speaks from the ranks, in a tone of command, against an officer class 'whose business (I might have said *trade*) is to deceive us' (p. 131). His power of organising an argument and developing a case is exhibited at greater length when he writes on Priestley. Even here, where the target is himself a radical, the language is plebeian and the appeal democratic: Cobbett's scorn for the middle-class Priestley's library, laboratory, and educated pursuits reeks of the philistinism of the common man, and compares pungently with Burke's more convoluted anti-intellectualism. Though not a central figure in the English Revolution debate, Cobbett illustrates one of its most important strands of feeling, and no one better demonstrates that writing can be both democratic and meaningful. 'Let us leave the sentiments and decisions of this virtuous assembly [the House of Commons] to those who have the management of them, and form a judgment for ourselves' (p. 131).

Amongst the many curious manoeuvres of the present Administration, I do not reccollect one that marks more strongly its character than the late alteration in the pay and establishment of the Army. The augmentation (as they would insinuate it is) of the pay of the Private Soldiers, is represented as arising from a consideration of the wretchedness of their situation; and the pretended reduction of the foot forces is held out to the Public as an act of œconomy. The People, I am much afraid, are satisfied with this: I say, I am afraid of it, for I shall always be sorry to see them satisfied with anything short of truth. The situation of the Privates in our marching regiments of foot was really so miserable, that every one, endued with the least compassion, must rejoice to find that a *morsel of bread* has been, by any means, added to their scanty meal; and the enormous load of taxes, that press out the very vitals of the People, ensures a favourable reception to every reduction, or pretended reduction, of public expence, let it be ever so

trifling or absurd. If we add to these considerations the little knowledge that the People in general have of military affairs, we shall not be
surprised to find them satisfied with the plausible delusions held out
to them on this occasion. But it certainly becomes us to look a little
deeper into things, and not to trust men on their bare words, whose
business (I might have said *trade*) is to deceive us.

I propose to make a few observations on the alteration that has
taken place in the Soldiers's pay; in doing which, although I shall be
very concise, I have the vanity to think, I shall discover a little better
information on the subject than the Secretary at War did at his
opening of it in the House of Commons; when he observed (after
having stated the saving that would arise from the reduction in the
infantry) that "against this saving he had to mention an increase that
had been made to the pay of the Private Soldiers, to the amount of
23,000l. The situation of the Privates had long been admitted to
have been extremely hard. It had *in former years* been a regulation, that
a Soldier should receive three shillings a week for his subsistence. It
has *of late years so happened*, that he had not had for that purpose above
eighteen pence or two shillings. This was evidently too little for the
bare purpose of existence. By the late regulation, his pay was to be
made adequate to the subsistence the common Soldier *formerly
enjoyed*, an object which he was confident would meet with the warm
approbation of every man."[2]

Upon hearing this, one might with great propriety have cried out in
the language of the *Clown* to *Malvolio* – "are you not mad indeed, or
do you but counterfeit?"[3] If anything done in that wise and equal
representation of the People, called the House of Commons, were
worth a thought from a man of sense; if any weakness or absurdity of
theirs could at this day possibly create the least astonishment, one
might think it wonderful, that Members should sit, and silently hear
their understandings thus insulted, and see their acts as it were
trampled under foot before their faces! But let us leave the sentiments
and decisions of this *virtuous* assembly to those who have the management of them, and form a judgment for ourselves.

As the Secretary observed, "the situation of the Privates had long
been admitted to have been extremely hard;" but people had not the
least notion that "*it had so happened* of late years, that the Soldier had
had only *eighteen pence* or *two shillings* a week for his subsistence." Men
of humanity thought the Soldier's situation hard, but every one
thought that he received *three shillings a week* for his subsistence; and
why any man, unacquainted with the abuses of the Army, should
think otherwise I cannot imagine, seeing that there is an act of

pound = / pence

Parliament, a law of the land, that declares it shall be so. "It was *formerly* a regulation, that a Soldier should receive three shillings a week for his subsistence." Why formerly? Has it not been a regulation, a law of the land, for these fifty or a hundred years, and does it not continue so to this moment? Was it not enacted, no longer ago than last year, by the very Parliament to whom this impudent absurdity was delivered, – "That, if any Officers having received their Soldiers' pay, shall refuse to pay each respective non-commissioned Officer and Soldier their respective pay, when it shall become due, at the rate of six shillings *per* week for each Serjeant, four shillings and sixpence *per* week for each Corporal and Drummer, and *three shillings per week for each Soldier* of any marching regiment of foot or independent company; – and at the end of every two months to account for one shilling *per* week to each Serjeant, two pence *per* week to each Corporal and Drummer, and sixpence *per* week to each Foot Soldier; – the said one shilling *per* week, two pence *per* week, and sixpence *per* week, being the remainder of the subsistence of each Serjeant, Corporal, Drummer and Foot Soldier; then, upon proof thereof before a Court-martial as aforesaid, to be for that purpose held and summoned by his Majesty's order, every such Officer so offending shall be discharged from his employment, and shall forfeit to the informer, upon conviction before the said Court-martial, one hundred pounds, to be levied as aforesaid; and the informer, if a Soldier (if he demands it) shall be, and is hereby discharged from all further service; any thing in this act contained to the contrary notwithstanding." This clause is to be found in every *Mutiny Bill* that ever was framed in this kingdom: it is not only *a law*, but it is a law that is renewed every year, and therefore must be understood by every Member of Parliament. Yet, notwithstanding this law, which so positively declares that the Foot Soldier shall receive three shillings *per* week subsistence, it has "so happened of late years that he has had only eighteen pence or two shillings!" It has "*so happened!*" and for years too! astonishing! It has "so happened" that an act of Parliament has been most notoriously and shamefully disobeyed for years, to the extreme misery of thousands of deluded wretches (our countrymen), and to the great detriment of the nation at large; it has "so happened," that not one of the offenders have been brought to justice for this disobedience, even now it is fully discovered; and it has "so happened," that the hand of power has made another dive into the national purse, in order – not to add to what the Soldier ought to have received; not to satisfy *his* hunger and thirst; but to gratify the whim or the avarice of his capricious and plundering superiors.

15. *The Soldier's Friend*

But *how* has this "happened?" The Secretary did not think proper to explain this; perhaps he could not, for the secrets of the Army are something like those of Free Masonry; it is absolutely necessary to become a brother of the blade before you can become at all acquainted with the *arcana* of the profession. . . . if the Soldier had only eighteen pence or two shillings a week for his subsistence, what became of the rest? – In the first place, a shilling a week was retained as arrears in room of sixpence; and, before we go any further, let us see how this shilling a week was disposed of. The sixpence a week, I will maintain, was quite sufficient to supply a Private Soldier with every thing *necessary* for his wear, if he were besides regularly provided with a complete dress annually, which always was, or, at least, always ought to have been the case. But it has "so happened of late years", that the Officers, to whose wisdom and honour the interest of one faction or another has committed the care of our Soldiers, have not been content with their men dressing according to their rank and ability; they have obliged them to purchase articles of dress unheard of in former Armies, all of them far too expensive, and most of them totally useless. It may seem difficult to account for a conduct like this; why should Officers take a delight in extorting the poor wretches' pay from them with no other view than that of merely fooling it away? To give them their due, this was not the case. The world is often deceived in those jovial, honest looking fellows, the Officers of the Army: I have known very few of them but perfectly well know how to take care of themselves in peace or war; and I could mention characters in this *honourable* profession that would shine amongst *the Seed of Abraham*, or do honour to the society of Stock Jobbers. Their industry and care is in nothing more conspicuous than in the management of the above-mentioned shilling a week, the arrears of the Private Soldier. Every one, who is in the least acquainted with the Army, knows that the expenditure of the Soldier's arrears is not left to himself; he has no choice when, or in what manner it shall be laid out; indeed, it is a matter that his Officer saves him the trouble of thinking about, by laying it all out – not for the Soldier's benefit, but for his own. This he thus manages: A little while before the time arrives when he is to account to the Soldier for his arrears, he makes up his account so far as to be able to see what credit the man will have; then he purchases something, no matter what, gives it the man, and brings his account to a balance. I have, indeed, heard of some tender conscienced Officers, who, to avoid the sin of extortion, have charged their men no more for articles thus purchased than the prices stated in the tradesmens' bills; but then they never failed to receive from the said tradesmen a pretty handsome *discount*. . . . The quality of the goods is never regarded; it is a matter totally out of the question; the red-coated *retailer* will take them to his company, by whom any rotten, moth-eaten rubbish must be received not only without grumbling, but with thanks. Now, whoever considers the discount on a shilling is twice as much as that on sixpence, and takes a strict survey of the ingenious process made use of in extracting the said discount from the pay of a poor half-starved wretch, will, I hope, be ready to acknowledge, that the whole is a master-piece in its kind; and that it entirely exonerates the *Gentlemen* of the Army from the general charge brought against them; viz. that of being *senseless, idle, hearty, honest fellows*.

This sixpence then, being, in direct disobedience to the Mutiny Act, added to the arrears, left the Soldier two shillings and sixpence a week; and out of that two and sixpence he was obliged to supply himself with brushes, combs, powder bag, puff, and all the nonsensical apparatus of foppery, besides being at perhaps eightpence or ninepence a week expence for flour, grease, soap, etc, to plaister his head with, when at the same time he was almost starved to death.[4]

Thus the poor fellow has, as the Secretary at War observed, "of late years, not had above eighteen pence or two shillings a week;" but this was not for want of a *new regulation*; it was not because his pay, as established by law, was insufficient; it was because his superior Officer was suffered to break the law with impunity, to answer the very worst of ends: to make a Soldier a fop, to deform him, to render his person as much unlike any thing human as possible; or to draw into the pockets of the commission Officers a few dirty beggarly pence. To this we may attribute all the robberies committed by the Soldiery (I mean those only committed by the *lower* orders of them), and the desertions which have been the disgrace of the British Army for several years past. And now, when it is at last found out that the act of Parliament, made to guard the rights of the Soldier, has been, and is, most notoriously disobeyed, and that the poor wretch has not, and does not receive enough "for the bare purpose of existence"; now, when it is perhaps become necessary to humour the abused Soldier a little for *some purpose* or other,[5] what one would naturally suppose to be the only just and rational method of putting things to rights has never once been thought of; that is, bringing the Officers to justice, and enforcing obedience in future to the Mutiny Act. No; this would not do, this would affront the Officers, the *Aristocracy of the Army*; and, therefore, the public purse, "the common Hack", has been again sweated for 23,000l. per annum, by which means the Soldiers are pleased, and the Officers not displeased.

This is certainly the most curious mode of rectifying abuses that ever was heard of; and it points out in the clearest light the close connection that exists between the *ruling Faction* in this Country and the military Officers: and this connection ever must exist while we suffer ourselves to be governed by *a Faction*. If any other body of men had thus impudently set the laws of the land at defiance, if a *gang of robbers*, unornamented with red coats and cockades, had plundered their fellow citizens, what would have been the consequence? They would have been brought to justice, hanging or transportation would have been their fate; but, it seems, the Army is become a *sanctuary* from the power of the law. – Nor shall we be at all surprised at this, if we consider that a standing Army is the great instrument of oppression, and that a very numerous one may in a little time be necessary. I am not, therefore, blaming the Ministry for this proceeding, I really think they have acted with a great deal of prudence in procuring this 23,000l. for their supporters; but, (as it was all amongst friends) I think the business might have been opened in a more unequivocal manner; as thus, in the language of truth:

"The situation of the Privates has long been admitted to be extremely hard. It is a Law (which in former years was obeyed) that a Soldier shall receive three shillings a week for his subsistence. It has so happened, of late years, the Officers have thought proper to despise this Law, and to give the Soldier only eighteen pence or two shillings. This is evidently too little for the bare purpose of existence; and, though he has subsisted on it of late years, and might with our good will have done so to the day of judgment, as there now is a necessity to humour the wretch a little, *for reasons best known to ourselves*; we have, by a late regulation, made his pay adequate to what he always ought to have enjoyed; an object, that we are confident must meet the warm approval of our majority in this House. The public burden will, indeed, be increased by this, but it is certainly much better to tax the people to their last farthing than to wound *the honour* of our *trusty and well beloved* the Officers of the Army, by any odious and *ungentleman-like* investigation of their conduct."

It particularly becomes you, the *British Soldier*, to look upon this matter in its proper light. . . . I would have you observe here, and observe it well too, how partially the military law is made to operate. If you should have the fortune to become a non-commissioned Officer, and were to deduct but a penny from a man unlawfully, you know, the consequence would be breaking and flogging, and refunding the money so deducted; but here you see your Officers have been guilty of the practice for years, and now it is found out, not a hair of one of their heads is touched; they are even permitted to remain in the practice, and a sum of money is taken from the public to coax you with, now it seems likely that you may be wanted. You know but too well that the military Law has not of late years been softened towards you; if you commit the most trifling offence you are flogged for it; if your gait or shape be not exactly according to the fancy of your driver, you are beaten with a stick; how comes it then that the Law is so softened towards your officers? Because the ruling Powers look upon your Officers as Gentlemen, and upon you as Beasts.

Soldiers are taught to believe every thing they receive, *a gift from the Crown*; – cast this notion from you immediately, and know, that there is not a farthing that you receive but comes out of the *Public Purse*. What you call your *King's Bounty*, or *Queen's Bounty*, is no bounty from either of them; it is twelve shillings, and two pence a year of the public money, which no one can withhold from you; it is allowed you by an Act of Parliament, while you are taught to look upon it as a present from the King or Queen! I feel an indignation at this I cannot describe. – I would have you consider the nature of your situation, I would have you know that you are not the servant of *one man* only; a British Soldier never can be that. You are a servant of the whole nation, of your countrymen, who pay you, and from whom you can have no separate interests. I would have you look upon nothing that you receive as a *Favour* or a *Bounty* from Kings, Queens, or Princes; you receive the wages of your servitude; it is your property, confirmed to you by Acts of the Legislature of your Country, which property, your rapacious Officers ought never to seize on, without meeting with a punishment due to their infamy.

16. *Observations on the Emigration of Dr. Joseph Priestley, and on the Several Addresses Delivered to him on his Arrival at New York* (Philadelphia, 1794), from *Selections from Cobbett's Political Works*, by John M. Cobbett and James P. Cobbett (6 vols., 1835–7),

vol. I, pp. 15–24, with cuts

Cobbett's pamphlet against Priestley, initially anonymous, is the first of his writings which he afterwards acknowledged. The occasion was Dr Priestley's arrival in New York as an emigrant on 4 June 1794, the welcoming addresses by two pro-French groups there, the Democratic Society and the Republican Natives of Great Britain and Ireland resident in New York, and Priestley's reply. The tone of these remarks brought out the patriot in Cobbett, who was now living in Philadelphia. He had been an assiduous reader of newspapers during his two years in America, and his pamphlet reflects his close interest in events in England and France. It is in the spirit of a reporter that he recalls the scenes in Birmingham in July 1791, during the celebrated riots in which Priestley's meeting-house and home, with its laboratory, were burnt (see p. 84). Cobbett challenges the interpretation put upon the facts by the radicals: that a good man was persecuted, and that the authorities condoned the activities of the rioters. In Cobbett's hands, Priestley becomes a covert politician, whose apparent professions, religion and learning, need not be taken seriously. But he is even more anxious to impress upon his American readers his portrait of England, as a moderate, tolerant society – how different from France – in which the mob avoids violence to the person, and the law protects a Priestley.

Opinion at Philadelphia, as at New York, was pro-French, and Cobbett had difficulty in getting his pro-British pamphlet published. Thomas Bradford eventually published it, in August 1794, with both Cobbett's name and his own left off the title-page, and the opening words of the title also dropped – 'The Tartuffe Detected'. But the pamphlet was a success: there were five Philadelphia editions, and editions in New York, Birmingham, and London.[6]

[Dr. Priestley's] answers to the addresses of the New York Societies are evidently calculated to mislead and deceive the people of the United States. He there endeavours to impose himself on them for a sufferer in the cause of liberty; and makes a canting profession of moderation, in direct contradiction to the conduct of his whole life.

He says he hopes to find here "that protection from violence which laws and government promise in all countries, but which he has not found in his own." He certainly must suppose that no European intelligence ever reaches this side of the Atlantic, or that the inhabitants of these countries are too dull to comprehend the sublime events that mark his life and character. Perhaps I shall show him that it is not the people of England alone who know how to estimate the merit of Doctor Priestley.

Let us examine his claims to our compassion; let us see whether his charge against the laws and government of his country be just or not.

On the 14th of July 1791, an unruly mob assembled in the town of Birmingham, set fire to his house and burnt it, together with all it contained.[7] This is the subject of his complaint, and the pretended cause of his emigration. The fact is not denied; but in the relation of facts, circumstances must not be forgotten. To judge of the Doctor's charge against his country, we must take a retrospective view of his conduct, and of the circumstances that led to the destruction of his property.

It is about twelve years since he began to be distinguished among the dissenters from the established church of England. He preached up a kind of *deism* which nobody understood, and which it was thought the Doctor understood full as well as his neighbours. This doctrine afterwards assumed the name of Unitarianism, and the *religieux* of the order were called, or rather they called themselves, Unitarians.[8]. . .

Those who know any thing of the English Dissenters, know that they always introduce their political claims and projects under the mask of religion. The Doctor was one of those who entertained hopes of bringing about a revolution in England upon the French plan; and for this purpose he found it would be very convenient for him to be at the head of a religious sect. Unitarianism was now revived, and the society held regular meetings at Birmingham. . . .

Nothing was neglected by this branch of the Parisian *propagande* to excite the people to a general insurrection. Inflammatory hand-bills, advertisements, federation dinners, toasts, sermons, prayers; in short, every trick that religious or political duplicity could suggest, was played off to destroy a constitution which has borne the test and attracted the admiration of ages; and to establish in its place a new system, fabricated by themselves.

The 14th of July, 1791, was of too much note in the annals of modern regeneration to be neglected by these regenerated politicians. A club of them, of which Doctor Priestley was a member, gave public notice of a feast, to be held at Birmingham, in which they intended to celebrate the French revolution. Their endeavours had hitherto excited no other sentiments in what may be called the people of England, than those of contempt. The people of Birmingham, however, felt, on this occasion, a convulsive movement. They were scandalized at this public notice for holding in their town a festival, to celebrate events which were in reality a subject of the deepest horror; and seeing in it at the same time an open and audacious attempt to destroy the constitution of their country, and with it their happiness, they thought their understandings and loyalty insulted, and prepared to avenge themselves by the chastisement of the English revolutionists, in the midst of their scandalous orgies. The feast nevertheless took place; but the Doctor, knowing himself to be the grand projector, and consequently the particular object of his townsmen's vengeance, prudently kept away. The cry of *Church and King* was the

Unitarianism

signal for the people to assemble, which they did to a considerable number, opposite the hotel where the *convives* were met. The club dispersed, and the mob proceeded to breaking the windows, and other acts of violence, incident to such scenes; but let it be remembered, that no personal violence was offered. Perhaps it would have been well, if they had vented their anger on the persons of the revolutionists, provided they had contented themselves with the ceremony of the horse-pond or blanket. Certain it is, that it would have been very fortunate if the riot had ended this way; but when that many-headed monster, a mob, is once roused and put in motion, who can stop its destructive steps?

From the *hotel of the federation* the mob proceeded to Doctor Priestley's meeting-house, which they very nearly destroyed in a little time. Had they stopped here, all would yet have been well. The destruction of this temple of sedition and infidelity would have been of no great consequence; but, unhappily for them and the town of Birmingham, they could not be separated before they had destroyed the houses and property of many members of the club. Some of these houses, among which was Doctor Priestley's, were situated at the distance of some miles from town: the mob were in force to defy all the efforts of the civil power, and, unluckily, none of the military could be brought to the place till some days after the 14th of July.[9] In the mean time many spacious and elegant houses were burnt, and much valuable property destroyed; but it is certainly worthy remark, that during the whole of these unlawful proceedings, not a single person was killed or wounded, either wilfully or by accident, except some of the rioters themselves. At the end of four or five days, this riot, which seemed to threaten more serious consequences, was happily terminated by the arrival of a detachment of dragoons; and tranquillity was restored to the distressed town of Birmingham.

The magistrates used every exertion in their power to quell this riot in its very earliest stage, and continued to do so to the last.[10] . . . Eleven of the rioters were . . . indicted; seven of them were acquitted, four found guilty, and of these four two *suffered death*.[11] These unfortunate men were, according to the law, prosecuted on the part of the King; and it has been allowed by the Doctor's own partisans, that the prosecution was carried on with every possible enforcement, and even rigour, by the judges and counsellors. . . .

Some time after the riots, the Doctor and the other revolutionists who had had property destroyed, brought their actions for damages against the town of Birmingham, or rather against the hundred of which that town makes a part. The Doctor laid his damages at 4122l.

11s. 9d. sterling, of which sum 420l. 15s. was for works in manuscript, which, he said, had been consumed in the flames. The trial of
this cause took up nine hours: the jury gave a verdict in his favour, but
curtailed the damages to 2502l. 18s. It was rightly considered that the
imaginary value of the manuscript works ought not to have been
included in the damages; because the Doctor being the author of
them, he in fact possessed them still, and the loss could be little more
than a few sheets of dirty paper. Besides, if they were to be estimated
by those he had published for some years before, their destruction was
a benefit instead of a loss, both to himself and his country. The sum,
then, of 420l. 15s. being deducted, the damages stood at 370il. 16s.
9d.; and it should not be forgotten, that even a great part of this sum
was charged for an apparatus of philosophical instruments, which, in
spite of the most unpardonable gasconade of the philosopher, can be
looked upon as a thing of imaginary value only, and ought not to be
estimated at its cost, any more than a collection of shells or insects, or
any other of the *frivola* of a virtuoso. . . .

If he had been the very best subject in England, in place of one of
the very worst, what could the laws have done more for him? Nothing
certainly can be a stronger proof of the independence of the courts of
justice, and of the impartial execution of the laws of England, than the
circumstances and result of this cause. A man who had for many years
been the avowed and open enemy of the Government and constitution, had his property destroyed by a mob who declared themselves
the friends of both, and who rose up against him because he was not.
This mob were pursued by the Government, whose cause they
thought they were defending; some of them suffered death, and the
inhabitants of the place where they assembled were obliged to
indemnify the man whose property they had destroyed. It would be
curious to know what sort of protection this *reverend* Doctor, this
"friend of humanity," wanted. Would nothing satisfy him but the
blood of the whole mob? Did he wish to see the town of Birmingham,
like that of Lyons, razed, and all its industrious and loyal inhabitants
butchered, because some of them had been carried to commit unlawful excesses, from their detestation of his wicked projects? BIRMING-
HAM HAS COMBATED AGAINST PRIESTLEY. BIRMINGHAM IS NO
MORE. This, I suppose, would have satisfied the charitable modern
philosopher, who pretended, and who the Democratic Society say,
did "return to his enemies blessings for curses." Woe to the wretch
that is exposed to the benedictions of a modern philosopher! His
"*dextre vengresse*" is ten thousand times more to be feared than the
bloody poniard of the assassin: the latter is drawn on individuals only,

the other is pointed at the human race. Happily for the people of Birmingham, these blessings had no effect; there was no National Convention, Revolutionary Tribunal, or guillotine, in England. . . .

Let us see, a little, how mobs have acted under the famous Government that the Doctor so much admires. . . . Does the Doctor remember having heard anything above the glorious achievements of the 10th of August 1792?[12] Has he ever made an estimate of the property destroyed in Paris on that and the following days? Let him compare the destruction that followed the steps of that mob, with the loss of his boasted apparatus; and when he has done this, let him tell us, if he can, where he would now be, if the Government of England had treated him and his friends as the National Assembly did the sufferers in the riots of the 10th of August. But, perhaps, he looks upon the events of that day as a glorious victory, a new emancipation, and of course will say, that I degrade the *heroes* in calling them a mob. I am not for disputing with him about a name; he may call them the heroes of the 10th of August, if he will: "The heroes of the 14th of July," has always been understood to mean, a gang of blood-thirsty cannibals, and I would by no means wish to withhold the title from those of the 10th of August.

From scenes like these, the mind turns for relief and consolation to the riot at Birmingham. That riot, considered comparatively with what Dr. Priestley and his friends wished and attempted to stir up, was peace, harmony and gentleness. Has this man any reason to complain? He will perhaps say, he did not approve of the French riots and massacres; to which I shall answer, that he did approve of them. His public celebration of them was a convincing proof of this; and if it were not, his sending his son to Paris in the midst of them, to request the *honour* of becoming a French citizen, is a proof that certainly will not be disputed.[13] If, then, we take a view of the riots of which the Doctor is an admirer, and of those of which he expresses his detestation, we must fear that he is very far from being that "*friend of human happiness*," that the Democratic Society pretend to believe him. In short, in whatever light we view the Birmingham riots, we can see no object that excites our compassion, except the inhabitants of the hundred, and the unfortunate rioters themselves.

Samuel Horsley

(1733–1806)

Burke connection

17. A Sermon, Preached Before the Lords Spiritual and Temporal, in the Abbey Church of St. Peter, Westminster, on . . . January 30, 1793: Being the Anniversary of the Martyrdom of King Charles I[1] (1793),

2nd edn, 1793, pp. 1–3, 21–5

The conservative case against the radical pamphleteers was at first made by politicians in Parliament, in speeches duly reported in the newspapers. But after 1792, the leading *writers* on the orthodox side, after Burke, were a group of Bishops of the Church of England. The Established Church was profoundly affected by the social changes which transformed English society between 1780 and 1850. Its leaders were almost all conservatives, especially at the outset, but the crisis of the 1790s involved them urgently in events, and so played its part in changing the standard clerical attitude towards clerical responsibility. Within the Church of the 1790s were Evangelicals to whom religion was primarily a matter of personal conviction, an inward experience of sin and of redemption, and High Church bishops panicked by the ruin which revolution had visited upon Church and State across the Channel. It was more particularly the example of France that brought them to the defence of the old order early in 1793, following the execution of Louis XVI (21st January), and at the outbreak (1 February) of war with France.

Samuel Horsley, successively Bishop of St David's (from 1788), of Rochester (from 1793) and of St Asaph (from 1802), was a pluralistic High Churchman and one of the most fervent and anxious opponents of the Revolution. Beginning with the sermon of 30 January 1793, he waged an often hysterical, occasionally millenarian thirteen-year campaign to teach the people their duty. Man was intended to live in a civil society, which derived its authority from the divine will; his subjection to authority was not a voluntary compact, but 'a conscientious submission to the will of God'.[2] Schemes mounted by individuals to alter civil society, perhaps on behalf of the people, 'we abominate and reject, as wicked and illegitimate'.[3] Another reply to Price, and indebted to Burke, the Bishop's *Sermon* represents a style of pulpit oratory wholly different from the tone of rational Dissent – though Coleridge, the Unitarian brought up an Anglican, and the son of an Anglican clergyman, sounds not unlike Horsley (see p. 199).

Romans XIII.I
Let every soul be subject unto the higher powers

The freedom of dispute, in which, for several years past, it hath been the folly in this country to indulge, upon matters of such high importance as the origin of Government, and the authority of Sovereigns; . . . this forwardness to dispute about the limits of the Sovereign's power, and the extent of the People's rights, with this evident desire, to set civil authority upon a foundation on which it cannot stand secure; argues, it should seem, that something is forgotten, among the Writers, who have presumed to treat these curious questions. . . . It surely is forgotten, that . . . the Christian is possessed of a written rule of conduct, delivered from on high. . . .

From these records it appears, that the Providence of God was careful to give a beginning to the Human Race, in that particular way, which might for ever bar the existence of the whole, or of any large portion of mankind, in that state which hath been called the State of Nature. Mankind, from the beginning never existed otherwise, than in Society, and under Government. Whence follows this important consequence: that to build the authority of Princes, or of the chief Magistrate under whatever denomination, upon any compact or agreement between the individuals of a multitude, living previously in the state of nature, is in truth to build a reality upon a fiction. . . . Our Constitution exempts her Kings from the degrading necessity of being accountable to the subject. She invests them with the high attribute of political Impeccability. She declares, that wrong, in his public capacity, a King of Great Britain cannot do; and thus unites the most perfect security of the Subject's Liberty, with the most absolute inviolability of the sacred person of the Sovereign.

Such is the British Constitution. Its Basis, Religion; its End, Liberty; its principal means and safe-guard of Liberty, the Majesty of the Sovereign. In support of it, the King is not more interested than the Peasant.

It was a signal instance of God's mercy, not imputing to the people of this land the atrocious deed of a desperate faction; it was a signal instance of God's mercy, that the goodly fabric was not crushed, in the middle of the last century, ere it had attained its finished perfection, by the phrensy of that fanatical banditti, which took the life of the First

Samuel Horsley (1733–1806)

Charles. In the madness and confusion, which followed the shedding of that blood, our History holds forth an edifying example of the effects, that are ever to be expected – in that example, it gives warning of the effects, that ever are INTENDED, by the dissemination of those infernal maxims, that Kings are the servants of the people, punishable by their Masters. The same lesson is confirmed by the horrible example, which the present hour exhibits, in the unparalleled misery of a neighbouring Nation; once great in Learning, Arts and Arms! Now torn by contending factions! Her Government demolished! Her Altars overthrown! Her First-born despoiled of their Birth right! Her Nobles degraded! Her best Citizens exiled! Her riches, sacred and profane, given up to the pillage of sacrilege and rapine! Atheists directing her Councils! Desperadoes conducting her Armies! Wars of unjust and chimerical ambition consuming her Youth! Her Granaries exhausted! Her Fields uncultivated! Famine threatening her multitudes! Her Streets swarming with Assassins, filled with violence, deluged with blood!

Is the picture frightful? Is the misery extreme? the guilt horrid? Alas, these things were but the prelude of the tragedy. Public Justice poisoned in its source! profaned, in the abuse of its most solemn forms, to the foulest purposes! A monarch deliberately murdered! A monarch – whose only crime it was, that he inherited a sceptre, the thiry-second of his illustrious stock, – butchered on a public scaffold, after the mockery of arraignment, trial, sentence! Butchered, without the merciful formalities of the vilest malefactor's execution! The sad privilege of a last farewel to the surrounding populace refused! Not the pause of a moment allowed for devotion! Honourable interment denied to the corpse! The Royal Widow's anguish imbittered by the rigour of a close imprisonment! with hope, indeed, at no great distance, of release – of such release as hath been given to her Lord!

This foul murther, and these barbarities, have filled the measure of the guilt and infamy of France. O my Country! Read the horror of thy own deed in this recent heightened imitation! Lament and weep, that this black French treason should have found its example, in the crime of thy unnatural sons! Our contrition for the guilt that stained our hand, our gratitude to God, whose mercy so soon restored our Church and Monarchy; our contrition for our own crime, and our gratitude for God's unspeakable mercy, will be best expressed by us all, by setting the example of a dutiful submission to government in our own conduct, and by inculcating upon our children and dependants, a loyal attachment to a King, who hath ever sought his own glory in the virtue and prosperity of his people. . . .

Richard Watson, Bishop of Llandaff

(1737–1816)

18. Appendix to A Sermon Preached before the Stewards of the Westminster Dispensary . . . April 1785 (1793),

pp. 26–9, 31–3

of Paine)

A liberal Whig, who owed his clerical advancement to the patronage of Whig grandees, Watson was never a typical figure on the bench of bishops. First a Professor of Chemistry (1764), next Regius Professor of Divinity (1771) at Cambridge, he owed his elevation to the Bishopric of Llandaff in 1782 to an old pupil, the Duke of Rutland, who recommended him to the Prime Minister, Shelburne. Watson was guilty of most of the malpractices endemic in the Church of his day: he was a pluralist (sixteen livings), a nepotist, and a non-resident. He nevertheless also pioneered reform of the Church from within: in his *Letter to his Grace the Archbishop of Canterbury* (1783), he advocates a more equitable disposal of Church revenue, so that bishops will be encouraged to live in their diocese, and so learn to co-operate with parish clergy 'in the great work of amending the Morals of His Majesty's subjects, and of feeding the flock of Christ.'[1] Given this background, it is not surprising that Watson, alone among the bishops, supported the Dissenters' cause in Parliament, and, with some cautions, welcomed the French Revolution in two pamphlets of 1790 and 1791.[2] Like many other Whigs, however, he was deeply disturbed by the increasingly violent and popular nature of the Revolution, and equally so by Paine, to whom his *Appendix* of January 1793 (to a previously published *Sermon*) is in large part a reply. Later in 1793, he issued his earlier pamphlets on poverty under the general title, *The Wisdom and Goodness of God in Having made both Rich and Poor*.

Watson's *Appendix* is a lucid, temperate, elegantly presented statement of the classic Whig view of the British Constitution. His attractive manner and unusual moderation (unusual, that is, for a bishop) earned him over the years a number of replies from radicals, including Wordsworth (p. 224) and Wakefield (p. 220).

And are there any men in this kingdom, except such as find their account in public confusion, who would hazard the introduction of such scenes of rapine, barbarity, and bloodshed, as have disgraced France and outraged humanity, for the sake of obtaining – What? –

145

Liberty and Equality. – I suspect that the meaning of these terms is not clearly and generally understood: it may be of use to explain them.

The liberty of a man in a state of nature consists in his being subject to no law but the law of nature; – and the liberty of a man in a state of society consists in his being subject to no law, but to the law enacted by the general will of the society to which he belongs. – And to what other law is any man in Great Britain subject? The king, we are all justly persuaded, has not the inclination; and we all know that if he had the inclination, he has not the power, to substitute his will in the place of the law. The house of lords has no such power; the house of commons has no such power; the church has no such power; the rich men of the country have no such power. The poorest man amongst us, the beggar at our door, is governed – not by the uncertain, passionate, arbitrary will of an individual – not by the selfish insolence of an aristocratic faction – not by the madness of democratic violence – but by the fixed, impartial, deliberate voice of law, enacted by the general suffrage of a free people. – Is your property injured? Law, indeed, does not give you property; but it ascertains it. – Property is acquired by industry and probity; by the exercise of talents and ingenuity; and the possession of it is secured by the laws of the community. Against whom think you is it secured? It is secured against thieves and robbers; against idle and profligate men, who, however low your condition may be, would be glad to deprive you of the little you possess. It is secured, not only against such disturbers of the public peace, but against the oppression of the noble, the rapacity of the powerful and the avarice of the rich. The courts of British justice are impartial and incorrupt; they respect not the persons of men: the poor man's lamb is, in their estimation, as sacred as the monarch's crown; with inflexible integrity they adjudge to every man his own. Your property under their protection is secure. – If your personal liberty be unjustly restrained, though but for an hour, and that by the highest servants of the crown – the crown cannot screen them; the throne cannot hide them; the law, with an undaunted arm, seizes them, and drags them with irresistible might to the judgment of whom? – of your equals – of twelve of your neighbours. In such a constitution as this, what is there to complain of on the score of liberty?

The greatest freedom that can be enjoyed by man in a state of civil society; the greatest security that can be given him with respect to the protection of his character, property, personal liberty, limb, and life, is afforded to every individual by our present constitution.

The equality of men in a state of nature, does not consist in an

quality of bodily strength or intellectual ability, but in their being
equally free from the dominion of each other. – The equality of men in
a state of civil society does not consist in an equality of wisdom,
honesty, ingenuity, industry, – nor in an equality of property resulting from a due exertion of these talents; but in being equally subject
to, equally protected by the same laws. . . .

But some one may think, and indeed, it has been studiously
inculcated into the minds of the multitude, that a monarchy, even a
limited one, is a far more expensive mode of civil government than a
republic; that a civil-list of a million a year, is an enormous sum, which
might be saved to the nation.[3] Supposing that every shilling of this
sum could be saved, and that every shilling of it was expended in
supporting the dignity of the crown – both which suppositions are
entirely false – still should I think the liberty, the prosperity, the
tranquillity, the happiness of this great nation cheaply purchased by
such a sum; still should I think that he would be a madman in politics
who would, by a change of the constitution, risk these blessings (and
France supplies us with a proof that infinite risk would be run) for a
paltry saving of expense. I am not, nor have ever been, the patron of
corruption. So far as the civil-list has a tendency to corrupt the
judgment of any member of either house of parliament, it has a bad
tendency, which I wish it had not; but I cannot wish to see the
splendour of the crown reduced to nothing, lest its proper weight in
the scale of the constitution should be thereby destroyed. A great
portion of this million is expended in paying the salaries of the judges,
the interpreters of our law, the guardians of our lives and properties!
Another portion is expended in maintaining ambassadors at different
courts, to protect the general concerns of the nation from foreign
aggression; another portion is expended in pensions and donations to
men of letters and ingenuity; to men who have, by naval, military, or
civil services, just claims to the attention of their country; to persons
of respectable families and connections, who have been humbled and
broken down by misfortunes. I do not speak with accuracy, nor on
such a subject is accuracy requisite; but I am not far wide of truth in
saying, that a fifth part of the million is more than sufficient to defray
the expenses of the royal household. What a mighty matter is it to
complain of, that each individual contributes less than sixpence a year
towards the support of the monarchy!

That the constitution of this country is so perfect as neither to
require or admit of any improvement, is a proposition to which I
never did or ever can assent; but I think it far too excellent to be
amended by peasants and mechanics. I do not mean to speak of

Richard Watson (1737–1816)

peasants and mechanics with any degree of disrespect; I am not so ignorant of the importance, either of the natural or social chain by which all the individuals of the human race are connected together, as to think disrespectfully of any link of it. Peasants and mechanics are as useful to the State as any other order of men; but their utility consists in their discharging well the duties of their respective stations: it ceases when they affect to become legislators; when they intrude themselves into concerns for which their education has not fitted them. The liberty of the press is a main support of the liberty of the nation; it is a blessing which it is our duty to transmit to posterity; but a bad use is sometimes made of it; and its use is never more pernicious than when it is employed to infuse into the minds of the lowest orders of the community disparaging ideas concerning the constitution of their country. No danger need be apprehended from a candid examination of our own constitution, or from a display of the advantages of any other; it will bear to be contrasted with the best: but all men are not qualified to make the comparison; and there are so many men, in every community, who wish to have no government at all, that an appeal to them on such a point ought never to be made.

148

William Godwin

(1756–1836)

[handwritten: defensive strategies]

[handwritten: p. 11]

19. Enquiry Concerning Political Justice, and its Influence on Morals and Happiness (1793),

3rd edn, 2 vols., 1798; vol. I, pp. 15–50, 125–9, 229–36, 242–6, 267–74, 288–90; vol. II, pp. 124–40, 210–12, 500–10

Godwin, the son of a Dissenting minister, was educated at Hoxton Academy under the radical Dissenter Andrew Kippis, influenced in youth by the Calvinist creed of Sandemanianism (in which Thomas Spence was brought up), and himself became a Dissenting minister at Ware, Hertfordshire (1778), and then at Stowmarket, Suffolk (1779). Moving rapidly towards Deism under the influence of d'Holbach, Rousseau, and Helvetius (and shortly afterwards, Priestley), he gave up the ministry in 1782 and earned his living thereafter by writing. During the 1780s he wrote Whiggish propaganda (*A Life of Chatham*, 1783, and *A Defence of the Rockingham Party*, 1783) and moralistic novels. He moved in Joseph Johnson's London circle, but it was another Dissenting publisher, George Robinson, who paid him the advance he needed to enable him to write *Political Justice*, which he published in February 1793.

Political Justice is Godwin's major literary achievement, along with the novel *Caleb Williams* (1794), which is a kind of rider to it.[1] He was working on *Political Justice* for sixteen months, throughout the period of high radical optimism, but by the time it appeared *Rights of Man*, Part I, had already been out for two years. Many of the positions and gestures, even some of the phrases, of *Political Justice* would thus already seem familiar to the reader of Paine's work. The reader would have been likely to notice such connections, since *Political Justice* emerged into a fraught atmosphere, in which hysteria over Paine made one large element, the execution of the French King and the declaration of war with France another (see pp. 7–10). Though nowadays often discussed as though it were an academic treatise, *Political Justice* addresses the topic of *The Rights of Man*: it is another hostile analysis of aristocratic society, which Godwin sees as upheld by a deliberate fraud, or imposition, of the governors upon the governed.

At the same time, *Political Justice* is also a more deeply considered, researched, academic book than *The Rights of Man*, and the programme of reading Godwin undertook for it, in the French *philosophes* and in the Anglo-Scottish empiricists, marks it out as a work intended for the educated

149

minority rather than for the masses. (Godwin and his friends believed that it was not prosecuted by Pitt's government only on account of its price: thirty-six shillings for the first edition, a quarto – not three guineas, as in early versions of the story – and fourteen shillings for the later octavo editions.) Godwin's theorisings explain the social mechanism in terms more satisfactory to the educated reader than Paine's. He is subtler than Paine, and more sustained than Tooke, in probing the influence of aristocracy not merely over institutions like Parliament and the Law, but also over ideas and culture. Through institutions, oppression is systematised; through ideology, it is all-pervasive and almost irresistible – 'the opinions of men [are], for the most part, under the absolute control of political institutions' (p. 155). The particular educated reader for whom Godwin writes would seem to be a member of one of the overlapping circles, of active reforming Dissenters like Kippis, or of artist-intellectuals like Fuseli and Holcroft, in which Godwin moved and, as his diary shows, debated in 1791–3. Though secular in its language, the book derives from a Protestant concern with the individual conscience, an originally religious preference for private judgment over external, state authority.

Political Justice is sometimes called a clumsy book – timidly chairbound when it should have been activist, or tediously abstract just when Paine had shown how writing on intellectual topics could be done plainly and pithily. These charges are not unfair. Godwin's social ambience was far narrower than Paine's or Burke's, and in approaching their common task – a portrait of the Aristocrat, of the Common (middle-class) Man, and of the struggle between the two – he writes as though his knowledge of aristocrats is notional, or from books. Godwin's inexperience also results in a curious failure of proportion or of common sense. It is easy to laugh at him when, in illustrating the proposition that we should think justly rather than partially, he suggests that if Fénelon and Fénelon's servant were caught in a fire, and we could save only one of them, we should save Fénelon – even if the servant were our mother (3rd edn has father).[2] Another frequently caricatured passage suggests that, when the hierarchical state withers away, we shall all need to work for only two hours a day and can spend the rest of our waking hours philosophising with our friends.[3] Views like these emerged, surely, in the trustful, sympathetic atmosphere engendered within a group of idealists. Yet elsewhere in his book Godwin, like Paine in *The Age of Reason*, introduces a bitterly divisive note, and gives hostages to the enemies of reform, when he appears to recommend free love in preference to marriage (p. 168).

The relentless, humourless air of specialisation that led Lamb to dub Godwin 'the Professor' does not obscure the full topical significance of *Political Justice*, a profoundly political book. The complete answer to Burke's idiosyncratic, emotional *Reflections* must present its case dispassionately. Under the repressed and awkward style, Godwin's approach is inventive, imaginative. While Burke thinks what it would be like to be outcast and alienated, Godwin shows, no less plausibly, what it is like to be terrorised within existing society, by the very father-figures whom Burke idealises. For Burke, we are and should be children, guided by our kings and priests – 'We know that we have made no discoveries. . .'. For Godwin, 'we should divest ourselves . . . of the shackles of infancy . . . human life should not be one eternal childhood . . . men should judge for themselves, unfettered by the prejudices of education, or the institutions of their country' (p. 158).

Political Justice engages in a dialogue with Burke's *Reflections*. As Burke's book is essentially an apology for aristocracy, Godwin's is a critique of it, with the direct discussion of aristocratic government again, as in Burke (see p. 34), centrally placed in the book. Ten days after finishing the treatise, Godwin began his novel, *Caleb Williams*, which acts out the relations, in a stylised England, between a representative aristocratic master (Falkland) and a plebeian Everyman (Caleb). Falkland stands generically for the Aristocrat and is not a portrait of Burke, but he is often given Burke's arguments and tone, and his hold over Caleb is a brilliantly personalised version of the aura Burke bestows on patriarchal society in the *Reflections*. Caleb has presumed to enquire into his master's affairs, an act of intellectual independence which aristocracy forbids. (In *Political Justice* Godwin refers to 'the imposture, that would persuade us there is a mystery in government, which uninitiated mortals must not presume to penetrate'.)[4] In writing the novel, Godwin came to a maturer understanding of the bind into which we are led by imposition, and his novel persuades precisely because Caleb, the narrator, is so imperfectly rational, so insidiously betrayed into reverence for his 'master'. After the experience of writing *Caleb Williams*, many of Godwin's revisions to *Political Justice* deepen, one way or another, the exploration of how hierarchical societies work: the study of aristocracy (i.e., the prevailing European political system) is for example expanded by two substantially new chapters on 'Obedience' and 'Forms of Government' (see below, pp. 157–60).

The most fundamental revision was made in 1795, to take effect in the second edition of 1796. Put summarily, these alterations take Godwin more deeply into the consequences for individuals of living under existing political constraints: a number of discussions become more psychological, subjective, apparently personal. The changes reflect not only Godwin's further unaided thought, but the helpful criticisms which the immense prestige of *Political Justice* attracted from fellow-intellectuals. On the crest of a wave of literary success, Godwin comes to know more, and more varied, individuals, and his book benefits in subtlety. Yet the years of his rise, 1793–5, saw splits within his optimistic, idealistic, tight-knit Dissenting discussion-group, while radical action passed into the hands of the organisers of mass societies and orators at mass meetings, contexts in which the individual writer lost his prestige and influence. Godwin now spells out more clearly than in his first edition how far the individual should go in his pursuit of autonomy: above all, can violent revolution be justified? This is a profoundly awkward topic for the radical: it is more or less equally fatal to recommend armed resistance, and to state that it should never be resorted to. With characteristic tactlessness and bravery, Godwin faces the issue, and half-justifies revolution because of the people's suffering (p. 161), before moving more decisively than in the first edition towards recommending passivity. The most lasting reforms will be achieved gradually (which does not mean what 'gradualism' often means, that the political structure will be left untouched). Government needs political opinion to uphold it; once men's minds are free of imposition, no political institution will be strong enough to prevent the utopian withering-away of the state (p. 166). Nevertheless, for the present he comes out firmly against the two main instruments of radical action – political associations, and the political lecturing of Thelwall.[5] It could be said that the model for a radical hero ceases to be an activist like Thelwall, and becomes instead a philosopher like Godwin. With time, Godwin becomes more explicit about the virtue of political quietism. As yet, his compensatory belief in enlightenment – a process which his writings are part of – gives the individual thinker a power which is not at all incompatible with the optimism and genuine radicalism of 1790–2. The philosopher who sets out, like Caleb or like Godwin himself, to tear the veil off imposition, does so with the practical intention of altering the present system and is thus, strictly, a revolutionary. It was for this brand of intellectual radicalism that Shelley admired the Godwin of *Political Justice*, and became his lifelong disciple.

Some students of Godwin would argue that we should read the first edition, because they believe it to be the most radical, and see the later modifications as a yielding to political pressure. But each of the three versions responds to events, to the literary environment within which Godwin worked, and to the notional readership for which his book was intended: this was characteristic of the political writing of the 1790s. Because the analysis of aristocratic ascendancy gains in detail, originality, and cogency, *Political Justice* becomes in its successive stages a somewhat better intellectual performance. The only way to judge the issue is to examine the different versions fully, which can conveniently be done with the help of F. E. L. Priestley's facsimile of the third edition, to which he has added a volume of commentary.[6] The end note indicated at the end of each chapter that follows gives the date the material appeared in substantially its present form.

From Book I, chapter III: Spirit of Political Institutions

It is to be observed, that, in the most refined states of Europe, the inequality of property has risen to an alarming height. Vast numbers of their inhabitants are deprived of almost every accommodation that can render life tolerable or secure. Their utmost industry scarcely suffices for their support. The women and children lean with an insupportable weight upon the efforts of the man, so that a large family has in the lower orders of life become a proverbial expression for an uncommon degree of poverty and wretchedness. If sickness or some of those casualties which are perpetually incident to an active and laborious life, be added to these burthens, the distress is yet greater.

It seems to be agreed that in England there is less wretchedness and distress than in most of the kingdoms of the continent. In England the poors' rates amount to the sum of two millions sterling per annum. It has been calculated that one person in seven of the inhabitants of this country derives at some period of his life assistance from this fund. If to this we add the persons, who, from pride, a spirit of independence, or the want of a legal settlement, though in equal distress receive no such assistance, the proportion will be considerably increased.

I lay no stress upon the accuracy of this calculation; the general fact is sufficient to give us an idea of the greatness of the abuse. The consequences that result are placed beyond the reach of contradiction. A perpetual struggle with the evils of poverty, if frequently ineffectual, must necessarily render many of the sufferers desperate. A painful feeling of their oppressed situation will itself deprive them of the power of surmounting it. The superiority of the rich, being thus unmercifully exercised, must inevitably expose them to reprisals; and the poor man will be induced to regard the state of society as a state of war, an unjust combination, not for protecting every man in his rights and securing to him the means of existence, but for engrossing all its advantages to a few favoured individuals, and reserving for the portion of the rest want, dependence and misery. . . .

In many countries justice is avowedly made a subject of solicitation, and the man of the highest rank and most splendid connections almost infallibly carries his cause against the unprotected and friendless. In countries where this shameless practice is not established, justice is frequently a matter of expensive purchase, and the man with the longest purse is proverbially victorious. A consciousness of these facts must be expected to render the rich little cautious of offence in his dealings with the poor, and to inspire him with a temper overbearing, dictatorial and tyrannical. Nor does this indirect oppression satisfy his despotism. The rich are in all such countries directly or indirectly the legislators of the state; and of consequence are perpetually reducing oppression into a system, and depriving the poor of that little commonage of nature, which might otherwise still have remained to them. . . . legislation is in almost every country grossly the favourer of the rich against the poor. Such is the character of the game-laws, by which the industrious rustic is forbidden to destroy the animal that preys upon the hopes of his future subsistence, or to supply himself with the food that unsought thrusts itself in his path. Such was the spirit of the late revenue-laws of France, which in several of their provisions fell exclusively upon the humble and industrious, and exempted from their operation those who were best able to support it. Thus in England the land-tax at this moment produces half a million less than it did a century ago, while the taxes on consumption have experienced an addition of thirteen millions per annum during the same period. This is an attempt, whether effectual or no, to throw the burthen from the rich upon the poor, and as such is an example of the spirit of legislation. Upon the same principle robbery and other offences, which the wealthier part of the community have no temptation to commit, are treated as capital crimes, and attended with the most rigorous, often the most inhuman punishments. The rich are encouraged to associate for the execution of the most partial and oppressive positive laws; monopolies and patents are lavishly dispensed to such as are able to purchase them; while the most vigilant policy is employed to prevent combinations of the poor to fix the price of labour, and they are deprived of the benefit of that prudence and judgment which would select the scene of their industry. . . . The administration of law is not less iniquitous than the spirit in which it is framed. Under the late government of France the office of judge was a matter of purchase, partly by an open price advanced to the crown, and partly by a secret douceur paid to the minister. . . . In England the criminal law is administered with greater impartiality so far as regards the trial itself; but the number of capital offences, and of consequence the frequency of pardons, open a wide door to favour and abuse. In causes relating to property the practice of law is arrived at such a pitch as to render its nominal impartiality utterly nugatory. The length of our chancery suits, the multiplied appeals from court to court, the enormous fees of counsel, attornies, secretaries, clerks, the drawing of briefs, bills, replications and rejoinders, and what has sometimes been called the "glorious uncertainty" of the law, render it frequently more advisable to resign a property than to contest it, and particularly exclude the impoverished claimant from the faintest hope of redress.[7]

From Book I, chapter IV: The Characters of Men originate in their external circumstances

Thus far we have argued from historical facts, and from them have collected a very strong presumptive evidence, that political institutions have a more powerful and extensive influence, than it has been generally the practice to ascribe to them.

But we can never arrive at precise conceptions relative to this part of the subject, without entering into an analysis of the human mind, and endeavouring to ascertain the nature of the causes by which its operations are directed. Under this branch of the subject I shall attempt to prove two things; first, that the actions and dispositions of mankind are the offspring of circumstances and events, and not of any original determination that they bring into the world; and, secondly, that the great stream of our voluntary actions essentially depends, not upon the direct and immediate impulses of sense, but upon the decisions of the understanding. If these propositions can be sufficiently established, it will follow that the happiness men are able to attain, is proportioned to the justness of the opinions they take as guides in the pursuit; and it will only remain, for the purpose of applying these premises to the point under consideration, that we should demonstrate the opinions of men to be, for the most part, under the absolute control of political institution. . . .

It remains to be considered what share political institution and forms of government occupy in the education of every human being. Their degree of influence depends upon two essential circumstances.

First, it is nearly impossible to oppose the education of the preceptor, and the education we derive from the forms of government under which we live, to each other; and therefore, however powerful the former of these may be, absolutely considered, it can never enter the lists with the latter upon equal terms. Should any one talk to us of rescuing a young person from the sinister influence of a corrupt government by the power of education, it will be fair to ask, who is the preceptor by whom this task is to be effected? Is he born in the ordinary mode of generation, or does he descend among us from the skies? Has his character been in no degree modified, by that very influence he undertakes to counteract?. . . As long as parents and teachers in general shall fall under the established rule, it is clear that politics and modes of government will educate and infect us all. They poison our minds, before we can resist, or so much as suspect their malignity. Like the barbarous directors of the Eastern seraglios, they deprive us of our virility, and fit us for their despicable employment from the cradle. So false is the opinion that has too generally prevailed, that politics is an affair with which ordinary men have little concern.[8]

From Book II, chapter II: 'Of Justice'

From what has been said it appears, that the subject of our present enquiry is strictly speaking a department of the science of morals. Morality is the source from which its fundamental axioms must be drawn, and they will be made somewhat clearer in the present instance, if we assume the term justice as a general appellation for all moral duty. . . .

Considerable light will probably be thrown upon our investigation, if, quitting for the present the political view, we examine justice merely as it exists among individuals. Justice is a rule of conduct originating in the connection of one percipient being with another. A comprehensive maxim which has been laid down upon the subject is, "that we should love our neighbour as ourselves." But this maxim, though possessing considerable merit as a popular principle, is not modelled with the strictness of philosophical accuracy.

In a loose and general view I and my neighbour are both of us men; and of consequence entitled to equal attention. But, in reality, it is probable that one of us, is a being of more worth and importance than the other. A man is of more worth than a beast; because, being possessed of higher faculties, he is capable of a more refined and genuine happiness. In the same manner the illustrious archbishop of Cambray[9] was of more worth than his valet, and there are few of us that would hesitate to pronounce, if his palace were in flames, and the life of only one of them could be preserved, which of the two ought to be preferred.

But there is another ground of preference, beside the private consideration of one of them being further removed from the state of a mere animal. We are not connected with one or two percipient beings, but with a society, a nation, and in some sense with the whole family of mankind. Of consequence that life ought to be preferred which will be most conducive to the general good. In saving the life of Fénelon, suppose at the moment he conceived the project of his immortal Telemachus, I should have been promoting the benefit of thousands, who have been cured by the perusal of that work, of some error, vice and consequent unhappiness. Nay, my benefit would extend further than this; for every individual, thus cured, has become a better member of society, and has contributed in his turn to the happiness, information and improvement of others.

Suppose I had been myself the valet; I ought to have chosen to die, rather than Fénelon should have died. The life of Fénelon was really preferable to that of the valet. But understanding is the faculty that perceives the truth of this and similar propositions; and justice is the principle that regulates my conduct accordingly. It would have been just in the valet to have preferred the archbishop to himself. To have done otherwise would have been a breach of justice.[10]

Suppose the valet had been my brother, my father or my benefactor. This would not alter the truth of the proposition. The life of

Fénelon would still be more valuable than that of the valet; and justice, pure, unadulterated justice, would still have preferred that which was most valuable. Justice would have taught me to save the life of Fénelon at the expence of the other. What magic is there in the pronoun "my," that should justify us in over-turning the decisions of impartial truth? My brother or my father may be a fool or a profligate, malicious, lying or dishonest. If they be, of what consequence is it that they are mine?

"But to my father I am indebted for existence; he supported me in the helplessness of infancy." When he first subjected himself to the necessity of these cares, he was probably influenced by no particular motives of benevolence to his future offspring. Every voluntary benefit however entitles the bestower to some kindness and retribution. Why? Because a voluntary benefit is an evidence of benevolent intention, that is, in a certain degree, of virtue. It is the disposition of the mind, not the external action separately taken, that entitles to respect. But the merit of this disposition is equal, whether the benefit were conferred upon me or upon another. [11]

From Book III, chapter VI: 'Of Obedience'

The greatest mischief that can arise in the progress of obedience, is, where it shall lead us, in any degree, to depart from the independence of our understanding, a departure which general and unlimited confidence necessarily includes. In this view, the best advice that could be given to a person in a state of subjection, is, "Comply, where the necessity of the case demands it; but criticise while you comply. Obey the unjust mandates of your governors; for this prudence and a consideration of the common safety may require; but treat them with no false lenity, regard them with no indulgence. Obey; this may be right; but beware of reverence. Reverence nothing but wisdom and skill: government may be vested in the fittest persons; then they are entitled to reverence, because they are wise, and not because they are governors: and it may be vested in the worst. Obedience will occasionally be right in both cases: you may run south, to avoid a wild beast advancing in that direction, though you want to go north. But be upon your guard against confounding things, so totally unconnected with each other, as a purely political obedience, and respect. Government is nothing but regulated force; force is its appropriate claim upon your attention. It is the business of individuals to persuade; the tendency of concentrated strength, is only to give consistency and permanence to an influence more compendious than persuasion.". . .

William Godwin (1756–1836)

One of the lessons most assiduously inculcated upon mankind in all ages and countries, is that of reverence to our superiors. If by this maxim be intended our superiors in wisdom, it may be admitted, but with some qualification. But, if it imply our superiors in station only, nothing can be more contrary to reason and justice. . . . Why reverence a man because he happens to be born to certain privileges; or because a concurrence of circumstances (for wisdom, as we have already seen, gives a claim to respect utterly distinct from power) has procured him a share in the legislative or executive government of our country? Let him content himself with the obedience which is the result of force; for to that only is he entitled. . . .

The reverence which is due from a child to his parent, or rather to his senior in age and experience, falls under the same rules as have already been delivered. Wherever I have good reason to believe, that another person knows better than myself what is proper to be done, there I ought to conform to his direction. But the advantage which he possesses, must be obvious, otherwise I shall not be justified in my proceeding. . . . The deference of a child becomes vicious, whenever he has reason to doubt that the parent possesses essential information, of which he is deprived. Nothing can be more necessary for the general benefit, than that we should divest ourselves, as soon as the proper period arrives, of the shackles of infancy; that human life should not be one eternal childhood; but that men should judge for themselves, unfettered by the prejudices of education, or the institutions of their country.[12] *1796*

From Book III, chapter VII: 'Of Forms of Government'

Government, in particular, is founded in opinion; nor can any attempt to govern men, otherwise than in conformity to their own conceptions, be expected to prove salutary. A project therefore to introduce abruptly any species of political institution, merely from a view to its absolute excellence, and without taking into account the state of the public mind, must be absurd and injurious. The best mode of political society, will, no doubt, be considered by the enlightened friend of his species, as the ultimate object of his speculations and efforts. But he will be on his guard against precipitate measures. The only mode for its secure and auspicious establishment, is through the medium of a general preference in its favour. . . .

It follows, however, from the principles already detailed, that the interests of the human species require a gradual, but uninterrupted change. He who should make these principles the regulators of his conduct, would not rashly insist upon the instant abolition of all existing abuses. But he would not nourish them with false praise. He would show no indulgence to their enormities. He would tell all the truth he could discover, in relation to the genuine interests of mankind. Truth, delivered in a spirit of universal kindness, with no narrow resentments or angry invective, can scarcely be dangerous, or fail, so far as relates to its own operation, to communicate a similar spirit to the hearer. Truth, however unreserved be the mode of its enunciation, will be sufficiently gradual in its progress. It will be fully comprehended, only by slow degrees, by its most assiduous votaries; and the degrees will be still more temperate, by which it will pervade so considerable a portion of the community, as to render them mature for a change of their common institutions.

Again: if conviction of the understanding be the compass which is to direct our proceedings in the general affairs, we shall have many reforms, but no revolutions.[13] As it is only in a gradual manner that the public can be instructed, a violent explosion in the community, is by no means the most likely to happen, as the result of instruction. Revolutions are the produce of passion, not of sober and tranquil reason. There must be an obstinate resistance to improvement on the one side, to engender a furious determination of realising a system at a stroke on the other. The reformers must have suffered from incessant counteraction, till, inflamed by the treachery and art of their opponents, they are wrought up to the desperate state of imagining that all must be secured in the first favourable crisis, as the only alternative for its being ever secured. It would seem therefore, that the demand of the effectual ally of the public happiness, upon those who enjoy the privileges of the state, would be, "Do not give us too soon; do not give us too much; but act under the incessant influence of a disposition to give us something."

Government, under whatever point of view we examine this topic, is unfortunately pregnant with motives to censure and complaint. Incessant change, everlasting innovation, seem to be dictated by the true interests of mankind. But government is the perpetual enemy of change. What was admirably observed of a particular system of government,[14] is in a great degree true of all: They "lay their hand on the spring there is in society, and put a stop to its motion." Their tendency is to perpetuate abuse. Whatever was once thought right and useful, they undertake to entail to the latest posterity. They reverse the genuine propensities of man, and, instead of suffering us to proceed, teach us to look backward for perfection. They prompt us to seek the public welfare, not in alteration and improvement, but in a timid reverence for the decisions of our ancestors, as if it were the nature of the human mind always to degenerate, and never to advance.[15]

Man is in a state of perpetual mutation. He must grow either better or worse, either correct his habits or confirm them. The government under which we are placed, must either increase our passions and prejudices by fanning the flame, or, by gradually discouraging, tend to extirpate them. In reality, it is impossible to conceive a government that shall have the latter tendency. By its very nature positive institution has a tendency to suspend the elasticity and progress of mind. Every scheme for embodying imperfection must be injurious. That which is to-day a considerable melioration, will at some future period, if preserved unaltered, appear a defect and disease in the body politic. It is earnestly to be desired, that each man should be wise enough to govern himself, without the intervention of any compulsory restraint; and, since government, even in its best state, is an evil, the object principally to be aimed at is, that we should have as little of it, as the general peace of human society will permit.[16]

From Book IV, chapter II: 'Of Revolutions'

Revolution is engendered by an indignation against tyranny, yet is itself evermore pregnant with tyranny. The tyranny which excites its indignation, can scarcely be without its partisans; and, the greater is the indignation excited, and the more sudden and vast the fall of the oppressors, the deeper will be the resentment which fills the minds of the losing party. What more unavoidable, than that men should entertain some discontent, at being violently stripped of their wealth and their privileges? What more venial, than that they should feel some attachment, to the sentiments in which they were educated, and which, it may be, but a little before, were the sentiments of almost every individual in the community? Are they obliged to change their creed, precisely at the time at which I see reason to alter mine? . . .

Revolution is instigated by a horror against tyranny, yet its own tyranny is not without peculiar aggravations. There is no period more at war with the existence of liberty. The unrestrained communication of opinions has always been subjected to mischievous counteraction, but upon such occasions it is trebly fettered. . . . Where was there a revolution, in which a strong vindication of what it was intended to abolish, was permitted, or indeed almost any species of writing or argument, that was not, for the most part, in harmony with the opinions which happened to prevail? An attempt to scrutinise men's thoughts, and punish their opinions, is of all kinds of despotism the most odious; yet this attempt is peculiarly characteristic of a period of revolution. . . .

Perhaps no important revolution was ever bloodless. It may be useful in this place, to recollect in what the mischief of shedding blood consists. The abuses which at present exist in political society are so enormous, the oppressions which are exercised so intolerable, the ignorance and vice they entail so dreadful, that possibly a dispass-ionate enquirer might decide that, if their annihilation could be purchased, by an instant sweeping of every human being now arrived at years of maturity, from the face of the earth, the purchase would not be too dear. It is not because human life is of so considerable value, that we ought to recoil from the shedding of blood. Alas! the men that now exist, are for the most part poor and scanty in their portion of enjoyment, and their dignity is no more than a name. Death is in itself among the slightest of human evils. An earthquake, which should swallow up a hundred thousand individuals at once, would chiefly be to be regretted for the anguish it entailed upon survivors; in a fair estimate of those it destroyed, it would often be comparatively a trivial event. The laws of nature which produce it, are a fit subject of investigation; but their effects, contrasted with many other events, are scarcely a topic of regret. The case is altogether different, when man falls by the hand of his neighbour. Here a thousand ill passions are generated. The perpetrators, and the witnesses of murders, become obdurate, unrelenting and inhuman. Those who sustain the loss of relations or friends by a catastrophe of this sort, are filled with indignation and revenge. Distrust is propagated from man to man, and the dearest ties of human society are dissolved. It is impossible to devise a temper, more inauspicious to the cultivation of justice, and the diffusion of benevolence.

To the remark, that revolutions can scarcely be unaccompanied with the shedding of blood, it may be added that they are necessarily crude and premature. Politics is a science. The general features of the nature of man are capable of being understood, and a mode may be delineated which, in itself considered, is best adapted to the condition of man in society. . . . Imperfect institutions, as has already been shown,[17] cannot long support themselves, when they are generally disapproved of, and their effects truly understood. There is a period, at which they may be expected to decline and expire, almost without an effort. Reform, under this meaning of the term, can scarcely be considered as of the nature of action. Men feel their situation; and the restraints that shackled them before, vanish like a deception. When

William Godwin (1756–1836)

such a crisis has arrived, not a sword will need to be drawn, not a finger
to be lifted up in purposes of violence. The adversaries will be too few
and too feeble, to be able to entertain a serious thought of resistance
against the universal sense of mankind.

Under this view of the subject then it appears, that revolutions,
instead of being truly beneficial to mankind, answer no other purpose,
than that of marring the salutary and uninterrupted progress, which
might be expected to attend upon political truth and social improvement. They disturb the harmony of intellectual nature. They propose
to give us something, for which we are not prepared, and which we
cannot effectually use. They suspend the wholsome advancement of
science, and confound the process of nature and reason.[18] *1796*

From Book IV, chapter III: 'Of Political Associations'

If we would arrive at truth, each man must be taught to enquire and
think for himself. If a hundred men spontaneously engage the whole
energy of their faculties upon the solution of a given question, the
chance of success will be greater, than if only ten men are so employed.
By the same reason, the chance will also be increased, in proportion as
the intellectual operations of these men are individual, and their
conclusions are suggested by the reason of the thing, uninfluenced by
the force either of compulsion or sympathy. But, in political associations, the object of each man, is to identify his creed with that of his
neighbour. We learn the Shibboleth of a party. We dare not leave our
minds at large in the field of enquiry, lest we should arrive at some
tenet disrelished by our party. We have no temptation to enquire.
Party has a more powerful tendency, than perhaps any other circumstance in human affairs, to render the mind quiescent and stationary.
Instead of making each man an individual, which the interest of the
whole requires, it resolves all understandings into one common mass,
and subtracts from each the varieties, that could alone distinguish him
from a brute machine. Having learned the creed of our party, we have
no longer any employment for those faculties, which might lead us to
detect its errors. We have arrived, in our own opinion, at the last page
of the volume of truth; and all that remains, is by some means to effect
the adoption of our sentiments, as the standard of right to the whole
race of mankind. . . . In fine, from these considerations it appears, that
associations, instead of promoting the growth and diffusion of truth,
tend only to check its accumulation, and render its operation, as far as
possible, unnatural and mischievous.

There is another circumstance to be mentioned, strongly calculated

to confirm this position. A necessary attendant upon political associations, is harangue and declamation. A majority of the members of
any numerous popular society, will look to these harangues, as the
school in which they are to study, in order to become the reservoirs of
practical truth to the rest of mankind. But harangues and declamation, lead to passion, and not to knowledge. The memory of the
hearer is crowded with pompous nothings, with images and not
arguments. He is never permitted to be sober enough, to weigh
things with an unshaken hand. It would be inconsistent with the art of
eloquence, to strip the subject of every meretricious ornament.
Instead of informing the understanding of the hearer by a slow and
regular progression, the orator must beware of detail, must render
every thing rapid, and from time to time work up the passions of his
hearers to a tempest of applause. Truth can scarcely be acquired in
crowded halls and amidst noisy debates. Where hope and fear,
triumph and resentment, are perpetually afloat, the severer faculties of
investigation are compelled to quit the field. Truth dwells with
contemplation. We can seldom make much progress in the business of
disentangling error and delusion, but in sequestered privacy, or in the
tranquil interchange of sentiments that takes place between two
persons.[19] *1796*

From Book V, chapter XV: 'Of Political Imposture'

All the arguments that have been employed to prove the insufficiency
of democracy, grow out of this one root, the supposed necessity of
deception and prejudice for restraining the turbulence of human
passions. Without the assumption of this principle the argument
could not be sustained for a moment. The direct and decisive answer
would be, "Are kings and lords intrinsically wiser and better than their
humbler neighbours? Can there be any solid ground of distinction,
except what is founded in personal merit? Are not men, really and
strictly considered, equal, except so far as what is personal and
inalienable, establishes a difference?" To these questions there can be
but one reply, "Such is the order of reason and absolute truth, but
artificial distinctions are necessary for the happiness of mankind.
Without deception and prejudice the turbulence of human passions
cannot be restrained." Let us then examine the merits of this
theory. . . .

How many arts, and how noxious to those towards whom we
employ them, are necessary, if we would successfully deceive? We
must not only leave their reason in indolence at first, but endeavour to

supersede its exertion in any future instance. If men be, for the present, kept right by prejudice, what will become of them hereafter, if, by any future penetration, or any accidental discovery, this prejudice shall be annihilated? Detection is not always the fruit of systematical improvement, but may be effected by some solitary exertion of the faculty, or some luminous and irresistible argument, while every thing else remains as it was. If we would first deceive, and then maintain our deception unimpaired, we shall need penal statutes, and licensers of the press, and hired ministers of falshood and imposture. Admirable modes these for the propagation of the wisdom and virtue!

There is another case. . . upon which much stress has been laid by political writers. "Obedience," say they, "must either be courted or compelled. We must either make a judicious use of the prejudices and the ignorance of mankind, or be contented to have no hold upon them but their fears, and to maintain social order entirely by the severity of punishment. To dispense us from this painful necessity, authority ought carefully to be invested with a sort of magic persuasion. Citizens should serve their country, not with a frigid submission that scrupulously weighs its duties, but with an enthusiasm that places its honour in its loyalty. For this reason, our governors and superiors must not be spoken of with levity. They must be considered, independently of their individual character, as deriving a sacredness from their office. They must be accompanied with splendour and veneration.[20] . . .

This is still the same argument under another form. It takes for granted, that a true observation of things, is inadequate to teach us our duty; and, of consequence, recommends an equivocal engine, which may, with equal ease, be employed in the service of justice and injustice, but would surely appear somewhat more in its place in the service of the latter. It is injustice that stands most in need of superstition and mystery, and will most frequently be a gainer by the imposition. This hypothesis proceeds upon an assumption, which young men sometimes impute to their parents and preceptors. It says, "Mankind must be kept in ignorance: if they know vice, they will love it too well; if they perceive the charms of error, they will never return to the simplicity of truth." And, strange as it may appear, this bare-faced and unplausible argument, has been the foundation of a very popular and generally received hypothesis. It has taught politicians to believe, that a people, once sunk into decrepitude, as it has been termed, could never afterwards be endued with purity and vigour.[21] . . .

19. *Enquiry Concerning Political Justice*

The system of political imposture divides men into two classes, one of which is to think and reason for the whole, and the other to take the conclusions of their superiors on trust. This distinction is not founded in the nature of things; there is no such inherent difference between man and man, as it thinks proper to suppose. Nor is it less injurious, than it is unfounded. The two classes which it creates, must be more and less than man. It is too much to expect of the former, while we consign to them an unnatural monopoly, that they should rigidly consult for the good of the whole. It is an iniquitous requisition upon the latter, that they should never employ their understandings, or penetrate into the essences of things, but always rest in a deceitful appearance. It is iniquitous, to deprive them of that chance for additional wisdom, which would result, from a greater number of minds being employed in the enquiry, and from the disinterested and impartial spirit that might be expected to accompany it. . . .

With respect to the multitude, in this system, they are placed in the middle between two fearful calamities, suspicion on one side, and infatuation on the other. . . . Sometimes they suppose their governors to be the messengers and favourites of heaven, a supernatural order of beings; and sometimes they suspect them to be a combination of usurpers to rob and oppress them. For they dare not indulge themselves in solving the dilemma, because they are held in awe by oppression and the gallows.

Is this the genuine state of man? Is this a condition so desirable, that we should be anxious to entail it upon posterity for ever? Is it high treason to enquire whether it may be meliorated? Are we sure, that every change from such a situation of things, is severely to be deprecated? Is it not worth while, to suffer that experiment, which shall consist in a gradual, and almost insensible, abolition of such mischievous institutions?

It may not be uninstructive to consider what sort of discourse must be held, or book written, by him who should make himself the champion of political imposture. He cannot avoid secretly wishing that the occasion had never existed. What he undertakes is to lengthen the reign of "salutary prejudices." For this end, he must propose to himself the two opposite purposes, of prolonging the deception, and proving that it is necessary to deceive. By whom is it that he intends his book should be read? Chiefly by the governed; the governors need little inducement to continue the system. But, at the same time that he tells us, we should cherish the mistake as mistake, and the prejudice as prejudice, he is himself lifting the veil, and destroying his own system. While the affair of our superiors and the enlightened, is simply, to impose upon us, the talk is plain and intelligible. But, the moment they begin to write books, to persuade us that we ought to be willing to be deceived, it may well be suspected that their system is upon the decline. It is not to be wondered at, if the greatest genius, and the sincerest and most benevolent champion, should fail in producing a perspicuous or very persuasive treatise, when he undertakes so hopeless a task.[22]

From Book V, chapter XXIV: 'Of the Dissolution of Government'

In proportion as the spirit of party was extirpated, as the restlessness of public commotion subsided, and as the political machine became simple, the voice of reason would be secure to be heard. . . .

At first, we will suppose, that some degree of authority and violence would be necessary. But this necessity does not appear to arise out of the nature of man, but out of the institutions by which he has been corrupted. Man is not originally vicious. He would not refuse to listen to, or to be convinced by, the expostulations that are addressed to him, had he not been accustomed to regard them as hypocritical, and to conceive that, while his neighbour, his parent, and his political governor, pretended to be actuated by a pure regard to his interest or pleasure, they were, in reality, at the expence of his, promoting their own. Such are the fatal effects of mysteriousness and complexity. Simplify the social system, in the manner which every motive, but those of usurpation and ambition, powerfully recommends; render the plain dictates of justice level to every capacity; remove the necessity of implicit faith; and we may expect the whole species to become reasonable and virtuous. It might then be sufficient for juries to recommend a certain mode of adjusting controversies, without assuming the prerogative of dictating that adjustment. It might then be sufficient for them to invite offenders to forsake their errors. . . .

The reader has probably anticipated the ultimate conclusion from these remarks. If juries might at length cease to decide, and be contented to invite, if force might gradually be withdrawn and reason trusted alone, shall we not one day find, that juries themselves, and every other species of public institution, may be laid aside as unnecessary? Will not the reasonings of one wise man, be as effectual as those of twelve? Will not the competence of one individual to instruct his neighbours, be a matter of sufficient notoriety, without the formality of an election? Will there be many vices to correct, and much obstinacy to conquer? This is one of the most memorable stages of human improvement. With what delight must every well informed

friend of mankind look forward, to the auspicious period, the dissolution of political government, of that brute engine, which has been the
only perennial cause of the vices of mankind, and which, as has
abundantly appeared in the progress of the present work, has mischiefs of various sorts incorporated with its substance, and no otherwise removable than by its utter annihilation![23]

*From Book VIII, chapter VIII, Appendix: 'Of Co-operation, Cohabitation
and Marriage'*

. . . individuality is of the very essence of intellectual excellence. . . .
The truly venerable, and the truly happy, must have the fortitude to
maintain his individuality. . . .

From these principles it appears, that every thing that is usually
understood by the term cooperation, is, in some degree, an evil. . . .
In society he will find pleasure; the temper of his mind will prepare
him for friendship and for love. But he will resort with a scarcely
inferior eagerness to solitude; and will find in it the highest com-
placence and the purest delight.

Another article which belongs to the subject of cooperation, is
cohabitation. The evils attendant on this practice, are obvious. In
order to the human understanding's being successfully cultivated, it is
necessary, that the intellectual operations of men should be independent of each other.[24] We should avoid such practices as are calculated
to melt our opinions into a common mould. Cohabitation is also
hostile to that fortitude, which should accustom a man, in his actions,
as well as in his opinions, to judge for himself, and feel competent to
the discharge of his own duties. Add to this, that it is absurd to expect
the inclinations and wishes of two human beings to coincide, through
any long period of time. To oblige them to act and to live together, is
to subject them to some inevitable portion of thwarting, bickering
and unhappiness. . . .

The subject of cohabitation is particularly interesting, as it includes
in it the subject of marriage. It will therefore be proper to pursue the
enquiry in greater detail. The evil of marriage, as it is practised in the
European countries, extends further than we have yet described. The
method is, for a thoughtless and romantic youth of each sex, to come
together, to see each other, for a few times, and under circumstances
full of delusion, and then to vow eternal attachment. What is the
consequence of this? In almost every instance they find themselves
deceived. They are reduced to make the best of an irretrievable
mistake. They are led to conceive it their wisest policy, to shut their

William Godwin (1756–1836)

eyes upon realities, happy, if, by any perversion of intellect, they can persuade themselves that they were right in their first crude opinion of each other. Thus the institution of marriage is made a system of fraud; and men who carefully mislead their judgments in the daily affair of their life, must be expected to have a crippled judgment in every other concern.

Add to this, that marriage, as now understood, is a monopoly, and the worst of monopolies. So long as two human beings are forbidden, by positive institution, to follow the dictates of their own mind, prejudice will be alive and vigorous. So long as I seek, by despotic and artificial means, to maintain my possession of a woman, I am guilty of the most odious selfishness. . . .

The abolition of the present system of marriage, appears to involve no evils. We are apt to represent that abolition to ourselves, as the harbinger of brutal lust and depravity. But it really happens, in this, as in other cases, that the positive laws which are made to restrain our vices, irritate and multiply them. Not to say, that the same sentiments of justice and happiness, which, in a state of equality, would destroy our relish for expensive gratifications, might be expected to decrease our inordinate appetites of every kind, and to lead us universally to prefer the pleasures of intellect to the pleasures of sense.

It is a question of some moment, whether the intercourse of the sexes, in a reasonable state of society, would be promiscuous, or whether each man would select for himself a partner, to whom he will adhere, as long as that adherence shall continue to be the choice of both parties. Probability seems to be greatly in favour of the latter. Perhaps this side of the alternative is most favourable to population. . . . It is the nature of the human mind, to persist, for a certain length of time, in its opinion or choice. The parties therefore, having acted upon selection, are not likely to forget this selection when the interview is over. Friendship, if by friendship we understand that affection for an individual which is measured singly by what we know of his worth, is one of the most exquisite gratifications, perhaps one of the most improving exercises, of a rational mind. Friendship therefore may be expected to come in aid of the sexual intercourse, to refine its grossness, and increase its delight. All these arguments are calculated to determine our judgment in favour of marriage as a salutary and respectable institution, but not of that species of marriage, in which there is no room for repentance, and to which liberty and hope are equally strangers.

Admitting these principles therefore as the basis of the sexual commerce, what opinion ought we to form respecting infidelity to this attachment? Certainly no ties ought to be imposed upon either party, preventing them from quitting the attachment, whenever their judgment directs them to quit it.[25]

20. *Cursory Strictures on the Charge Delivered by Lord Chief Justice Eyre to the Grand Jury, October 2, 1794* (1794),

pp. 3–9, 12–14, 24–6

Though not a member of the radical associations on principle (see p. 162), Godwin knew many of the middle-class radicals prosecuted in the series of trials which began with Paine's in December 1792. In early 1794, when he was finishing *Caleb Williams*, Godwin frequently saw one of radicalism's martyrs, Joseph Gerrald, at first as he awaited sentence, latterly in Newgate before he was transported to Botany Bay.[26] The emotional sense in the novel of oppression, of indignant identification with the law's victims, was won at first hand. As Godwin was finishing *Caleb Williams*, in May of that year, twelve London radicals, among them Hardy, Tooke and Godwin's friend Holcroft, were arrested, three to be tried later that year on the capital charge of High Treason. Godwin's outspoken Preface to *Caleb Williams*, in which he emphasises that it is a novel about injustice, is pointedly dated the day of Hardy's arrest, 12 May 1794, and alludes to the newly formulated crime of 'constructive treason'. Before the trial in October, Godwin wrote his *Cursory Strictures*, a twelve-thousand-word article on behalf of the defendants, which appeared first in the *Morning Chronicle* of 21 October, and was afterwards published by D. I. Eaton from the shop he now provocatively called the Cock and Swine (see below, p. 185). The pamphlet met with difficulties, as a prefatory note explained:

The following Work was originally published By Mr. KEARSLEY, who, on receiving a menace from the Treasury, discontinued its sale: – DANIEL ISAAC EATON, who does not, perhaps, consider a menace from that place in the same way as Mr. Kearsley, – but believes that a TREASURY MANDATE is not yet generally adopted as the law of the land, was *thereby* induced upon application made to him, not only to sell what remained of the first edition, but also to offer to the public, at half price, a work, which as its only crime is, perhaps, the containing more law than the Charge on which it animadverts, cannot but be very acceptable to those who would rather expend six-pence than a shilling. And as posterity may need every proof that a charge, so fraught with labour and invention, was ever given, the Charge itself is annexed at the same reduced price.

Godwin was afterwards proud of this performance, and boasted that it was much admired; understandably so, for it is calculated to secure support. This is an unusually judicious and worldly Godwin, the liberal Whig propagandist of the 1780s, who had learnt his craft from the Burke of the American war, and the young Pitt of the same era. The hero of the tale is the English Constitution, with its laws guaranteeing freedom of thought and expression, and safeguarding the individual citizen from the arbitrary tyranny of his betters. It is interesting to compare Godwin's description here of the law of treason, 'one of the great palladiums of the English constitution',[27] with the grim portrait he had just drawn in *Caleb Williams* of the workings of the law. Yet in the *Cursory Strictures* too, Godwin's tongue is in his cheek when he writes of the law and lawyers; unlike the ordinary Whig orator on the Constitution, he seems to marvel at the 'careful, lenient and unbloody' law of treason, especially when he thinks about judges. Only in his preamble (and then briefly) does Mr. Justice Eyre sound as if he might try the case leniently, let alone impartially. Godwin's real impression of the English law is kept severely in check, however, to emerge startlingly in the *coup de théâtre* of the final paragraph, when he allows the medieval sentence for treason, so very different from the medieval definition of it, to speak for the barbarity of what his friends are actually threatened with.

Godwin's own estimation, that his pamphlet secured the acquittal of Hardy, Tooke, and Thelwall, the only three brought to trial, cannot be proved, and overlooks the equally admirable conduct of the defence in court by Thomas Erskine. But the vociferousness of the Foxite Whigs in Parliament a year later, when Grenville and Pitt were pushing through their two Sedition Bills, demonstrates that this continued to be the most telling liberal issue for upper- and middle-class moderates; the defence of liberty could still, given the occasion and the rhetorician, outweigh fears for property, and muster in the opposition some sense of a common cause.

A special Commission was opened on the Second day of October for the trial of certain persons apprehended upon suspicion of High Treason, the greatest part of whom were taken into custody in the month of May 1794. Upon this occasion a charge was delivered to the Grand Jury, by Sir James Eyre, Lord Chief Justice of the Court of Common Pleas.[28]

It is one of the first privileges of an Englishman, one of the first duties of a rational being, to discuss with perfect freedom, all principles proposed to be enforced upon general observance, when those principles are first disclosed, and before they have, by any solemn and final proceeding, been made part of a regular established system. The Chief Justice, in his Charge to the Jury, has delivered many new and extraordinary doctrines upon the subject of Treason. These doctrines, now when they have been for the first time stated, it is fit we should examine. . . .

Among the various branches of the English Constitution that have for centuries been a topic of unbounded praise, there is none, that has been more, or more deservedly, applauded, than that which relates to the law of Treason. "The crime of High Treason," says Chief Justice Eyre, "though the greatest crime against faith, duty, and human society, and though the public is deeply interested in every well founded prosecution of this kind, has yet, at the best times, been the object of considerable jealousy, in respect of the prosecutions instituted against it: they are State prosecutions." It is therefore of the utmost consequence, that the crime of High Treason should be clearly defined, and the exquisite jealousy allayed, which must otherwise arise in every benevolent mind. This has been done by the act 25 Edward III, one of the great palladiums of the English constitution. This law has been sanctioned by the experience of more than four centuries; and, though it has been repeatedly attacked by the encroachments of tyrannical princes, and the decisions of profligate judges, Englishmen have always found it necessary in the sequel to strip it of mischievous appendages and artificial glosses, and restore it to its original sim- plicity and lustre. By this law all treason, exclusively of a few articles of little general concern, is confined to the "levying war against the King within the realm, and the compassing or imagining the death of the King." Nay, the wise framers of the law were not contented to stop here: they not only shut out the mischief of arbitrary and constructive treason for themselves, but inserted a particular clause, providing that "if in any future time it might be necessary to declare any new treasons, that should only be done by a direct proceeding of parlia- ment for that special purpose."

It is obvious upon the face of this wise and moderate law, that it made it extremely difficult for a bad king, or an unprincipled adminis- tration, to gratify their resentment against a pertinacious opponent by instituting against him a charge of treason. Such kings and ministers would not fail to complain, that the law of Edward III shut up the crime within too narrow bounds; that a subtle adversary of the public peace would easily evade these gross and palpable definitions; and that crimes of the highest magnitude, and most dangerous tendency, might be committed, which could never be brought under these dry, short, and inflexible clauses. It is not to be denied, that some mischief might arise from so careful, lenient, and unbloody a provision. No doubt offences might be conceived, not less dangerous to the public welfare, than those described in the act under consideration. But our ancestors exposed themselves to this inconvenience, and found it by no means such as was hard to be borne. They experienced a substantial benefit, a proud and liberal security, arising out of this statute, which amply compensated for the mischief of such subterfuges as might occasionally be employed by a few insignificant criminals. If we part with their wisdom and policy, let us beware that we do not substitute a mortal venom in its stead.

The Chief Justice has thought proper to confine himself to that article of the statute of King Edward III which treats of "compassing and imagining the death of the King." This compassing and imagining, he very properly observes, "requires that it should be manifested by overt acts";[29] and he adds, "that they who aim directly at the life of the King, are not the only persons who may be said to compass or imagine his death. The entering into measures, which in the nature of things do *obviously* tend to bring the life of the King into danger, is also compasssing and imagining the death of the King; and the measures which are taken, will be at once evidence of the compassing and overt acts of it. The instances which are put under this head by Sir Michael Foster[30] and Sir Matthew Hale,[31] and upon which there have been adjudged cases, are [principally four, viz.] of a conspiracy to depose the King, to imprison him, to get his person into the power of the conspirators, and to procure an invasion of the kingdom."[32] He farther states "that occasions have unhappily but too frequently brought overt acts of this species of treason under consideration, in consequence of which we are furnished with judicial opinions upon many of them. We are also furnished with opinions drawn from these sources of text writers, some of the wisest and most enlightened men of their time, whose integrity has always been considered as the most prominent feature of their character, and whose doctrines do now form great land marks, by which posterity will be enabled to trace with considerable certainty the boundary line between High Treason, and offences of a lower order and degree. It is a fortunate circumstance," continues the Chief Justice, "that we are thus assisted. I can easily conceive that it must be a great relief to Jurors, placed in the responsible situation in which you now stand; and sure I am that it is a consolation and comfort to us, who have upon us the responsibility of declaring what the law is, in cases in which the public and the individual are so deeply interested."[33]

In all this preamble of the Chief Justice, there is certainly something extremely humane and considerate. I trace in it the language of a constitutional lawyer, a sound logician, and a temperate, discreet, and honest man. I see rising to my view by just degrees a judge, resting upon the law as it is, and determinedly setting his face against new, unprecedented, and temporizing constructions. I see a judge, that scorns to bend his neck to the yoke of any party, or any administration; who expounds the unalterable principles of justice, and is prepared to try by them, and them only, the persons that are brought before him. I see him taking to himself, and holding out to the Jury the manly consolation, that they are to make no new law, and force no new interpretations; that they are to consult only the statutes of the realm, and the decisions of those writers who have been the luminaries of England.

Meanwhile what would be said by our contemporaries and by our posterity, if this picture were to be reversed; if these promises were made, only to render our disappointment more bitter; if these high professions served merely as an introduction to an unparalleled mass of arbitrary constructions, of new fangled treasons, and doctrines equally inconsistent with history and themselves? I hope these appearances will not be found in the authentic charge. But whoever be the unprincipled impostor, that thus audaciously saps the vitals of human liberty and human happiness, be he printer, or be he judge, it is the duty of every friend to mankind to detect and expose his sophistries.

Chief Justice Eyre, after having stated the treasons which are most strictly within the act of Edward III as well as those which are sanctioned by high law authorities, and upon which there have been adjudged cases, proceeds to reason in the following manner.

"If a conspiracy to depose or imprison the King, to get his person into the power of the conspirators, or procure an invasion of the kingdom, involves in it the compassing and imagining his death, and if steps taken in prosecution of such a conspiracy, are rightly deemed overt acts of the treason of compassing the King's death," what ought to be our judgment, "if it should appear that it had entered into the heart of any man, who is a subject of this country, to design to overthrow the whole government of the country, to pull down and to subvert from its very foundations the British Monarchy, that glorious fabric, which it has been the work of ages to erect, maintain, and support; which has been cemented with the best blood of our ancestors; to design such a horrible ruin and devastation, which no king could survive?"[34]

Here we are presented with the question which is no doubt of the utmost magnitude and importance. Is the proceeding thus described matter of High Treason, or is it not? It confessedly does not come within the letter of 25 Edward III. It does not come within the remoter instances "upon which there have been adjudged cases." Chief Justice Eyre has already enumerated these, and, having finished that part of his subject, gone on to something confessedly different.

Are we reasoning respecting law, or respecting a state of society, which, having no fixed rules of law, is obliged to consult the dictates of its own discretion? Plainly the former. It follows therefore, that the aggravations collected by the Chief Justice, are totally foreign to the question he had to consider. Let it be granted, that the crime, in the eye of reason and discretion, is the most enormous, that it can enter into the heart of man to conceive, still I shall have a right to ask, Is it a crime against law? Show me the statute that describes it; refer me to the precedent by which it is defined; quote me the adjudged case in which a matter of such unparalleled magnitude is settled.

Let us know the ground upon which we stand. Are we to understand that, under Chief Justice Eyre, and the other Judges of the Special Commission, reasonings are to be adduced from the axioms and dictums of moralists and metaphysicians, and that men are to be convicted, sentenced, and executed, upon these? Are we to understand that henceforth the man most deeply read in the laws of his country, and most assiduously conforming his actions to them, shall be liable to be arraigned and capitally punished for a crime, that no law describes, that no precedent or adjudged case ascertains, at the arbitrary pleasure of the administration for the time being? Such a miserable miscellany of law and metaphysical maxims, would be ten thousand times worse, than if we had no law to direct our actions. The law in that case would be a mere trap to delude us to our ruin, creating a fancied security, an apparent clearness and definition, the better to cover the concealed pitfalls with which we are on every side surrounded.

The Chief Justice is by no means unaware of the tremendous consequences that would result from such an administration of criminal law. He speaks respecting it, when the subject is first started, with great temperance and caution. He says, "That the crime of conspiring to overthrow the monarchy, is such an one, as *no lawgiver in this country has ever ventured to contemplate in its whole extent*. If any man of plain sense, but not conversant with subjects of this nature, should feel himself disposed to ask, whether a conspiracy of this extraordinary nature is to be reached by the statute of treasons? whether it is a specific treason to compass and imagine the death of the King, and not a specific treason to conspire to subvert the Monarchy itself? I answer, that *the statute of Edward III, by which we are bound, has not declared this*, which undoubtedly in all just theory of treason is the greatest of all treasons, *to be a specific high treason*. I said, NO LAWGIVER HAD EVER VENTURED TO CONTEMPLATE IT IN ITS WHOLE EXTENT."[35]

The language here employed is no doubt strong and decisive. From hence it follows, with the most irresistible evidence, that that "which the statute by which we are bound, has not declared to be treason," that "which no lawgiver has ever ventured to contemplate," can never be construed into treason, till all law is annihilated, and all maxims of jurisprudence trampled under foot and despised. . . .

The first mode in which, according to Chief Justice Eyre, an association for Parliamentary Reform, may incur the penalties of High Treason, is, when "other purposes, besides those of Parliamentary Reform, and of the most traiterous nature, are hidden under this veil."[36] The purposes he may be supposed to mean, are those of his new-fangled treason, of "conspiring to subvert the Monarchy." Thus, in the first place we have an innocent purpose constituting the professed object of this supposed association; and behind that the Grand Jury are to discover, if they can, a secret purpose, totally unlike that which the associators profess; and this purpose Chief Justice Eyre declares to be treason, contrary, as he avowedly confesses, to all law, precedent, and adjudicated cases.

The second mode, in which the Chief Justice is willing to presuppose High Treason in an association for Parliamentary Reform is by such an association, not in its own nature, as he says, "simply unlawful, too easily degenerating, and becoming unlawful in the highest degree."[37]

It is difficult to comment upon this article with the gravity, that may seem due to a magistrate, delivering his opinions from a bench of justice. An Association for Parliamentary Reform may "degenerate, and become unlawful in the highest degree, even to the enormous extent of the crime of High Treason." Who knows not that? Was it necessary that Chief Justice Eyre should come in 1794, solemnly to announce to us so irresistible a proposition? An association for Parliamentary Reform may desert its object, and be guilty of High Treason. True: so may a card club, a bench of justices, or even a cabinet council. Does Chief Justice Eyre mean to insinuate, that there is something in the purpose of a Parliamentary Reform, so unhallowed, ambiguous and unjust, as to render its well wishers objects of suspicion, rather than their brethren and fellow subjects? What can be more wanton, cruel, and inhuman, than thus gratuitously to single out the purposes of Parliamentary Reform, as if it were of all others, most especially connected with degeneracy and treason?

But what is principally worthy of observation in both these cases, is, the easy and artful manner in which the idea of treason is introduced into them. First, there is a "concealed purpose," or an insensible "degeneracy" *supposed* to take place in these associations. Next, that "concealed purpose," or insensible "degeneracy," is *supposed* to tend directly to this end, the "subversion of the Monarchy." Lastly, a "conspiracy to subvert the Monarchy," is a treason, first discovered

William Godwin (1756–1836)

by Chief Justice Eyre in 1794, never contemplated by any lawgiver, or included in any statute. Deny the Chief Justice any one of his three assumptions, and his whole deduction falls to the ground. Challenge him, or any man living, to prove any of them; and you require of him an impossibility. And it is by this sort of logic, which would be scouted in the rawest graduate in either of our Universities, that Englishmen are to be brought under the penalties of treason! . . .

If these principles be established, utterly subversive as they are of the principles of the English government, who will say that we shall stop here? Chief Justice Eyre says to-day, "all men may, nay, all men must, if they possess the faculty of thinking, reason upon every thing, that sufficiently interests them to become an object of their attention; and among the objects of attention of freemen, the principles of government, the constitution of particular governments, and, above all, the constitution of the government under which they live, will naturally engage attention, and provoke speculation." But who will say how long this liberty will be tolerated, if the principles, so alarmingly opened in the charge to the Grand Jury, shall once be established? This is the most important crisis, in the history of English liberty, that the world ever saw. If men can be convicted of High Treason, upon such constructions and implications as are contained in this charge, we may look with conscious superiority upon the republican speculations of France, but we shall certainly have reason to envy the milder tyrannies of Turkey and Ispahan.

From what has been said it appears, that the whole proceedings intended in the present case, are of the nature of an *ex post facto* law.[a] This is completely admitted by the Chief Justice. In summing up the different parts of his charge, he enumerates three cases, in the first of which he directs the Grand Jury to throw out the bills, and in that of the two last to find them true bills. One of these two relates to Chief Justice Eyre's new treason of "a conspiracy to subvert the Monarchy," a treason which, he says, is not declared by the statute of Edward III and no lawgiver in this country has ever ventured to contemplate. The other, "that of overawing Parliament," he states to be a new and doubtful case, and recommends, that it should be "put into a judicial course of enquiry, that it may receive a solemn adjudication whether it will or will not amount to High Treason."

Thus it is fully admitted, respecting the persons now under accusation, that they could find no reason, either in the books of our law, or of any commentators of received authority, to suppose that they were

[a] An *ex post facto* law is a retrospective law that makes criminal what was not criminal when it was done.

incurring the guilt of treason. "The mark set upon this crime, the token by which it could be discovered, lay entirely concealed; and no human prudence, no human innocence, could save them from the destruction with which they are at present threatened."[38].

It is pretty generally admitted, that several of those persons, at least, were honest and well-intentioned, though mistaken men. Punishment is awarded in human Courts of Justice, either according to the intention, or the mischief committed. If the intention be alone to be considered, then the men of whom I speak, however unguarded and prejudicial their conduct may be supposed to have been, must on that ground be infallibly acquitted. If, on the other hand, the mischief incurred be the sole measure of the punishment, we are bound by every thing that is sacred to proceed with reluctance and regret. Let it be supposed, that there are cases, where it shall be necessary, that a well designing man should be cut off, for the sake of the whole. The least consideration that we can pay in so deplorable a necessity, is, to warn him of his danger, and not suffer him to incur the penalty, without any previous caution, without so much as the knowledge of its existence.

I anticipate the trials to which this Charge is the prelude. I know that the Judge will admit the good intention and honest design of several of the persons arraigned: it will be impossible to deny it; it is notorious to the whole universe. He has already admitted, that there is no law or precedent for their condemnation. If therefore he address them in the frank language of sincerity, he must say, "Six months ago you engaged in measures, which you believed conducive to the public good. You examined them in the sincerity of your hearts, and you admitted them with the full conviction of the understanding. You adopted them from this ruling motive, the love of your country and mankind. You had no warning that the measures in which you engaged were acts of High Treason: no law told you so; no precedent recorded it; no man existing upon the face of the earth could have predicted such an interpretation. You went to your beds with a perfect and full conviction, that you had acted upon the principles of immutable justice, and that you had offended no provision or statute that was ever devised. I, the Judge sitting upon the bench, you, Gentlemen of the Jury, every inhabitant of the island of Great Britain, had just as much reason to conceive they were incurring the penalties of the law, as the prisoners at the bar. This is the nature of the crime; these are the circumstances of the case."

"And for this, the Sentence of the Court [but not of the law] is, *That you, and each of you, shall be taken from the bar, and conveyed to the*

William Godwin (1756–1836)

place from whence you came, and from thence be drawn upon a hurdle to the place of execution, there to be hanged by the neck, but not until you are dead; you shall be taken down alive, your privy members shall be cut off, and your bowels shall be taken out and burnt before your faces; your heads shall be severed from your bodies, and your bodies shall then be divided into four quarters, which are to be at the King's disposal; and the Lord have mercy on your souls!"

Hannah More

(1745–1833)

21. *Village Politics. Addressed to all the Mechanics, Journeymen, and Day Labourers, in Great Britain.* By Will Chip, a Country Carpenter (Canterbury, 1793),

pp. 1–9, with cuts

In November 1792 John Reeves set up the Association for Preserving Liberty and Property against Republicans and Levellers, known for short as 'the Association'. Whether or not it began at the government's initiative, the Association had the support of powerful parliamentary figures like Pitt, Burke, and Windham, and its major enterprises, the publication and distribution of pamphlets and loyalist resolutions, were probably government-funded. By putting into circulation innumerable tracts, of which the *Liberty and Property* series (from 1793) were the most famous, the Association tried to reach the hearts and minds of the populace, in writing even more closely designed for a semi-literate readership than Paine's.

Hannah More's *Village Politics* is individually the most celebrated of the Association's tracts. It was distributed, probably free, by the East Kent and Canterbury Associations. It can also claim to be one of the best conceived for its proposed readership, since Hannah More writes a vivid vernacular English, can convey character through dialogue, and preserves a nice disinterestedness in her approach to rank: Jack Anvil the blacksmith is thoughtful and well informed, but the squire's wife is fantastical, or 'rantipolish' (see p. 182), and does good only by accident. By making both her interlocutors working men, Hannah More avoids the didactic and patronising impression left by innumerable pamphlets of the period, in which (perhaps on the model of dialogues for children between wise adults and their pupils) a gentleman soundly lectures a member of the lower orders.

Hannah More went on to depict a greater variety of character and situation in her *Cheap Repository Tracts* (1795–8), which cost between a penny and one and a half pence. By March 1796 the total number sold had already reached two million, making this the most remarkable feat of circulation of the decade. More was criticised for teaching the masses to read by her conservative Somerset neighbours, and by *The Antijacobin*, yet she impressed on the poor the Christian merit of submitting patiently to

179

one's lot in the world. Her religious convictions give depth to her writing for the semi-literate, which stylistically compares well with projects for the same readership by Eaton and Spence.

A DIALOGUE between JACK ANVIL the Blacksmith, and TOM HOD the Mason.

Jack. What's the matter, Tom? Why dost look so dismal?

Tom. Dismal indeed! Well enough I may.

Jack. What's the old mare dead? or work scarce?

Tom. No, no, work's plenty enough, if a man had but the heart to go to it.

Jack. What book art reading? Why dost look so like a hang dog?

Tom. (looking on his book.) Cause enough. Why I find here that I'm very unhappy, and very miserable; which I should never have known if I had not had the good luck to meet with this book. O 'tis a precious book!

Jack. A good sign tho'; that you can't find out you're unhappy without looking into a book for it. What is the matter?

Tom. Matter? Why I want liberty.

Jack. Liberty! What has any one fetched a warrant for thee? Come man, cheer up, I'll be bound for thee. – Thou art an honest fellow in the main, tho' thou dost tipple and prate a little too much at the Rose and Crown.

Tom. No, no, I want a new constitution.

Jack. Indeed! Why I thought thou hadst been a desperate healthy fellow. Send for the doctor then.

Tom. I'm not sick; I want Liberty and Equality, and the Rights of Man.

Jack. O now I understand thee. What thou art a leveller and a republican I warrant. . . .

Tom. I'm a friend to the people. I want a reform. . . . I want freedom and happiness, the same as they have got in France.

Jack. What, Tom, we imitate them? We follow the French! Why they only begun all this mischief at first, in order to be just what *we* are already. . . .

Tom. . . . Down with the jails, I say; all men should be free.

Jack. Harkee, Tom, a few rogues in prison keep the rest in order, and then honest men go about their business, afraid of nobody; that's the way to be free. And let me tell thee, Tom, thou and I are tried by our peers as much as a lord is. Why the *king* can't send me to prison if I do no harm, and if I do, there's reason good why I should go there. I may go to law with Sir John, at the great castle yonder, and he no more dares lift his little finger against me than if I were his equal. A lord is hanged for hanging matter, as thou or I should be; and if it will be any comfort to thee, I myself remember a Peer of the Realm being hanged for killing his man, just the same as the man wou'd have been for killing *him*.[1]

Tom. Well, that is some comfort. – But have you read the Rights of Man?

Jack. No, not I. I had rather by half read the *Whole Duty of Man*.[2] I have but little time for reading, and such as I should therefore only read a bit of the best.

Tom. Don't tell me of those old fashioned notions. Why should not we have the same fine things they have got in France? I'm for a *Constitution*, and *Organization*, and *Equalization*. . . .

Jack. I'll tell thee a story. When Sir John married, my Lady, who is a little fantastical, and likes to do every thing like the French, begged him to pull down yonder fine old castle, and build it up in her frippery way. No, says Sir John, what shall I pull down this noble building, raised by the wisdom of my brave ancestors; which outstood the civil wars, and only underwent a little needful repair at the Revolution; and which all my neighbours come to take a pattern by – shall I pull it all down, I say, only because there may be a dark closet or an inconvenient room or two in it? My Lady mumpt and grumbled; but the castle was let stand, and a glorious building it is, though there may be a trifling fault or two, and tho' a few decays may want stopping; so now and then they mend a little thing, and they'll go on mending, I dare say, as they have leisure, to the end of the chapter, if they are let alone. But no pull-me-down works. What is it you are crying out for, Tom?

Tom. Why for a perfect government.

Jack. You might as well cry for the moon. There's nothing perfect in this world, take my word for it. . . .

Tom. But I say all men are equal. Why should one be above another?

Jack. If that's thy talk, Tom, thou dost quarrel with Providence and not with government. For the woman is below her husband, and the children are below their mother, and the servant is below his master.

Tom. But the subject is not below the king; all kings are "crowned ruffians;"[3] and all governments are wicked. For my part, I'm resolved I'll pay no more taxes to any of them.

Jack. Tom, Tom, this is thy nonsense; if thou didst go oftner to church, thou wou'dst know where it is said, "Render unto Cesar the things that are Cesar's";[4] and also, "Fear God, honour the king."[5]

Hannah More (1745–1833)

Tom. I don't see why one man is to ride in his coach and six, while another mends the highway for him.

Jack. I don't see why the man in the coach is to *drive over* the man on foot, or hurt a hair of his head. And as to our great folks, that you levellers have such a spite against; I don't pretend to say they are a bit better than they should be; but that's no affair of mine; let them look to that; they'll answer for that in another place. To be sure, I wish they'd set us a better example about going to church, and those things; but still *hoarding's* not the sin of the age; they don't lock up their *money* – away it goes, and every body's the better for it. They do spend too much, to be sure, in feasting and fandangoes, and if I was a parson I'd go to work with 'em in another kind of a way; but as I am only a poor tradesman, why 'tis but bringing more grist to my mill. It all comes among the people – Their coaches and their furniture, and their buildings, and their planting, employ a power of tradespeople and labourers. – Now in this village; what shou'd we do without the castle? Tho' my Lady is too rantipolish,[a] and flies about all summer to hot water and cold water, and fresh water and salt water, when she ought to stay at home with Sir John; yet when she does come down, she brings such a deal of gentry that I have more horses than I can shoe, and my wife more linen than she can wash. Then all our grown children are servants in the family, and rare wages they have got. Our little boys get something every day by weeding their gardens, and the girls learn to sew and knit at Sir John's expence; who sends them all to school of a Sunday.[6]

Tom. Aye, but there's not Sir Johns in every village.

Jack. The more's the pity. But there's other help. 'Twas but last year you broke your leg, and was nine weeks in the Bristol 'Firmary, where you was taken as much care of as a lord, and your family was maintained all the while by the parish. No poor-rates in France, Tom; and here there's a matter of two million and a half paid for them, if 'twas but a little better managed.

Tom. Two million and a half!

Jack. Aye, indeed. Not translated into ten-pences, as your French millions are, but twenty good shillings to the pound. But, when this levelling comes about, there will be no 'firmaries, no hospitals, no charity-schools, no sunday-schools, where so many hundred thousand poor souls learn to read the word of God for nothing. For

---

[a] *Rantipole*: first citation, *O.E.D.* 1700; a romp, a wild, ill-behaved, or reckless person. The argument that aristocratic vice benefits the poor goes back to Bernard Mandeville's *Fable of the Bees* (1714).

who is to pay for them? *equality* can't afford it; and those that may be willing won't be able. . . .

Tom. What then dost thou take French *liberty* to be?

Jack. To murder more men in one night, than ever their poor king did in his whole life.

Tom. And what dost thou take a *Democrat* to be?

Jack. One who likes to be governed by a thousand tyrants, and yet can't bear a king.

Tom. What is *Equality*?

Jack. For every man to pull down every one that is above him, till they're all as low as the lowest.

Tom. What is *the new Rights of Man*?

Jack. Battle, murder, and sudden death.

Tom. What is it to be an *enlightened people*?

Jack. To put out the light of the gospel, confound right and wrong, and grope about in pitch darkness.

Tom. What is *Philosophy*, that Tim Stannish talks so much about?

Jack. To believe that there's neither God, nor devil, nor heaven, nor hell. . . . Tom! I have got the use of my limbs, of my liberty, of the laws, and of my Bible. The two first, I take to be my *natural* rights; the two last my *civil* and *religious*; these, I take it, are the *true Rights of Man*, and all the rest is nothing but nonsense and madness and wickedness. My cottage is my castle; I sit down in it at night in peace and thankfulness, and "no man maketh me afraid."[7] Instead of indulging discontent, because another is richer than I in this world, (for envy is at the bottom of your equality works,) I read my bible, go to church, and think of a treasure in heaven.

Tom. Aye; but the French have got it in *this* world.

Jack. Tis all a lye, Tom. Sir John's butler says his master gets letters which *say* 'tis all a lye. 'Tis all murder, and nakedness, and hunger; many of the poor soldiers fight without victuals, and march without clothes. These are your *democrats*! Tom.

Tom. And what mean the other hard words that Tim talks about – *organisation* and *function*, and *civism* and *incivism*, and *equalization*, and *inviolability*, and *imperscriptible*?

Jack. Nonsense, gibberish, downright hocus-pocus. . . .

Tom. Let me sum up the evidence, as they say at 'sizes – Hem! To cut every man's throat who does not think as I do, or hang him up at a lamp-post! – Pretend liberty of conscience, and then banish the parsons only for being conscientious! – Cry out liberty of the press, and hang up the first man who writes his mind! – Lose our poor laws! – Lose one's wife perhaps upon every little tiff! – March without clothes, and fight without victuals! – No trade! – No bible! – No sabbath nor day of rest! – No safety, no comfort, no peace in this world – and no world to come! – Jack, I never knew thee tell a lie in my life.

Jack. Nor wou'd I now, not even against the French.

Tom. And thou art very sure we are not ruined.

Jack. I'll tell thee how we are ruined. We have a king so loving, that he wou'd not hurt the people if he cou'd; and so kept in, that he cou'd not hurt the people if he wou'd. We have as much liberty as can make us happy, and more trade and riches than allows us to be good. We have the best laws in the world, if they were more strictly enforced; and the best religion in the world, if it was but better followed. While Old England is safe, I'll glory in her and pray for her, and when she is in danger, I'll fight for her and die for her.

Tom. And so will I too, Jack, that's what I will. (sings.)

"O the roast beef of Old England!"

Jack. Thou art an honest fellow, Tom.

Daniel Isaac Eaton

(d. 1814)

22. *Politics for the People*, or *Hog's Wash*,

from no. VIII (16 November 1793)

The intrepid bookseller D. I. Eaton was arrested six times between 1792 and 1795, but the prosecution found it hard to get juries to convict: on the fable of Thelwall's which was the subject of one charge (see below), the jury found that he had published the material but without malicious intent. He continued in business despite the passing of the Two Acts (see p. 249 n. 16) in December 1795, and was finally convicted of seditious libel in 1796. After publishing a further edition of Paine's *Age of Reason*, he fled to America, but returned in 1803 and was arrested and jailed for fifteen months for his earlier offences. In 1812 and 1813 he was convicted again, but excused from serving the second sentence because of his age. Like Spence, he died in 1814, too soon to see the next radical dawn.

Eaton and Spence launched similar weekly journals for a popular readership during 1793, in an attempt to counter the mass distribution of simply written tracts by John Reeves's loyalist Association (see p. 179). Their experience illustrates not only the personal hazards faced by those trying to write for the people during the reaction to Paine, but the technical difficulties in the way of doing it effectively. The title-page of *Hog's Wash, or a Salmagundy for Swine* indicates that it is a mélange of the kind of fare pioneered by the Association's tracts, and by provincial newspapers (see p. 11): 'Consisting of the choicest Viands, contributed by the Cooks of the present day, and of the highest flavoured delicacies, composed by the Caterers of former Ages'. The original title alludes to Burke's notorious offhand reference to 'a swinish multitude' (see p. 46); it was changed during November 1793 to the more dignified *Politics for the People*. The intention was from the outset to challenge Burke's assumptions about the stupidity and non-intellectuality of the masses, by offering them classic texts on politics and commentaries on public affairs. But the style and tone are uncertain, especially in the early numbers, which harp monotonously on the pig joke (as in 'Remonstrance of the Swinish Multitude to the Chief and Deputy Swineherds', no. V), and rely on the staples of chapbook literature, allegories, and fables. Sometimes these appear to originate with Eaton himself; sometimes, as in the fable of Chaunticleer, they are borrowed from someone else. The later numbers use more up-to-date selections, refer more frequently and

Daniel Isaac Eaton (d. 1814)

boldly to current affairs, and (a great strength in a journal) carry more material sent in by readers.

KING CHAUNTICLERE;
or, THE FATE OF TYRANNY:
An Anecdote, related by Citizen Thelwall, at the Capel Court Society, during the discussion of a Question, relative to the comparative Influence of the Love of Life, of Liberty, and of the fair Sex, on the Actions of Mankind.

We have been told, Citizen Chairman! by a learned orator,[1] who seems very fond of life, and who has drawn so depraved and contemptible a picture of human nature, that one must almost be ashamed of having lived to witness it, that the love of life must certainly have the strongest influence on the actions of mankind. And to prove this, he tells us a cock and bull story of Caractacus, at Rome;[2] who, when he had *lost his liberty*, thought it was better to have *life and love*, with a *prospect of regaining his liberty*, than to *die and have no such prospect at all*. He has told also another melancholy tale of a poor tortured slave in the West Indies. . . . This poor kidnapped negro, we are told, (for there are pressgangs to make men *slaves of labour* as well as *slaves of war*) having had his hands and feet chopped off, by order of his tyrant masters, on account of some *seditious* attempt to regain his freedom, was afterwards put into a large frying pan over the fire, that he might expiate, by his tortures, that impious love of liberty which he had the audacity to entertain. In the midst of his torments, we are told, that one of his companions, more compassionate than the rest, rushed towards him, and, aiming a blow with his cudgel, would have dashed out his brains, had not the poor mutilated wretch conceived (such is the curious reasoning that is offered to us by the tame advocates of life without liberty) that the tortures of the frying pan were preferable to instant death, and therefore lifted his poor bleeding stumps, with sudden terror, and broke the force of the blow.[3] Now, if this magnanimous advocate for the *frying pan of despotism*, had happened to have reflected a little on the physical laws of the animal frame, he would have known that this motion of the arms was merely involuntary, and that neither love, nor fear, nor liberty, nor any other preference of the judgment, had any thing at all to do with it – it being natural to all animals, after they have been long used to perform certain actions in consequence of any particular stimulus, applied either to the sight or any other of the senses, to continue those actions, by mere mechanical impulse, whenever the usual objects are presented, without ever reflecting what it is they are doing: just as men, of base and abject minds, who have been long used to cringe and tremble at the names of kings and lords, for fear they should be clapped up in bastiles, or turned out of their shops, continue to cringe and tremble, when neither shops nor bastiles happen to be present to their imaginations

But in order to set this difference between mental and muscular action, in a clearer point of view before you, I will tell you Citizen President! a little anecdote concerning a youthful exploit of my own. – You must know then, that I used, together with a variety of youthful attachments, to be very fond of birds and poultry; and among other things of this kind, I had a very fine majestic kind of animal, a game cock: a haughty, sanguinary tyrant, nursed in blood and slaughter from his infancy – fond of foreign wars and *domestic rebellions*, into which he would sometimes drive his subjects, by his oppressive obstinacy, in hopes that he might increase his power and glory by their suppression. Now this haughty old tyrant would never let my farmyard be quiet; for, not content with devouring by far the greater part of the grain that was scattered for the morning and evening repast, and snatching at every little treasure that the toil of more industrious birds might happen to scratch out of the bowels of the earth, the restless despot must be always picking and cuffing at the poor doves and pullets, and little defenceless chickens, so that they could never eat the scanty remnant, which his inordinate taxation left them, in peace and quietness. Now, though there were some aristocratic prejudices hanging about me, from my education, so that I could not help looking, with considerable reverence, upon the majestic decorations of the person of king Chaunticlere – such as his ermine spotted breast, the fine gold trappings about his neck and shoulders, the flowing robe of plumage tucked up at his rump, and, above all, that fine ornamented thing upon his head there – (his crown, or *coxcomb*, I believe you call it – however the distinction is not very important) yet I had even, at that time, some lurking principles of aversion to barefaced despotism struggling at my heart, which would sometimes whisper to me, that the best thing one could do, either for cocks and hens, or men and women, was to rid the world of tyrants, whose shrill martial clarions (the provocatives to fame and murder) disturbed the repose and destroyed the happiness of their respective communities. So I believe, if guillotines had been in fashion, I should have certainly guillotined him: being desirous to be merciful, even in the stroke of death, and knowing, that the instant the brain is separated from the heart, (which, with this instrument, is done in a moment,) pain and consciousness are at end – while the lingering torture of the rope may procrastinate the pang for half an hour. However, I managed the business very well; for I caught Mr. Tyrant by the head, and dragging him immediately to the block, with a heavy knife in my hand, separated his neck at a blow: and what will surprise you very much, when his fine trappings were stripped off, I found he was no better than a common tame scratch-dunghill pullet: no, nor half so good, for he was tough, and oily, and rank with the pollutions of his luxurious vices. But that which it is particularly my duty to dwell upon, as applicable to the story of the poor mutilated negro, is the continuance of the habitual muscular motion after (by means of the loss of his head) he was no longer capable of knowing what he was about. In short, having been long in the habit of flying up, and *striking* with his spurs, and cuffing about with his *arms* – or his *wings*, if you please (for anatomists can tell you, that arms are only wings without feathers, and wings are nothing but feathered arms) he still continued the same hostile kind of action, bouncing, and flapping, and spurring, and scuffling about, till the muscular energy (as they call it) was exhausted; so that if the gentleman had been there, with his club stick, attempting to knock the mutilated tyrant down, he might have concluded, every time that he flapped up his wings against the stick, that this effort of King Chaunticlere proceeded from the conviction that life was worth preserving even after he had lost his head: which, in my opinion, would be just about as rational as supposing that it can be worth preserving to that man who is writhing about in *the frying pan of despotism*.

This story was received with almost unanimous applause, as was also the whole speech, till Citizen Thelwall, alluding to the wonderful exertions, which Liberty was stimulating the French to make against the whole united force of Europe, he was interrupted by some of the members of the committee; and though, upon appeal to a shew of hands, five or six to one appeared in his favour, the chairman refused to hear him; declared the society adjourned, and quitted the chair. This produced considerable confusion; and, on the part of the committee, much insolent abuse; and even an attempt from one individual to do personal violence to the speaker, by coming behind him, and attempting to fling him down. Notwithstanding which he continued to harrangue the people; and was at last conducted away with shouts of triumph by the greater part of the company.

Thomas Spence

(1750–1814)

23. *The Meridian Sun of Liberty; or the Whole Rights of Man Displayed and most Accurately Defined.* In a Lecture read at the Philosophical Society in Newcastle, on the 8th of November, 1775, for printing of which the Society did the Author the honor to expel him. To which is now first prefixed, by way of Preface, a most important Dialogue between the Citizen Reader and the Author (1796),

pp. 2–3, 8–12

One of nineteen children of a netmaker and shoemaker, Spence was taught his letters from the Bible by his father. The family lived in Newcastle, centre of a mining region with an artisan presence in its politics, and belonged to a religious sect known as the Sandemanians or 'Glassites', which believed in a community of goods among members of the same church. In 1775 Spence read to a Newcastle Philosophical Society a paper on the parochial ownership of land, which in the 1790s he reissued on a number of occasions, including it in *Pig's Meat* as 'The Real Rights of Man' (vol. II, pp. 220–9), and publishing it separately for one penny as *The Meridian Sun of Liberty* (see below). Also in 1775, Spence published his *Grand Repository of the English Language*, a pioneer argument for phonetic orthography (see above, p. 14). While he remained in Newcastle he published these works himself, but earned his living principally as a schoolmaster.

Spence moved to London in the revolutionary year 1792, in order to propagate his radical ideas. He set up a bookstall in Chancery Lane (later opening a shop in Little Turnstile, off High Holborn, called 'At the Hive of Liberty'), and by 1793 was issuing a penny weekly for working people called *Pig's Meat, or Lessons for the Swinish Multitude.* Spence's journal resembles Eaton's, except that it has more character: even the selections from Harrington, Locke, Swift, Voltaire, and others smack of Spence's own experience, as his title-page claims – 'Collected by the Poor Man's Advocate (an old Veteran in the Cause of Freedom) in the Course of his Reading for more than Twenty Years'. His own verse and prose, the other main ingredient, are of the same vintage, for Spence was not prolific, and his thought did not develop as it

189

might have done if he had mixed with other radicals. But what it lacks in variety, *Pig's Meat* makes up for in originality, and occasional humour. Spence evidently took much pleasure in the transcript of the proceedings at the Old Bailey on 24 February 1794, when Eaton was tried for sedition for publishing his fable of Chaunticleer (see preceding excerpt). The offending pamphlet was published entire, garnished with the prosecution's explanations of its political application: 'I had a very fine majestic kind of animal, a Game cock (*meaning thereby to denote and represent our said Lord the King*), a haughty, sanguinary tyrant. . . .' Spence promptly issued a new fable in the same style: 'The Lion (*not meaning our Sovereign Lord the King*) and several other beasts (*not meaning the continental Kings and Powers*) . . . . having made a sort of excursion (*not meaning in France*) by way of hunting, they took a very fine, large fat deer (*not meaning Dunkirk, Toulon, or any other place taken from the French*), which was divided into four parts. . . .' (*Pig's Meat*, vol. II, pp. 14–15). Spence had learnt a useful lesson, for at his own trial for sedition in 1801 he caused the pamphlet at issue, *The Restorer of Society to its Natural State*, to be read out in court, so that it would be published, with impunity, as part of the court record.

Though his career as a bookseller is similar to Eaton's, Spence is distinguished from Eaton and indeed from other radicals by his single-hearted pursuit of his main doctrine, the parish ownership of land – which is, in effect, a form of agrarian socialism. Between 1792 and 1795 he was arrested four times, and was in jail again in 1798 and 1801: the first offence was selling Paine's *Rights of Man*, but after that Spence was always charged with propagating his own doctrines. His message is addressed to the landless poor in plain language, which varies, like Tom Paine's, from direct, forceful appeals, or insults, to a workmanlike list of practical propositions. Spence differs from other radicals in never seeming to conciliate middle-class opinion, or to obscure the threat his ideas represent to existing owners of land. An eccentric and a 'loner', he lived on in London in great proverty. His cause and his personal example made him a hero to a small band of devoted Spensonians, headed by Thomas Evans, through whom his ideas became part of the stock of nineteenth-century British radicalism.

PREFACE *(added, 1796)*

Citizen Reader. Pray what is all this you make ado about Landlords, and Tenants, and Parishes? We don't understand you.

Author. That is surprising. I thought I had been very plain. But none are so blind as those who will not see. But the reason why I trouble you with my little publications, is, that I wish to teach you the Rights of Man.

Reader. Rights of Man! What? – Don't we yet know enough of the Rights of Man?

Author. No.

Reader. No! do you say? After all that Paine, Thelwall, and other

23. *The Meridian Sun of Liberty*

Philosophers, and the French Republic have taught us, do we not yet
know the Rights of Man?

Author. No.

Reader. Does not the whole Rights of Man consist in a fair, equal
and impartial representation of the People in a Parliament?

Author. No. Nobody ought to have right of suffrage or representation in a society wherein they have no property. As none are suffered
to meddle in the affairs of a benefit society or corporation, but those
who are members, by having a property therein, so none have a right to
vote or interfere in the affairs of the government of a country who have
no right to the soil; because such are and ought to be accounted
strangers.

Reader. Do you then account men born in a country as strangers to
it, and unworthy of suffrage, that unfortunately may have no title to
landed property?

Author. Most certainly I do. Especially such men as being afraid to
look their rights in the face, have disfranchised and alienated themselves, by denying and renouncing all claim to the soil of their birth,
and profess to be content with the "Right of property in the fruits of
their industry, ingenuity and good fortune." This is the right of
property that a Hottentot, a Chinese, or a native of the Moon may
claim among us, as well as you! Wherefore, as you are content with the
property of a foreigner, pray do likewise be content with the privileges
of a foreigner.

Reader. I tell you, we have a right to universal suffrage, as well as to
the fruits of our labour.

Author. And I tell you, that such Lacklanders as you have no right to
suffrage at all. . . .

Text (original version, 1775)

Let it be supposed then, that the whole people in some country, after
much reasoning and deliberation, should conclude, that every man has
an equal property in the land in the neighbourhood where he resides.
They therefore resolve, that if they live in society together, it shall only
be with a view, that every one may reap all the benefits from their
natural rights and privileges possible. Therefore, a day is appointed on
which the inhabitants of each parish meet, in their respective parishes,
to take their long-lost rights into possession, and to form themselves
into corporations. So, then each parish becomes a corporation, and all
the men who are inhabitants become members or burgers. The land
with all that appertains to it, is in every parish, made the property of the

corporation or parish, with as ample power to let, repair or alter all, or any part thereof, as a lord of the manor enjoys over his lands, houses &c. but the power of alienating the least morsel, in any manner, from the parish, either at this or any time hereafter, is denied. For it is solemnly agreed to, by the whole nation, that a parish that shall either sell, or give away, any part of its landed property, shall be looked upon with as much horror and detestation, and used by them as if they had sold all their children to be slaves, or massacred them with their own hands. Thus are there no more nor other landlords, in the whole country than the parishes; and each of them is sovereign landlord of its own territories.

O hearken! ye besotted sons of men. By this one bold resolve your chains are eternally broken, and your enemies anihilated. By this one resolve the power, the pride, and the arrogance of the landed interest, those universal and never ceasing scourges and plunderers of your race, are instantaneously and for ever broken and cut off. For being thus deprived and shorn of their revenues, they become like shorn Sampson, as weak as other men; weak as the poor dejected wretches whom they have so long been grinding and treading under foot.[1]

There you may behold the rent, which the people have paid into the parish treasuries employed by each parish in paying the government so much per pound to make up the sum, which the parliament or national representation at any time think requisite; in maintaining and relieving its own poor, and people out of work; in paying the necesary Officers their salaries; in building, repairing, and adorning its houses, bridges, and other structures; in making and maintaining convenient and delightful streets, highways, and passages both for foot and carriages; in making and maintaining canals, and other conveniences for trade and navigation; in planting and taking in waste grounds; in providing and keeping up a magazine of ammunition and all sorts of arms sufficient for all its inhabitants in case of danger from enemies; in premiums for the encouragement of agriculture, or any thing else thought worthy of encouragement; and, in a word, in doing whatever the people think proper; and not as formerly, to support and spread luxury, pride, and all manner of vice. As for corruption in elections, it has now no being or effect among them; all affairs to be determined by voting either in a full meeting of a parish, its committees, or in the house of Representatives, are done by balloting, so that votings, or elections among them, occasion no animosities, for none need to let another know for which side he votes; all that can be done, therefore, to gain a majority of votes for any thing, is to make it appear in the best light possible by speaking or writing.

23. *The Meridian Sun of Liberty*

Among them government does not meddle in every trifle but on the contrary, allows to each parish the power of putting the laws in force in all cases, and does not interfere, but when they act manifestly to the prejudice of society, and the rights and liberties of mankind as established in their glorious constitution and laws. For the judgment of a parish may be as much depended upon as that of a house of lords, because they have as little to fear from speaking or voting according to truth, as they.

A certain number of neighbouring parishes, chuse delegates to represent them in Parliament, Senate, or Congress: and each of them pays equally towards their maintainance. They are chosen thus: all the candidates are proposed in every parish on the same day, when the election by balloting immediately proceeds in all the parishes at once, to prevent too great a concourse at one place, and they who are found to have the majority on a proper survey of the several pole books are acknowledged to be their representatives.

A man by dwelling a whole year in any parish becomes a parishioner, or member of its corporation; and retains that privilege, till he lives a full year in some other, when he becomes a member in that parish, and immediately loses all his right to the former for ever, unless he chuse to go back and recover it, by dwelling again a full year there. Thus none can be a member of two parishes at once; and yet a man is always a member of one, though he move ever so oft.

If in any parish should be dwelling strangers from foreign nations, or people from distant parishes, who by sickness or other casualties should become so necessitous as to require relief before they have acquired a settlement by dwelling a full year therein; then this parish, as if it were their proper settlement, immediately takes them under its humane protection, and the expence thus incurred by any parish in providing for those not properly their own poor, being taken an account of, is deducted by the parish, out of the first payment made to the state. Thus poor strangers being the poor of the State, are not looked upon by their new neighbours where they have come to reside with an envious evil eye lest they should become burdensome; neither are the poor harassed about in the extremity of distress, and perhaps in a dying condition, to gratify the litigiousness of parishes.

All the men in the parish, at times, of their own chusing, repair together to a field for that purpose, with their officers, arms, banners, and all sorts of martial music, in order to learn or retain the complete art of war; there they become soldiers! Yet not to molest their neighbours unprovoked, but to be able to defend what none have a right to dispute their title to the enjoyment of; and woe be to them who occasion them to do this! they would use them worse than highwaymen, or pirates, if they got them in their power.

There is no army kept in pay among them, in times of peace; as all have a property in their country to defend, they are alike ready to run to arms when their country is in danger: and when an army is to be sent abroad, it is soon raised, of ready trained soldiers, either as volunteers, or by casting lots in each parish for so many men.

Besides, as each man has a vote in all the affairs of his parish, and for his own sake must wish well to the public, the land is let in very small farms, which makes employment for a greater number of hands, and makes more victualling of all kinds be raised.

There are no tolls or taxes of any kind paid among them, by native or foreigner, but the aforesaid rent. The government, poor, roads, &c. &c. as said before, are all maintained by the parishes with the rent: on which account, all wares, manufactures, allowable trade, employments, or actions, are entirely duty-free. Freedom to do any thing whatever cannot there be bought; a thing is either entirely prohibited as theft or murder; or entirely free to every one without tax or price.

When houses, lands, or any tenements become vacant they are let publicly by the parish officers in seven year leases to the best bidder. This way prevents collusion to the prejudice of the parish revenue and likewise prevents partiality.

Methinks I now behold the parish republics, like fraternal or benefit societies each met at quarter-day to pay their rents and to settle their accounts as well with the state as with all their parochial officers and workmen, their several accounts having been examined some days before. . . . Though I have only spoke of parishioners receiving dividends, which may be understood as if men only were meant to share the residue of the rents, yet I would have no objection, if the people thought proper, to divide it among the whole number of souls, male and female, married and single, in a parish, from the infant of a day old to the second infantage of hoary hairs.[2] For as all of every age, legitimate and illegitimate, have a right to live on the public common, and as that common, for the sake of cultivation, must be let out for rent, that rent, then, ought to be equally enjoyed by every human being, instead of the soil which they are thus deprived of.

But what makes this prospect yet more glorious is, that after this empire of right and reason is thus established it will stand for ever. Force and corruption attempting its downfall shall equally be baffled, and all other nations struck with wonder and admiration at its happiness and stability, shall follow the example; and thus the whole earth shall at last be happy and live like brethren.

Samuel Taylor Coleridge

(1772–1834)

24. *Conciones ad Populum, or Addresses to the People* (Bristol, 1795),

from Coleridge's *Collected Works*, vol. 1, Lectures 1795 on Politics and Religion, ed. Lewis Patton and Peter Mann (Princeton and London, 1971), pp. 65–70

The *Conciones ad Populum* were delivered as lectures in Bristol in February 1795, and printed there in December, with two lectures now combined to make a single essay, 'On the Present War'. Coleridge lectured from notes, probably in an upper room in the Corn Market, to modest audiences of the mainly converted, who each paid a shilling at the door to hear him. Reports of his manner range from the meteoric to the monotonous, but he acquired sufficient reputation in Bristol to earn financial backing over the next three years from Joseph Cottle the bookseller, the merchant Josiah Wade, the tanner Thomas Poole, and the two sons of the Staffordshire potter and industrialist, Josiah and Thomas Wedgwood. Most of these grew up in rational Dissent; a leading motive for such men to encourage Coleridge, with his brilliant intellectual gifts and personal magnetism, was the disorganisation of West Country and southern Midlands Dissent, and its need for a newspaper of the calibre of the *Sheffield Register* or the more genteel Norwich *Cabinet* (see above, pp. 11 and 84). The following year Cottle, Wade, and another Bristol bookseller, Reed, helped Coleridge to set up his own weekly, *The Watchman*, an enterprise for which he recruited readers by travelling through the Midlands strongholds of Dissent as far north as Sheffield and Manchester.

The Watchman failed after ten issues, which carried rather too little news and contributions from others, and rather too much by the eccentric editor himself. His apprentice journalistic work in 1795 conveys the merits and demerits of his manner – brilliantly animated, as rich in its range of reference as Burke's, and for that reason relatively inaccessible to the ordinary newspaper reader. Coleridge never intended to appeal to the masses, for rational Dissenters were middle class and propertied; his topics – religious toleration, humane sympathy for the poor and for slaves, opposition to the war, liberty of expression – are standard issues for the opposition, Whigs as well as radicals; Pitt himself, let alone Fox and Sheridan, was on record supporting some of them. The Coleridge of the 1790s is not essentially a political thinker, still less a popular agitator, but a preacher of sermons always more reminiscent of the Anglican Bishop Horsley (and to a lesser extent of Burke) than of Priestley or Price. The personal difficulties that went with great talent and the early loss of his father, an Anglican clergyman, can be followed in his *Letters* and *Notebooks*. They help to explain why Coleridge was affected so painfully by the schism among the radicals, between the secularists – atheists or Deists like Godwin and Paine – and the Christian civic humanism of Priestley, which first brought Coleridge to radicalism (see pp. 83 and 122).

If they, who mingled the cup of bitterness, drank its contents, we might look with a calm compassion on the wickedness of great Men. But alas! the storm which they raise, falls heaviest on the unprotected Innocent: and the Cottage of the poor Man is stripped of every Comfort, before the Oppressors, who send forth the mandate of Death, are amerced in one Luxury or one Vice. If a series of calamities succeed each, they deprecate the anger of Heaven by a FAST![1] – A word that implies, Prayers of Hate to the God of Love – and after these, a Turbot Feast for the rich, and their usual scanty Morsel to the poor, if indeed debarred from their usual labor they can procure even this. But if Victory be the event,[2]

> They o'er the ravag'd Earth,
> As at an Altar wet with human Blood
> And flaming with the Fires of Cities burnt,
> Sing their mad Hymns of Triumph, Hymns to God
> O'er the destruction of his gracious Works,
> Hymns to the Father o'er his slaughter'd Sons![3]

It is recorded in the shuddering hearts of Christians, that while Europe is reeking with Blood, and smoking with unextinguished Fires, in a contest of unexampled crimes and unexampled calamities, every Bishop but one voted for the continuance of the War.[4] They deemed the fate of their Religion to be involved in the contest! – Not the Religion of Peace, my Brethren, not the Religion of the meek and lowly Jesus, which forbids to his Disciples all alliance with the powers of this World – but the Religion of Mitres and Mysteries, the Religion of Pluralities and Persecution, the Eighteen-Thousand-Pound-a-Year[5] Religion* of Episcopacy. Instead of the Ministers of the Gospel,

---

* Wherever Men's temporal interests depend on the general belief of disputed tenets, we must expect to find hypocrisy and a persecuting Spirit, a jealousy of investigation, and an endeavor to hold the minds of the people in submissive Ignorance. That pattern of Christian meekness, Bishop Horsley, has declared it to be the vice of the age and government that it has suffered a free and general investigation of the most solemn Truths that regard Society[6] – and there is a remark in the last charge of the disinterested Bishop Prettyman, that the same busy spirit which inclines men to be Unitarians in Religion, drives them into Republicanism in Politics.[7] And truly, the most exalted Forms of Society are cemented and preserved by the purest Notions of Religion. But whatever I may deem of the justice of their Lordships' observations, the prudence and policy of them have

a Roman might recognize in these Dignitaries the High-priests of Mars – with this difference, that the Ancients fatted their Victims for the Altar, we prepare ours for sacrifice by leanness. War ruins our Manufactures; the ruin of our Manufactures throws Thousands out of employ; men cannot starve: they must either pick their country-men's Pockets – or cut the throats of their fellow-creatures, because they are Jacobins. If they chuse the latter, the chances are that their own lives are sacrificed: if the former, they are hung or transported to Botany Bay. And here we cannot but admire the deep and com-prehensive Views of Ministers, who having starved the wretch into Vice send him to the barren shores of new Holland to be starved back again into Virtue. It must surely charm the eye of humanity to behold Men reclaimed from stealing by being banished to a Coast, when there is nothing to steal, and helpless Women, who had been

Bold from despair and prostitute for Bread,[10]

find motives to Reformation in the sources of their Depravity, refined by Ignorance, and famine-bitten into Chastity. Yet even these poor unfortunates, these disinherited ones of Happiness, appear to me more eligibly situated than the wretched Soldier – because more innocently! Father of Mercies! if we pluck a wing from the back of a Fly, not all the Ministers and Monarchs in Europe can restore it – yet they dare to send forth their mandates for the Death of Thousands, and if they succeed call the Massacre Victory. They with all that majestic serenity, which the sense of personal safety fails not to inspire, can "Ride in the whirlwind and direct the storm,"[11] or rather like the gloomy Spirits in Ossian, "sit on their distant clouds and enjoy the Death of the Mariner."[12]

gained my immediate assent. Alas! what room would there be for Bishops or for Priests in a Religion where Deity is the only Object of Reverence, and our Immortality the only article of Faith – Immortality made probable to us by the Light of Nature, and proved to us by the Resurrection of Jesus. Him the High Priests crucified; but he has left us a Religion, which shall prove fatal to every HIGH PRIEST – a Religion, of which every true Christian is the Priest, his own Heart the Altar, the Universe its Temple, and Errors and Vices its only Sacrifices. Ride on, mighty Jesus! because of thy words of Truth, of Love, and EQUALITY! The age of Priesthood will soon be no more – that of Philosophers and of Christians will succeed, and the torch of Superstition be extinguished for ever. Never, never more shall we behold that generous Loyalty to rank, which is prodigal of its own virtue and its own happiness to invest a few with unholy Splendors; – that subordination of the Heart, which keeps alive the spirit of Servitude amid the empty forms of boasted Liberty! This dear-bought Grace of Cathedrals, this costly defence of Despotism, this nurse of grovelling sentiment and cold-hearted Lip-worship, will be gone – it will be gone, that sensibility to Interest, that jealous tenacity of Honors, which suspects in every argument a mortal wound; which inspires Oppression, while it prompts Servility; – which stains indelibly whatever it touches; and under which supple Dullness loses half its shame by wearing a Mitre where reason would have placed a Fool's-Cap![8] The age of Priesthood will be no more – Peace to its departing spirit! With delighted ears should I listen to some fierce Orator from St. Omers'[9] or from Bedlam, who should weep over its Pageantries rent and faded, and pour forth eloquent Nonsense in a funeral Oration.

Samuel Taylor Coleridge (1772–1834)

In former wars the victims of Ambition had crowded to the standard from the influence of national Antipathies; but this powerful stimulant has been so unceasingly applied, as to have well nigh produced an exhaustion. What remains? Hunger. Over a recruiting place in this city I have seen pieces of Beef hung up to attract the half-famished Mechanic. It has been said, that GOVERNMENT, though not the best preceptor of Virtue, procures us security from the attack of the lower Orders. – Alas! why should the lower Orders attack us, but because they are brutalized by Ignorance and rendered desperate by Want? And does Government remove this Ignorance by Education? And does not GOVERNMENT increase their want by Taxes? – Taxes rendered necessary by those national assassinations called Wars, and by that worst Corruption and Perjury, which a reverend Moralist has justified under the soft title of "secret Influence!"[13] The poor Infant born in an English or Irish Hovel breathes indeed the air and partakes of the light of Heaven; but of its other Bounties he is disinherited.

25. The Plot Discovered; or An Address to the People, Against Ministerial Treason (Bristol, 1795),

from Collected Works, vol. I, pp. 285–6, 288–91, 296

The title of Coleridge's pamphlet derives from the subtitle of Thomas Otway's still-popular Restoration tragedy, *Venice Preserved*, which is about a political conspiracy. The recently married Coleridge was living in the country, at Clevedon in Somerset, when in mid November the furore over the repressive Two Bills brought him hastening into Bristol to speak at political meetings of protest. The following week, on 26 November, at the Pelican Inn, Thomas Street, he gave the lecture against the Two Bills that formed the basis of *The Plot Discovered*.

As a pamphlet protesting at a threat to freedom of speech, *The Plot Discovered* compares interestingly with Godwin's coolly detached approach to the same subject, *Considerations on Lord Grenville's and Mr. Pitt's Bills* (see p. 252 n. 16), or with Godwin's *Cursory Strictures* of the previous year (above, pp. 169 ff.). Coleridge's manner is far more allusive and emotive; turning to him from Godwin is like turning from the prose of Hume to that of Carlyle, with its pulpit thunders, its sudden shifts of perspective, and its millenarian vistas. Coleridge's is a more extraordinary performance than either of Godwin's, and as an argument it too makes some shrewd hits, but there is no echo here of Godwin's statesman-like effort to win the support of moderates. The beginning of the excerpt is the beginning of the pamphlet:

like Horsley, appropriately cited in the first sentence, Coleridge likes violence, clamour, the shock of beginning on a note so high that crescendo seems impossible.

"THE MASS OF THE PEOPLE HAVE NOTHING TO DO WITH THE LAWS, BUT TO OBEY THEM!"[14] – Ere yet this foul treason against the majesty of man, ere yet this blasphemy against the goodness of God be registered among our statutes, I enter my protest! Ere yet our laws as well as our religion be muffled up in mysteries, as a CHRISTIAN I protest against this worse than Pagan darkness! Ere yet the sword descends, the two-edged sword that is now waving over the head of Freedom,[15] as a BRITON, I protest against slavery! Ere yet it be made legal for Ministers to act with vigour beyond law, as a CHILD OF PEACE, I protest against civil war! This is the brief moment, in which Freedom pleads on her knees: we will join her pleadings, ere yet she rises terrible to wrench the sword from the hand of her merciless enemy! We will join the still small voice of reason, ere yet it be overwhelmed in the great and strong wind, in the earthquake, and in the fire! These detestable Bills I shall examine in their undiminished proportions, as they first dared shew themselves to the light, disregarding and despising all subsequent palliatives and modifications. From their first state it is made evident beyond all power of doubt, what are the wishes and intentions of the present Ministers; and their wishes and intentions having been so evidenced, if the legislature authorize, if the people endure one sentence of such Bills for such manifest conspirators against the Constitution, that legislature will by degrees authorize the whole, and the people endure the whole – yea, that legislature will be capable of authorising even worse, and the people will be unworthy of better.

The first of these Bills is an attempt to assassinate the Liberty of the Press: the second, to smother the Liberty of Speech.[16] And first of the first, which we shall examine clause by clause. – The outrage offered to his Majesty is the pretext[17] – which outrage is ascribed to "the multitude of seditious pamphlets and speeches daily printed, published and dispersed, with unremitting industry and with a transcendant boldness."[18]. . . The ostensible reason of the present Bill we have heard; the real reason will not elude the search of common sagacity. The existing laws of Treason were too clear, too unequivocal. Judges indeed (what will not Judges do?) Judges might endeavour to transfer to these laws their own flexibility; Judges might make strange interpretations. But English Juries could not, would not understand them. Hence instead of eight hecatombs of condemned traitors behold eight triumphant acquitted felons![19] Hinc illæ lacrymæ[a] – The present Bills were conceived and laid in the dunghill of despotism among the other yet unhatched eggs of the old Serpent. In due time and in fit opportunity they crawled into light. Genius of Britain! crush them!

The old Treason Laws are superseded by the exploded commentaries of obsequious Crown lawyers, the commentary has conspired against the text: a vile and useless slave has conspired to dethrone its venerable master. "If any person within the realm or without shall compass, imagine, invent, devise, or intend death or destruction, or any bodily harm tending to death or destruction, maim or wounding, imprisonment or restraint of the person of our sovereign Lord, the King, or if he levy war against his Majesty, or move or stir any foreigner or stranger to invasion – he shall be adjudged a traitor." We object not. But "whoever by printing, writing, preaching, or malicious and advised speaking, shall compass, or imagine, or devise to deprive or depose the King, or his heirs and successors from the style, power, and kingly name, of the imperial crown of this realm, he shall be adjudged a traitor." Here lurks the snake. To promulge what we believe to be truth is indeed a law beyond law; but now if any man should publish, nay, if even in a friendly letter or in social conversation any should assert a Republic to be the most perfect form of government, and endeavour by all argument to prove it so, he is guilty of High Treason: for what he declares to be the more perfect and the most productive of happiness, he recommends; and to recommend a Republic is to recommend an abolition of the kingly name. By the existing treason laws a man so accused would plead, It is the privilege of an Englishman to entertain what speculative opinions he pleases, provided he stir up to no present action. Let my reasonings have been monarchical or republican, whilst I act as a royalist, I am free from guilt. Soon, I fear, such excuse will be of no avail. It will be in vain to alledge, that such opinions were not wished to be realized, except as the result of progressive reformation and ameliorated manners; that the author or speaker never dreamed of *seeing* them realized; though he should expressly set forth, that they neither could be, nor would be, nor ought to be, realized in the present or the following reign; still he would be guilty of high Treason: for though he recommends not an attempt to depose his present Majesty from the kingly name, yet he evidently recommends the denial of it to some one of his distant successors. All political controversy is at an end. Those sudden

[a] 'Hence these tears' (Terence, *Andria*, l.125).

breezes and noisy gusts, which purified the atmosphere they disturbed, are hushed to deathlike silence. The cadaverous tranquillity of
depotism will succeed the generous order and graceful indiscretions
of freedom – the black moveless pestilential vapour of slavery will be
inhaled at every pore. But, beware, O ye rulers of the earth! For it was
ordained at the foundation of the world by the King of kings, that all
corruption should conceal within its bosom that which will purify;
and THEY WHO SOW PESTILENCE MUST REAP WHIRLWINDS.[20]

But not only are the exertions of living genius to be smothered by
the operation of this execrable clause! All names of past ages dear to
liberty are equally proscribed! He who prints and publishes against
monarchy, as well as he who writes against it, is a traitor. The future
editions will be treasonable. If the legislature can pass, if the people
can endure such a law, it will soon pass, they will easily endure a
domiciliary inquest, which will go through our private and our public
libraries with the expurgatorial besom! This has been already done in
Hanover; it was done by order of the government there in the course
of the last year.[21] We hope and struggle to believe, that the measure
proceeded entirely from the resident ministers; we hope and struggle
to believe, that the first magistrate of a free country, that a monarch
whose forefathers the bold discussion of political principles placed
and preserved on the throne of Great Britain, could not be the author
of an edict which assumes the infallibility of the Pope, and the power
of the inquisition. We hope and struggle to believe it, lest an
unbidden and unwelcome suspicion force its way into our bosoms,
that they, who ordered such a measure in Hanover, must wish it in
England. Sages and patriots that being dead do yet speak to us, spirits
of Milton, Locke, Sidney, Harrington![22] that still wander through
your native country, giving wisdom and inspiring zeal! the cauldron
of persecution is bubbling against you, – the spells of despotism are
being muttered! Blest spirits! assist us, lest hell exorcise earth of all
that is heavenly!

Our ancestors were wisely cautious in framing the bill of treason;
they would not admit words as sufficient evidences of intention. How
often does the tongue utter what the moment after the heart disapproves! these indiscretions are blameable in the individual, but the
frequency of them was honorable to the nation at large, as it demonstrated the unsuspecting spirit of a free government, too proud to be
jealous! – Besides, words are easily misstated without ill-intention;
how easily then, where POWER CAN PAY PERJURY?[23] Hired swearers
were not perhaps so numerous in former days, as (we may judge by
the state trials) they are now. But our ancestors however had read,

that when the rulers and high-priests were interested in making a man appear guilty, even the spotless innocence of the Son of God could not preserve him from false witnesses.[24]

But I hear it suggested, that the two Acts will not be administered in all their possible stretch of implication![25] Pale-hearted men, who cannot approve, yet who dare not oppose a most foul ministry, is it come to this, that Britons should depend on clemency not justice, that Britons should whine to Ministers to stand between them and the law? But if honest pride and burning indignation prevent not the question in you, experience answers – that wherever it shall suit the purposes of a corrupt and abandoned ministry, these Acts will be administered to the utmost stretch of possible implication. . . .

We proceed to the second Bill, for more effectually preventing seditious meetings and assemblies. At my first glance over it, it recalled to me by force of contrast the stern simplicity and perspicuous briefness of the Athenian laws. But our minister's meaning generally bears an inverse proportion to the multitude of his words. If his declaration consist of fifty lines, it may be compressed into ten; if it extend to five hundred, it may be compressed into five. His style is infinitely porous; deprived of their vacuities the $\tau o \ \pi a v$,[a] the universe of his bills and speeches would take up less room than a nutshell.[26] The Bill now pending is indeed as full-foliaged, as the Manchineel tree; (and like the manchineel, will poison those who are fools enough to slumber beneath it) but its import is briefly this – first that the people of England should possess no unrestrained right of consulting in common on common grievances: and secondly, that Mr. Thelwall should no longer give political lectures.

[a] 'The whole'.

Joseph Ritson

(1752–1803)

26. Robin Hood: A Collection of all the Ancient Poems, Songs and Ballads, now Extant, relative to that celebrated English Outlaw: to which are prefixed Historical Anecdotes of his Life (2 vols., 1795),

pp. v–vi, ix–x, xi–xiii

Ritson, born and raised at Stockton-on-Tees, came of respectable yeoman stock, but his father was a poor man and young Ritson worked as a menial servant before entering his main profession, in the law as a conveyancer. In his leisure time he became a learned and enthusiastic antiquarian, who engaged in fierce literary controversies with and about less meticulous scholars, including Johnson as an editor of Shakespeare, Thomas Warton as a historian of poetry, and Thomas Percy as a collector of ballads. Ritson was himself a fine ballad-collector and editor, whom the young Walter Scott consulted and liked, in spite of his crankiness and what for Scott were his uncongenial politics.

From 1775 Ritson lived and worked in London. Before going south he moved in the same Newcastle intellectual world as Thomas Spence. Like Spence, and also in the 1770s, he developed his own idiosyncratic, partly phonetic system of spelling (illustrated here), and he shared Horne Tooke's interest in the vernacular, with its democratic implications. He was in Paris observing the Revolution in 1791, and returned home a keen atheist and a republican. *Robin Hood*, Ritson's most popular book, was thought at the time (for example by Scott) to be over-annotated; yet Ritson's exhaustive approach to his subject was influential, as was his zeal to divest himself from educated preconceptions, and the dignified status his prefatory Life claims for the popular form. Here Ritson takes the people to have had both political attitudes and a culture of their own; and it is the ballad which hands down this alternative oral tradition. The influence of Ritson on Scott, both as a ballad-collector and as a novelist interested in the diversity of national experience, is obviously very great. Peacock uses both the ballads and the polemic for his anti-monarchical satire, *Maid Marian* (1822). Perhaps most interestingly, these reputable scholarly claims for the ballad as a popular, democratic form must also be a significant element in the intellectual ambience in which the *Lyrical Ballads* were written and received.

Joseph Ritson (1752–1803)

In these forests, and with this company, he for many years reigned like an independant sovereign; at perpepetual war, indeed, with the king of England, and all his subjects, with an exception, however, of the poor and needy, and such as were "desolate and oppressed," or stood in need of his protection. . . . It is not, at the same time, to be concluded that he must, in this opposition, have been guilty of manifest treason or rebellion; as he most certainly can be justly charged with neither. An outlaw, in those times, being deprived of protection, owed no allegiance: "his hand 'was' against every man, and every mans hand against him".[1] These forests, in short, were his territories; those who accompanyed and adhered to him his subjects;. . . and what better title king Richard could pretend to the territory and people of England than Robin Hood had to the dominion of Barnsdale or Sherwood is a question humbly submitted to the consideration of the political philosopher. . . .

That our hero and his companions, while they lived in the woods, had recourse to robbery for their better support is neither to be concealed nor to be denied. . . . In allusion, no doubt, to this irregular and predatory course of life, he has had the honour to be compared to the illustrious Wallace, the champion and deliverer of his country; and that, it is not a little remarkable, in the latters own time.[2]

Our hero, indeed, seems to have held bishops, abbots, priests, and monks, in a word, all the clergy, regular or secular, in decided aversion.

> These byshoppes and these archebyshoppes,
> Ye shall them bete and bynde,

was an injunction carefully impressed upon his followers: and, in this part of his conduct, perhaps, the pride, avarice, uncharitableness, and hypocrisy of these clerical drones, or pious locusts, (too many of whom are still permitted to prey upon the labours of the industrious, and are supported, in pampered luxury,[3] at the expence of those whom their useless and pernicious craft tends to retain in superstitious ignorance and irrational servility,) will afford him ample justification. . . .

Such was the end of Robin Hood: a man who, in a barbarous age, and under a complicated tyranny, displayed a spirit of freedom and independence, which has endeared him to the common people, whose cause he maintained (for all opposition to tyranny is the cause of the people,) and, in spite of the malicious endeavours of pitiful monks, by whom history was consecrated to the crimes and follies of titled ruffians and sainted idiots, to suppress all record of his patriotic exertions and virtuous acts, will render his name immortal. . . .

26. Robin Hood

As proofs of his universal and singular popularity: his story and exploits have been made the subject as well of various dramatic exhibitions,[4] as of innumerable poems, rimes, songs and ballads:[5] his service [has been preferred] to the word of god:[6]. . . and, though not actually canonized, (a situation to which the miracles wrought in his favour, as well in his lifetime as after his death, and the supernatural powers he is, in some parts, supposed to have possessed[7] give him an indisputable claim,) he obtained the principal distinction of saint-hood, in having a festival allotted to him, and solemn games instituted in honour of his memory, which were celebrated till the latter end of the sixteenth century; not by the populace only, but by kings or princes and grave magistrates; and that as well in Scotland as in England; being considered, in the former country, of the highest political importance, and essential to the civil and religious liberties of the people, the efforts of government to suppress them frequently producing tumult and insurrection.[8]

John Thelwall

(1764–1834)

27. The Tribune, a Periodical Publication, consisting chiefly of the Political Lectures of J. Thelwall (1796),

vol. II, pp. 232–5, with cuts; from no. XXV, delivered at Lecture Room, Beaufort Buildings [London], 9 Sept. 1795

John Thelwall was a central figure of the radical campaign of the 1790s. An ex-mercer, ex-tailor, unqualified lawyer, and minor poet, he was one of the three defendants brought to trial in November 1794, a fact which gave him public notoriety: he became, in William Windham's unpleasant phrase, an 'acquitted felon'.[1] His fame as an orator was such that the second of Pitt's two 'Gagging Acts' of December 1795, the Seditious Meetings Act, was thought to be designed especially to silence him. 'If my Lectures had been of that seditious and treasonable complexion which they have been described', declares the title-page of *The Tribune*, 'it must have been easy to have checked me in my career, and brought me to punishment, without putting a gag upon the nation at large, and annihilating the boasted liberties of the country.' For nearly two more years after the passing of this Act, which empowered magistrates to disperse crowds of more than fifty, Thelwall went on lecturing, though nominally on the subject of Roman History. His conversations were spied on, his meetings broken up by hired 'bludgeon men', and at Yarmouth he was threatened by a press-gang. The year 1796 was certainly Thelwall's finest hour, the point at which an admiring Coleridge sought his friendship (though Godwin advised him to be silent).[2] By late 1797 Thelwall too was defeated, and in search of a retired spot, away from politics, in which he could farm. He settled in a Welsh valley, at Llyswen, Breconshire, nor far from the haven Francis Kilvert found in the mid nineteenth century, but within two years he was driven back to London by the politically inspired venom of his neighbours.[3]

Thelwall began as a writer, and his literary *oeuvre* is quite extensive: several volumes of poetry, the verse-prose miscellany *The Peripatetic* (1793), and a constant stream of publications in his political *annus mirabilis*, including *The Tribune*, the more theoretical *Rights of Nature*, and *Sober Reflections*, his reply to Burke (see below). Hazlitt paid tribute to his effectiveness as a speaker – 'he was the model of a flashy, powerful demagogue . . . he seemed to rend and tear the rotten carcase of corruption with the indecent rage of a wild beast' –

but he added, truthfully, that Thelwall's oratorical energy does not transfer to the page. 'The most dashing orator I ever heard is the flattest writer I ever read.'4 Some idea of the spoken manner can be had from Eaton's report of it (pp. 186ff.). The written one hardly compares, as a vehicle for addressing the masses, with the nervous, pungent writing of Paine and Cobbett. Though Thelwall's first experience of politics was the Westminster election of 1790, when Horne Tooke was the radical candidate, he made little use of Tooke's hostile analysis of upper-class language, or implied preference for a plain Anglo-Saxon discourse as a vehicle for ideas. Thelwall later became a teacher of elocution – an ambivalent profession for a radical, since it suggests a teacher of 'correct' pronunciation and of established rhetorical devices – and his prose style, with its abstractions and its classical allusions (for example, below, to Ulysses and Polyphemus), conveys a similar aspiration – to merge with the received culture, rather than to establish an alternative one.

On Thelwall's behalf, it could be said that his grasp of practical politics is far surer than that of Godwin, Wollstonecraft, and others. When he pleads with his middle-class hearers for the truly poor, he shows both humanity and a full sensitivity to the fears of the propertied. Here he seems at his most likeable, direct, and effective, even his ordinariness more attractive than his occasional egotism elsewhere.

Citizens, I cannot part from you without saying a few words relative to the condition of the lower orders of society. You who listen to me are most of you persons who are raised, in some degree, above the misery which I have been condemned to view: but do not suppose, because you are a few steps higher on the ladder of society, that the lower steps can be broken away without securing your destruction.

Citizens, in the Isle of Wight, where Nature seems to have poured her beauties, her sublimity and her fertility with the most lavish hand, where the common average of production upon every acre of land is a third part more than the average of the other parts of Britain – in the midst of this fertility, in the midst of this abundance, in the midst of all the sublime beauties and romantic scenes which that enchanting country presents, how often has my heart ached to behold the beggared misery of the great body of the people. – *Great body!* No, there is no great body of people there. Population is wasting away. Turn wherever you will, you see cottages falling into ruin; you see mansions of luxury rising, the fine feelings of whose masters cannot endure the sight of wretchedness; and who, therefore, permit not a cottage to rise within their vicinity. There you may see the little farmhouse turned into the summer house of some gentleman or lady of quality; the grounds upon which the farmer lived turned into *Fermes Ornés*5 where the produce is grasped by the luxurious individual who has laid out the country for his pleasure and amusement. It is true it is better that they produce corn there than that they should lay it out entirely in articles of pleasure and luxury. But what is the consequence? The wealthy individual hoards up the grain. He has no calls for rent; he has no particular necessities to compel him to do justice to society, and bring his corn to a fair market; and therefore he speculates, and waits for an opportunity to take advantage of the artificial distresses of mankind: and to such a height are these speculations carried, that corn in the *Isle of Wight* has been sold this summer at 20l. and 24l. a load, standing on the ground: though in the memory of the oldest man alive in that island it was never 12l. before.

Citizens I have not concluded the picture. It happens that this island produces in one year, as is admitted by all the historians, as much grain and cattle as would maintain the inhabitants ten. It produces, also, the greatest abundance of shell fish, particularly crabs and lobsters, which are sent to the London market. The markets, also, of Portsmouth, Gosport and Southampton are supplied with vegetables from this spot – and boats, and even large vessels, are built in the ports and creeks. Yet with all this, except in a few particular spots, the country is almost a Desert in point of population; and sometimes they are reduced to the greatest distress to get in their harvest.

You will suppose, then, that the peasantry being so few, live in happiness and comfort; that they have decent apparel, decent education, eat a little meat twice or three times a week at least. But, alas! No such thing. Their wages are not sufficient for bread. Their children run in barefoot beggary in groupes, at the chariot wheels of their oppressors; and they will run for miles to get a halfpenny by opening a gate to let you pass through; save your servant the trouble of dismounting, as if the curse of Canaan had fallen upon them that servants unto servants they should be. And thus is the universal condition of the peasantry of that country. I have been grieved at my heart to see human beings thus brought up in ignorance. I have been grieved to my soul to see beings whom nature made my equals thus subjected by usurping man to cringing beggary: and doomed to play tricks and anticks to extort that from the levity of their beholders which compassion will not impart. I have grieved to see the finest forms in the world (for the rustic females of the island have peculiar advantages in point of person) climbing over rocks to collect lampets[a] – miserable shell fish that stick to the shelves and shingles, to sustain

---

[a] Limpets.

an existence destitute of comfort, destitute of intelligence, destitute of every enjoyment – nay of every decent necessary of life.

Oh citizens, reflect, I conjure you, that the common class of mankind and you are one! that you are one in nature! that you are one in interest! and that those who seek to *oppress the lower*, seek to *annihilate the intermediate orders*. It is their interest to have but two classes, the very high and the very low, that those they oppress may be kept at too great a distance – and in too much ignorance to be enabled to seek rec ess; and that those who partake of their favors may take as little as possible from them of the wages of corruption and iniquity.

I have generally been most anxious about the condition of the most distressed orders of society, because they have seldom an anxious advocate: we are apt to feel disgust at abject misery and wretchedness, and the sickly imagination turns away from such objects of contemplation. It is therefore that I dwell particularly upon their case. But it is not to one class of the people I wish to confine myself; I wish not to limit justice to a particular sphere. – I would have it extend throughout the universe, and be participated to every being, whatever be his condition, his colour, nation or his circumstances. It is universal, and not partial justice that I contend for: the rights and happiness of the universe, not the amelioration and benefit of a particular class.

Let me however conjure the middling orders of society to remember that they are particularly interested: that if we have not peace and reform in time, those who are now the middling, must soon be the lower orders; for oppression, though it begins with the poor and helpless mounts upwards from class to class till it devours the whole: and let it be remembered, even by the wealthy and unfeeling merchant, who is now but too often the ready instrument of ministerial tyranny, that the only favor reserved for him is like the favor of *Polyphemus* to *Ulysses* – "You have endeavoured to gladden my heart," said the one-eyed monster, "by the beverage you have imparted; and therefore when I have devoured your companions; when I have torn their limbs to pieces, and banquetted on their flesh, you shall be the *last sacrifice that shall be made to my rapacious maw*."[6]

28. *Sober Reflections on the Seditious and Inflammatory Letter of the Right Hon. Edmund Burke* (1796),

pp. 55–105, with cuts

Thelwall's reply to the personal attack on him in Burke's pamphlet (see above, p. 53) well illustrates his strategy of making his opponents into extremists, hysterics, and warmongers, while casting himself as the true constitutionalist. Like many of Burke's antagonists, he slips into Burke's insistent and emotive rhythms, and sometimes virtually into parody. Partly because he is speaking to Burke rather than to his accustomed audience, his manner is more 'literary' here even than in *The Tribune*, and the subject – how to rate the political contribution of philosophers – has a more limited appeal. Yet the growing preoccupation of Thelwall and his friends with their own kind, and their reputation in society, also has its political significance, and Thelwall's real distress at Godwin's attack on him tellingly illustrates the difficulties of intellectuals.[7]

Mr. *Burke*, it is true, modestly declines "the high distinction," and "the glory" of being considered as the exclusive "author of the war;"[8] and as I am not at all desirous of removing *responsibility* from the shoulders where the constitution has placed it, I am ready to exonerate him from the charge. I believe that the ministers of this country had resolved, from the first dawn of the *Revolution in France*, to seize the earliest opportunity of attacking that nation. I believe, that but for the ministers of this country, the profligate and fatal treaty of *Pilnitz*[9] never would have been signed; *France* and the Empire would not have been embroiled in war; the excesses which have disgraced the greatest and most glorious event in the annals of mankind, would never have been perpetrated; and that *Louis* XVI might, perhaps, to this day have continued "King of the French." I believe, also, that if no such man as Mr. *Burke* had been in existence, Mr. *Pitt* – or more properly speaking, Lord *Hawkesbury*,[10] would nevertheless have plunged us into this unhappy contest. Mr. *Burke* and his *dagger*[11] were therefore only instruments (powerful instruments, however,) in exciting that terror and alarm, which gave, among certain classes at least, a degree of popularity to the measure, without which the minister would have found it difficult to fulfil *his continental engagements!* . . .

Is Mr. *Burke* really so ignorant, or does he presume so far upon the ignorance of his fellow citizens – upon the "stupefaction of the dull English understanding," as to pretend that the *philosophers* and the *Septembrizers* of France were the same persons;[12] – that the promulgators of the humane, the incontrovertible, the glorious principles that breathed through the speeches and declarations of the National Assembly, and enlarged, at once, the boundaries of science and philanthropy, were also the perpetrators of those horrid massacres, and still more horrible executions, by which all principles, all humanity, all justice, were so outrageously violated? Reason, at once, revolts at such a conclusion. But, fortunately, this argument, so important to the human race, does not rest upon the conclusions of speculative reason. Fact – strong, stubborn, incontrovertible fact (so hateful to the juggling philosophers of *the old sect*) stares us in the face so openly, that one knows not how sufficiently to admire the confidence of the man who could so grossly misrepresent *events and affairs of yesterday*, or the supineness and voluntary ignorance of those whom such misrepresentations could deceive! . . .

But though the pretences of Mr. *Burke* for confounding together the *philosophy* and the *crimes of France* are thus completely refuted, I do not expect that the ground will be abandoned. It is too important a part of the permanent conspiracy against the liberties of mankind to be readily given up. Remove but this delusion from the eyes of the people, and the reign of Corruption could not last – "no, not for a twelvemonth." The principles of liberty are so consonant to the general good – the cause of the rotten borough-mongers is so destitute of all rational support, and the miseries produced by that system are so numerous, that nothing but the groundless terrors so artfully excited – nothing but the prejudices inspired against all speculation and enquiry, by confounding together things that have no connection, could possibly prevent the people of Britain shouting from every village, town, and street, with one unanimous and omnipotent voice –

"REFORM! REFORM! REFORM!!!"

Of this the faction in power are sufficiently aware; and therefore it is, that their hatred and persecution are principally directed, not against the furious and the violent, but against the enlightened and humane. Therefore it is, that they endeavour to confound together, by chains of connection slighter than the spider's web, every san-guinary expression, every intemperate action of the obscurest individual whose mind has become distempered by the calamities of the times, not with the oppressions and miseries that provoke them, but with the honest and virtuous labours of those *true sons of moderation and good order* who wish to render their fellow citizens firm and manly, that they may have no occasion to be tumultuous and savage; to spread the solar light of reason, that they may extinguish the grosser fires of vengeance; and to produce a timely and temperate reform, as the only means of averting an ultimate revolution. These are the men against whom the bitterest malice of persecution is directed. These are the men against whom every engine of abuse and misrepresentation is employed; to calumniate whom their "Briton," and their "Times,"[13] and their dirty Grub-street pamphleteers, are pensioned out of the public plunder – and against whom grave senators from their benches, and *pensioned Cicero's*[a] from their literary retreats, are not ashamed to pour forth their meretricious eloquence, in torrents of defamation, and to exhaust all the fury of inventive (or *deluded*) malice. These are the men for whose blood they thirst; and whom they endeavour to destroy by new doctrines, not only of accumulative and constructive treason, but of *treason by second sight*: making them accountable for actions they were never consulted upon, books they never read, and sentiments they never heard. These, in short, are the men for whose destruction laws are perverted, spies are employed, and perjurers are pensioned: and when all these artifices prove inadequate to the end, these are the men to stop whose mouths bills have been proposed, in parliament, subversive of every principle of the constitution, lest the nation at large should be in time convinced that they are not what they have been represented: but that *the friends of Liberty and Reform, are the true friends of Humanity and Order!* . . .

These are the principles I have endeavoured to inculcate, in political societies, at public meetings; in my pamphlets, in my conversations, and in that lecture-room, (that school of vice, as Mr. *Burke* is pleased to call it) at which he is so anxious to dissuade the *"grown* gentlemen and noblemen of our time from thinking of finishing whatever may have been left incomplete at the old universities of this country."[14]

If to have inculcated these principles with a diligence and perseverance which no difficulties could check, no threats nor persecutions could controul – if to have been equally anxious to preserve the spirit of the people, and the tranquillity of society – to disseminate the information that might conduct to reform, and to check the intemperance that might lead to tumult – if these are crimes dangerous to the existence of the state, the minister did right to place me at the bar of the Old Bailey: and, if perseverance in these principles is perseverance in crime, it may be necessary once more to place me in the same situation of disgrace and peril. If to assemble my fellow citizens for the purpose of political discussion – if to strip off the mask from state hypocrisy and usurpation – if to expose apostacy, confute the sophisms of court jugglers and ministerial hirelings, and drag forth to public notice the facts that demonstrate the enormity and rapid progress of that corruption under which we groan, and by means of which *the rich are tottering on the verge of bankruptcy, and the poor are sinking into the abyss of famine* – if this is to keep a public *school of vice and licentiousness*, then was it right in ministers to *endeavour* to seal up the doors of that school with an act of parliament; then was it right

[a] Burke.

that I should be held up to public odium and public terror, by the virulent pamphlets of the *Burkes* and *Reeveses*,[15] and the *conjectural defamations* of *Godwin*.[16] But upon what sort of pretence, even the inflamed and prejudiced mind of Mr. *Burke*, can regard me as "a wicked pander to avarice and ambition,"[17] I am totally at a loss to conjecture.

The Antijacobin

29. *The Antijacobin, or Weekly Examiner*
(Published weekly during the sitting of Parliament
from 20 Nov. 1797 to 9 July 1798, price 6d.),

from the Prospectus, and from Nos. I, II and V, 4th corr. edn,
2 vols., 1799: vol. I, pp. 4–7, 9, 31–4, 69–70

Although the political system in the eighteenth century was in the hands of a group of aristocrats, who governed by dispensing money and patronage through a network of 'friends', the government minded about public opinion, which it could not effectively manage; and it minded more than usual when it became engaged in the potentially unpopular French war. In 1790, there were still no national newspapers: London had thirteen morning daily papers, seven tri-weeklies and two bi-weeklies, and by 1811 the total of dailies and weeklies had risen to fifty-two. But until 1814 all papers were printed by hand, which means that by modern standards their print runs and readership were very small. What money newspapers made came from advertising rather than from sales, then as now, and proportionately news and comment made up a relatively small element. Ministers nevertheless feared the hostile comment and misinformation the press might carry, and spent substantial sums off the Secret Service list in order to buy newspaper support, and to reward individual writers. Aspinall calculates the total as at least £4,594 in 1790–1 and £4,893 the following year, 'amounts almost equal to the sums known to have been annually spent by Sir Robert Walpole during the last ten years of his premiership'.[1] Even so, a group of papers, of which the *Morning Chronicle* was the most prestigious, remained 'in the Whig [or Opposition] interest' in the 1790s; and in February 1793, Bland Burgess, the Under-Secretary of State for Foreign Affairs, could tell Lord Auckland that it was high time something was done about the press, since almost all the newspapers were 'in the pay of the jacobins'.[2] Burke, too, urged the establishment of a government newspaper, and two were indeed set up on 1 October 1792 – a morning paper, *The True Briton*, and an evening paper, *The Sun*.

But reading-matter for intellectuals remained during the 1790s at first overwhelmingly, and in mid decade disproportionately, 'liberal', because literary journals were run by booksellers, most of whom were Dissenters (see above, p. 6). Creative literature emanated from connected circles, and was published by the same men. Especially if the war taxes and the food shortages of 1793–7 are kept in mind, the favourite literary themes of the time have a marked oppositional bias. Quite apart from the works of avowed radicals like Godwin and Holcroft, a new young group of poets – Southey, Coleridge, Wordsworth – wrote sympathetically in mid decade about the sufferings of the poor, for which they repeatedly blamed war; they alluded to events in France; or they reverted to heroes of old anti-monarchical struggles, like Wat Tyler or the regicide Henry Marten.[3] The response of one of the most intelligent of the junior ministers, George Canning,[4] and of a group of his friends, was to strike back, through the literary means of satire and burlesque, at what looked to them like a cultural fifth column. They combined to write the short-lived and splendid satirical weekly, *The Antijacobin*, which had William Gifford[5] as its working editor, and a team of literary amateurs as contributors, headed by Canning, John Hookham Frere, George Ellis, and, very occasionally, the Prime Minister, William Pitt. *The Antijacobin* proper, this gentlemanly miscellany of politics and poetry, was succeeded by *The Antijacobin Review*, edited confusingly by John Gifford, which has a more conventional format of long review articles, most of them dully polemical – though the creative brilliance of the old *Antijacobin* is echoed in a series of cartoons against intellectuals by the finest caricaturist of the day, James Gillray.

The *Antijacobin* ought to be read for its parodic poems – 'The Friend of Humanity and the Knifegrinder', which takes off Southey's Painite politics and his Sapphic metre, 'The Rovers' (aimed at the sentimental German drama of Schiller, Goethe, and Kotzebue), 'The Loves of the Triangles' (from Darwin's 'Loves of the Plants'), 'The Progress of Man' (R. P. Knight's *Progress of Civil Society*), and the satire in Pope's manner, 'The New Morality'. But the prefatory matter of the Prospectus and first numbers, all thought to be Canning's, has its own interest as part of the ideological debate, and its own literary merit. The Prospectus, in which the rhythms of parliamentary rhetoric can be distinctly heard, enumerates the values dear to the counter-revolution – old-fashioned virtues, patriotism, piety, and 'the decencies of private life'. The lighter and more polished literary essays of the first numbers seem highly mindful of their own elegance, classical correctness, and 'ease': good literature, the message goes, is for, and by, the upper orders only. Cleverness and wit are intimidating qualities, not comforting to the socially inexperienced reader, but demanding his respectful assent. Here Canning proceeds with that blend of dazzling expertise and serious passion – his order is in *danger* – that marks Pope's Tory satire, the ultimate model for *The Antijacobin* in English.

From the Prospectus, preceding the first number:

We confess, whatever disgrace may attend such a confession, that We have not so far gotten the better of the influence of long habits and early education, not so far imbibed that spirit of liberal indifference, of diffused and comprehensive philanthropy, which distinguishes the candid character of the present age, but that We have our feelings, our preferences, and our affections, attaching on particular places, manners, and institutions, and even on particular portions of the human race.

It may be thought a narrow and illiberal distinction; but We avow ourselves to be *partial* to the COUNTRY *in which we live*, notwithstanding the daily panegyricks which we read and hear on the superior virtues and endowments of its rival and hostile neighbours. We are *prejudiced* in favour of *her* Establishments, civil and religious; though without claiming for either that ideal perfection, which modern philosophy professes to discover in the other more luminous systems which are arising on all sides of us. . . .

In MORALS We are equally old-fashioned. We have yet to learn the modern refinement of referring in all considerations upon human conduct, not to any settled and preconceived principles of right and wrong, not to any general and fundamental rules which experience, and wisdom, and justice, and the common consent of mankind have established, but to the internal admonitions of every man's judgment or conscience in his own particular instance.

We do not dissemble, – that We reverence LAW, – We acknowledge USAGE, – We look even upon PRESCRIPTION without hatred or horror. And We do not think these, or any of them, less safe guides for the moral actions of men, than that new and liberal system of ETHICS, whose operation is not to bind but to loosen the bands of social order; whose doctrine is formed not on a system of reciprocal duties, but on the supposition of individual, independent, and unconnected rights; which teaches that all men are pretty equally honest, but that some have different notions of honesty from others, and that the most received notions are for the greater part the most faulty. . . .

It is not in our creed, that ATHEISM is as good a faith as CHRISTIANITY, provided it be professed with equal sincerity; nor could we admit it as an excuse for MURDER, that the murderer was in his own mind conscientiously persuaded that the murdered might for many good reasons be better out of the way.[6]

Of all these and the like principles, – in one word, of JACOBINISM in all its shapes, and in all its degrees, political and moral, public and private, whether as it openly threatens the subversion of States, or gradually saps the foundations of domestic happiness, We are the avowed, determined, and irreconcileable enemies.

[George Canning]

29. The Antijacobin

In our anxiety to provide for the amusement as well as information of our readers, We have not omitted to make all the enquiries in our power for ascertaining the means of procuring Poetical assistance. And it would give us no small satisfaction to be able to report, that We had succeeded in this point, precisely in the manner which would best have suited out own taste and feelings, as well as those which We wish to cultivate in our Readers.

But whether it be that good Morals, and what we should call good Politics, are inconsistent with the spirit of true Poetry – whether *"the Muses still with freedom found"* have an aversion to *regular* governments, and require a frame and system of protection less complicated than King, Lords, and Commons: –

> "Whether primordial *nonsense* springs to life
> In the wild war of *Democratic* strife,"[7]

and there only – or for whatever other reason it may be, whether physical, or moral, or philosophical (which last is understood to mean something more than the other two, though exactly *what*, it is difficult to say), we have not been able to find one good and true Poet, of sound principles and sober practice, upon whom we could rely for furnishing us with a handsome quantity of sufficient and approved Verse – such Verse as our Readers might be expected to get by heart, and to sing, as MONGE[8] describes the little children of Sparta and Athens singing the songs of Freedom, in expectation of the coming of *the Great Nation.*

In this difficulty, We have had no choice but either to provide no Poetry at all, – a shabby expedient, – or to go to the only market where it is to be had good and ready made, that of the *Jacobins* – an expedient full of danger, and not to be used but with the utmost caution and delicacy.

To this latter expedient, however, after mature deliberation, we have determined to have recourse: qualifying it at the same time with such precautions as may conduce at once to the safety of our Readers' principles, and to the improvement of our own Poetry. . . .

It might not be unamusing to trace the springs and principles of this species of Poetry, which are to be found, some in the exaggeration, and others in the direct inversion of the sentiments and passions which have in all ages animated the breast of the favourite of the Muses, and distinguished him from the "vulgar throng."

The Poet in all ages has despised riches and grandeur.

The *Jacobin* Poet improves this sentiment into a hatred of the rich and the great.

The Poet of other times has been an enthusiast in the love of his native soil.

The *Jacobin* Poet rejects all restriction in his feelings. His love is enlarged and expanded so as to comprehend all human kind. . . .

The Old Poet was a Warrior, at least in imagination; and sung the actions of the Heroes of his Country in strains which "made Ambition Virtue," and which overwhelmed the horrors of War in its glory.

The *Jacobin* Poet would have no objection to sing battles too – but he would take a distinction. The prowess of Bonaparte indeed he might chaunt in his loftiest strain of exultation. *There* we should find nothing but trophies, and triumphs, and branches of laurel and olive, phalanxes of Republicans shouting victory, satellites of despotism biting the ground, and geniuses of Liberty planting standards on mountain-tops.

But let his own Country triumph, or her Allies obtain an advantage; – straightway the "beauteous face of War" is changed; the "pride, pomp, and circumstance" of Victory are kept carefully out of sight – and we are presented with nothing but contusions and amputations, plundered peasants, and deserted looms. Our poet points the thunder of his blank verse at the head of the Recruiting Serjeant, or roars in dithyrambics against the Lieutenants of Pressgangs.

No. II (Nov. 27, 1797)

Another principle no less devoutly entertained, and no less sedulously disseminated, is the *natural and eternal warfare of the* POOR *and the* RICH. In those orders and gradations of society, which are the natural result of the original difference of talents and of industry among mankind, the Jacobin sees nothing but a graduated scale of violence and cruelty. He considers every rich man as an oppressor, and every person in a lower situation as the victim of avarice, and the slave of aristocratical insolence and contempt. These truths he declares loudly, not to excite compassion, or to soften the consciousness of superiority in the higher, but for the purpose of aggravating discontent in the inferior orders.

A human being, in the lowest state of penury and distress, is a treasure to the reasoner of this cast. He contemplates, he examines, he turns him in every possible light, with a view of extracting from the variety of his wretchedness new topics of invective against the pride of property. He, indeed, (if he is a true Jacobin,) refrains from *relieving* the object of his compassionate contemplation; as well knowing that every diminution from the general mass of human misery must proportionably diminish the force of his argument. . . .

No. V (Dec. 11, 1797)

We have already hinted at the principle by which the followers of the Jacobinical Sect are restrained from the exercise of their own favourite Virtue of Charity. The force of this prohibition and the strictness with which it is observed, are strongly exemplified in the following Poem. . . . [by Southey]:

THE SOLDIER'S WIFE
DACTYLICS

Weary Way-wanderer, languid and sick at heart,
Travelling painfully over the rugged road;
Wild-visaged Wanderer! Ah! for thy heavy chance.

Sorely thy little ones drag by thee barefooted,
Cold is the baby that hangs at thy bending back –
Meagre and livid, and screaming its wretchedness.

Woe-begone mother, half anger, half agony,
As over thy shoulder thou lookest to hush the babe,
Bleakly the blinding snow beats in thy haggard face.[9] . . .

We think that we see him fumbling in the pocket of his blue pantaloons; that the splendid Shilling is about to make its appearance, and to glitter in the eyes, and glad the hearts of the poor Sufferer. But no such thing – the bard very calmly contemplates her situation, which he describes in a pair of very pathetical Stanzas; and . . . concludes by leaving her to Providence. . . .

We conceived that it would be necessary to follow up this general rule with the particular exception, and to point out one of those cases in which the Embargo upon Jacobin Bounty is sometimes suspended; with this view, we have subjoined the poem of

THE SOLDIER'S FRIEND[10]
DACTYLICS

Come, little Drummer Boy, lay down your knapsack here:
I am the Soldier's Friend – here are some Books for you;
Nice clever Books, by TOM PAINE, the Philanthropist.

Here's Half-a-crown for you – here are some Hand bills too –
Go to the Barracks, and give all the Soldiers some.
Tell them the Sailors are all in a Mutiny.

> [*Exit Drummer Boy, with hand-bills, and
> half-a-crown. Manet Soldier's Friend.*]

Gilbert Wakefield

(1756–1801)

30. A Reply to Some Parts of the Bishop of Landaff's Address to the People of Great Britain (1798),

2nd edn, 1798, pp. 26–37, 47–50

Wakefield was brought up an Anglican and ordained in that faith, but in early manhood he became a unitarian. He then taught as a classics tutor at the Dissenting Academy at Warrington, along with the leading Dissenting intellectuals Priestley, William Enfield and John Aiken. From 1791 he lived among the Dissenting community at Hackney, East London, and devoted himself to classical scholarship and radical polemic, though in 1795 he wrote a pamphlet dissociating himself from the freethinking tendency represented by Paine's *Age of Reason* (see above, p. 122). He was provoked by the Bishop of Llandaff's *Address to the People of Great Britain* (1798), a pamphlet designed to rally support for the war policy of Pitt's Administration, and to raise a patriotic spirit against the French. Watson, formerly sympathetic to the Dissenters, had included a temperate passage on reformers, 'whom it seems the fashion of the day to represent as the enemies of the state, to stigmatise, as republicans, levellers, jacobins':

They may, perhaps, be mistaken in believing an effectual reform practicable, without a revolution; but few of them, I am persuaded, would be disposed to attain their object with such a consequence accompanying it; and fewer still would wish to make the experiment under the auspices of a French invasion. [p. 18]

Wakefield's peppery and injudicious *Reply* maintains that, on the contrary, he at least has no objection to seeing the French victorious, as he shortly expects to do. Pro-government writers complained of the disloyalty of the opposition press, which, in the absence of war censorship, sometimes plainly tried to assist the enemy.[1] In 1798 the balance of the war had tilted in France's favour and, in the mood of national vulnerability, Pitt's Administration seized the opportunity Wakefield gave them to make an example of a leading polemicist, along with his bookseller Cuthell, and two leading radical publishers – J. S. Jordan (publisher of *The Rights of Man*) and the eminent Joseph Johnson (see above, pp. 6, 8, 15). Wakefield was tried separately in February 1799 and sentenced to two years in Dorchester Gaol, to the indignation not only of radicals but of his friends among the leading Whigs, Charles James Fox, Lord Holland, and the Duke of Bedford. Very lively and very impertinent, Wakefield's pamphlet exemplifies both the ability of radical writers to make a point, and their alienation from the temper of the mass of British people in a national crisis.

The tyrannical temper and the violent measures of the present administration, exemplified by a transgression of the liberal policy of our ancestors and the confessed principles of constitutional freedom in such numerous and momentous instances, form so great a contrast to the free energies of republican equality, as will not allow *me* to suppose for a single moment, that Mr. Pitt and his colleagues entertained a sincere wish of a hearty reconciliation and friendly intercourse with the French government. They must be sensible, how such a commerce, sooner or later, must dissolve an usurpation of power in which they have fenced themselves by a copious manufacture of their staple commodity, posts and peerages; by a diffusion of corrupt humours through every vein of the body politic, even to the evanescent ramifications of its capillary vessels; and by a prostitute majority of borough-mongers, loan-jobbers, military officers, pensioners, and official sycophants, in the lower house. . . . Is it for such a crew to wish and promote a pacific communication with the French republic? . . .

"And, were there even a bridge over the channel, France durst not make an incursion with half her numbers. She knows how ready her neighbours would be to revenge the injuries they have sustained, – how ready her own citizens would be to regain the blessings they have lost, could they once see all her forces occupied in a distant country" (p. 13).

If this feat were indeed accomplished,

> – and the mole immense wrought on
> Over the foaming deep high-arch'd, a bridge
> Of length prodigious;[2]

the most sanguine wishes of the republicans would be gratified. The solicitude, I trow, of Buonaparte and his columns (unrivalled captain! unconquerable heroes!) does not turn upon "what numbers we should oppose against him," but "how he can get at us." No great expectation will be formed of English prowess on its own ground, with all our swaggering pretensions, by those who recollect the adventures of about 9000 ragamuffin breechless loons from Scotland, but a few years ago.[3] Though the Bishop of Landaff will prove, I doubt not, a second Ulysses at the least, too many of us, I fear, will alas! resemble the Satyrs in Euripides, who had made loud and boastful profession of their readiness to assist the hero in burning the eye of Polyphemus, but miserably failed in the performance of their engagement, when the hour of experiment was come. "Do but see," says one: (a *city light-horseman*) what a long way I am off! It is impossible for me to reach him." – "Oh! what a sudden lameness has seized my poor leg!" says another: (a *supplementary militia-man*) "Aye! and mine too!" says a third: (a *voluntary cavalier*) "A most unaccountable spasm began to contract my feet, just as I was ready.". . . .

"Many honest men, I am sensible, have been alarmed into a belief, that were the French to invade this country, they would be joined by great numbers of discontented men. This is not my opinion" (pp. 16–17).

On the contrary, I am fully satisfied, that, if the French could land a considerable army in this country, to the number, suppose, of 60,000 or 70,000 men; (which, nevertheless, appears to me utterly impracticable, with our present naval superiority) the kingdom would be lost for ever. The same cause, which has facilitated the progress of the republicans on the continent, would operate as powerfully for them in this country also: namely, a degree of poverty and wretchedness in the lower orders of the community, which, especially in their present state of depravity and ignorance, will render the chances, even from confusion, of *any* change desirable. I believe from my soul, that within three miles of the house, where I am writing these pages, there is a much greater number of starving, miserable human beings, the hopeless victims of penury and distress, than on any equal portion of ground through the habitable globe. A fable of our old friend Æsop is extremely apposite on this occasion; which I shall present to the reader in the simple stile of Croxall:

> Plain truth, dear Murray! needs no flowers of speech;
> So take it in the very words of Creech.[4]

The Sensible Ass

An old fellow was feeding an ass in a fine green meadow; and, being alarmed with the sudden approach of the enemy, was impatient with the ass to put himself forward, and fly with all the speed that he was able. The ass asked him, Whether or no he thought the enemy would clap two pair of panniers upon his back? The man said, No; there was no fear of that. Why then, says the ass, I will not stir an inch: for what is it to me, who my master is, since I shall but carry my panniers, as usual?

The Application

This fable shews us, how much in the wrong the poorer sort of people most commonly are, when they are under any concern about the revolutions of a government. All the alteration, which they can feel, is, perhaps, in the name of their sovereign, or some such important trifle; but they cannot well be poorer, or made to work harder than they did before. . . .

If the French republic should continue firm and faithful to itself, there exists not, I believe, a thinking man in these kingdoms, who can persuade himself of a possible redemption to this country, on a supposition of a much longer continuance of the war. Now this war is hopeless: for in what quarter are the French vulnerable by us? And the enormity of our expenditure from a perpetual state of complete preparation to resist the menaced invasion, that I may omit to mention a boundless prodigality throughout every department of public office, is daily operating with aggravated and resistless pressure. Is it not fatuity then, is it not madness, for the nation at large to acquiesce in measures, which absolutely leave our destruction in the power of our enemies without the necessity of landing a single soldier on our coasts? And who are benefited by this frantic procedure, but a few greedy obstinate, baffled, tyrannical, and sanguinary men in office; the scourge of this nation, and the contempt of Europe?

William Wordsworth

(1770–1850)

31. 'A Letter to the Bishop of Landaff on the extraordinary avowal of his Political Principles contained in the Appendix to his late Sermon.' By a Republican (1793),

from *The Prose Works of William Wordsworth*, ed. W. J. B. Owen and Jane Worthington Smyser (Oxford, 1974), vol. I, pp. 38–9, 45–6

William Wordsworth, newly returned in December 1792 after more than a year in revolutionary France, and still in the winter of 1792–3 living in London, was stung by the Bishop of Llandaff's apparent defection from reformism to write a reply to the Bishop's pamphlet of February 1793 (see above, p. 145). Wordsworth's riposte to Bishop Watson remained unpublished in his lifetime, and obviously unpolished; it is a clumsy, youthful performance, probably written in or soon after February 1793. Perhaps its most interesting feature is that it reflects French experience rather than English. Its republicanism is theoretical and absolute. The notion of representation based on property along current English lines is dismissed, apparently in favour of the radical demand, from 1780, of universal (male) suffrage – yet Wordsworth simultaneously envisages his citizens attaining a utopian moral perfection – 'virtues, talents, and acquirements are all' that will be looked for. The qualities of the Swiss peasant, and of Père Gérard, appear, idealised, as sagacity and blunt honesty; the emblematised labourer is a herdsman with a staff in one hand and a book in the other. The lifestyle of the aristocrat, on the other hand, has neither dignity nor purpose. This clear-cut class animosity seems representative of France in 1792 (see above, pp. 105 and 243 n. 11) rather than of English radicalism; certainly the native English radical Dissenters Price and Priestley write for their own secure middle-class circles and generalise little about aristocrats or artisans. Interestingly, it is two other expatriates, the 'Americans' Paine and Cobbett, who come nearest in English to sharing Wordsworth's admiration for the labourer and contempt of the lord, though they express both more pungently.

Appearing as I do the advocate of republicanism, let me not be misunderstood. I am well aware from the abuse of the executive power in states that there is not a single European nation but what affords a melancholy proof that if at this moment the original authority of the people should be restored, all that could be expected from such restoration would in the beginning be but a change of tyranny. . . . I must add also that the coercive power is of necessity so strong in all the old governments that a people could not but at first make an abuse of that liberty which a legitimate republic supposes. The animal just released from its stall will exhaust the overflow of its spirits in a round of wanton vagaries, but it will soon return to itself and enjoy its freedom in moderate and regular delight.

But, to resume the subject of universal representation, I ought to have mentioned before that in the choice of its representatives a people will not immorally hold out wealth as a criterion of integrity, nor lay down as a fundamental rule that to be qualified for the trying duties of legislation a citizen should be possessed of a certain fixed property. Virtues, talents, and acquirements are all that it will look for.

Having destroyed every external object of delusion, let us now see what makes the supposition necessary that the people will mislead themselves. Your Lordship respects "peasants and mechanics when they intrude not themselves into concerns for which their education has not fitted them". Setting aside the idea of a peasant or mechanic being a legislator, what vast education is requisite to enable him to judge amongst his neighbours which is most qualified by his industry and integrity to be intrusted with the care of the interests of himself and of his fellow citizens? But leaving this ground, as governments formed on such a plan proceed in a plain and open manner, their administration would require much less of what is usually called talents and experience, that is of disciplined treachery and hoary machiavelism; and, at the same time, as it would no longer be their interest to keep the mass of the nation in ignorance, a moderate portion of useful knowledge would be universally disseminated. If your lordship has travelled in the democratic cantons of Switzerland you must have seen the herdsman with the staff in one hand and the book in the other. In the constituent assembly of France was found a peasant whose sagacity was as distinguished as his integrity, whose blunt honesty overawed and baffled the refinements of hypocritical patriots. The people of Paris followed him with acclamations, and the name of Père Gérard will long be mentioned with admiration and respect through the eighty-three departments.[1] . . .

I have another strong objection to nobility which is that it has a necessary tendency to dishonour labour, a prejudice which extends far beyond its own circle; that it binds down whole ranks of men to idleness while it gives the enjoyment of a reward which exceeds the hopes of the most active exertions of human industry. The languid tedium of this noble repose must be dissipated; and gaming with the tricking manoeuvres of the horse-race, afford occupation to hours, which it would be happy for mankind had they been totally unemployed. Reflecting on the corruption of the public manners, does your lordship shudder at the prostitution which miserably deluges our streets? You may find the cause in our aristocratical prejudices. Are you disgusted with the hypocrisy and sycophancy of our intercourse in private life? You may find the cause in the necessity of dissimulation which we have established by regulations which oblige us to address as our superiours, indeed as our masters, men whom we cannot but internally despise. Do you lament that such large portions of mankind should stoop to occupations unworthy the dignity of their nature? You may find in the pride and luxury thought necessary to nobility how such servile arts are encouraged. Besides where the most honourable of the land do not blush to accept such offices as groom of the bedchamber, master of the hounds, lords in waiting, captain of the honourable band of gentlemen pensioners, is it astonishing that the bulk of the people should not ask of an occupation, what is it? but what may be gained by it? If the long equestrian train of equipage should make your lordship sigh for the poor who are pining in hunger, you will find that little is thought of snatching the bread from their mouths to eke out the "*necessary* splendor" of nobility.

I have not time to pursue this subject farther, but am so strongly impressed with the baleful influence of aristocracy and nobility upon human happiness and virtue that if, as I am persuaded, monarchy cannot exist without such supporters, I think that reason sufficient for the preference I have given to the republican system.

32. Preface to the *Lyrical Ballads, With Other Poems. In Two Volumes* (London, 1800),

from 3rd edn (in which Preface was enlarged), 1802,
pp. vii–x, xxviii–xxx, xxxiii–xxxiv, xxxix–xliii

Wordsworth and Coleridge became neighbours in Somerset in 1797, and in November 1797 conceived the plan of jointly writing a collection of ballads. If Coleridge's later descriptions of the scheme are accepted, they were to attempt two classes of ballad: the supernatural, to which Coleridge was to impart psychological and emotional truth, and – Wordsworth's concern –

'poems chiefly on natural subjects taken from common life but looked at . . . through an imaginative medium'.[2]

Nineteen of the twenty-three poems in *Lyrical Ballads* (1798) are Wordsworth's, and the impetus behind the idea reads like his rather than Coleridge's. If Coleridge was to give the medieval supernatural ballad contemporary currency by investing it with emotional realism, Wordsworth was more thorough-going in his claim that *his* poems were poems of today. His approach was basically unhistorical, for, unlike Percy and his imitators, he was no antiquarian. Goethe and Bürger in Germany, Lewis and (shortly) Scott in Britain, wrote pastiches of medieval ballads, with either an archaic or a timeless flavour. Ritson (see p. 203 above) saw the Robin Hood ballads as tied to specific historical circumstances, which politicised but also dated them. Wordsworth's ballads protest neither at the politics of the past nor – unlike Southey's *The Soldier's Wife* (p. 219 above) or his own *Salisbury Plain* – at the ills of the present. On one level this means that, compared with many poems written by the same authors in 1793–7, the *Lyrical Ballads* are de-politicised poems. This indeed was, and still is, an 'innocent' reading of them. Yet the essence of the theory behind them seems to emanate from the radical tradition, as Wordsworth explains his ideas in the Advertisement to the 1798 edition, in the Preface to the 1800 edition, and in additions to the Preface in 1802.

A distinctively radical theory of culture was available to Wordsworth, the one held for example by Ritson: namely, that the people have attitudes and art-forms of their own. A distinctively radical theory of language, enunciated by Horne Tooke (see above, p. 18), maintained the dignity of the vernacular, indeed its superiority over learned language as the medium of truth. These two essentially political positions of the 1790s are actually nearer to the sense of Wordsworth's Advertisement and to the opening pages of the Preface than are most sources and analogues cited nowadays by scholars, who often conflate Wordsworth's concept of simplicity with the specifically historical primitivism of the Scottish rhetoricians.[3] If Wordsworth set out to produce a democratic collection of poems, there is no need to go to Blair or to Macpherson's Ossian for a source, since Tooke, a political celebrity, was also the favourite grammarian of the radicals, had reissued *The Diversions of Purley*, vol. I, in 1798, and in 1800, while Wordsworth was writing the Preface, was being read with interest by Coleridge.

Among the radicals excerpted in this book, the Wordsworth of the 1790s was an unusually lonely figure, hardly as much a part of 'literary London' as was Coleridge, the former London schoolboy. Yet Wordsworth had met radicals, in early 1793 in the shop of the ubiquitous Joseph Johnson, who was then engaged in publishing his *Descriptive Sketches*; and, like even the most self-sufficient people, he drew on his ambience. Coincidentally, the Edgeworths, away in Ireland and thus geographically even more remote than Wordsworth in the West Country, were making observations about psychology and language that share some of Wordsworth's premises. Intellectually Wordsworth's poems concern themselves with unfamiliar thought-patterns, expressed in alien or immature language-systems, such as those of children ('We are Seven', 'Anecdote for Fathers', 'Idiot Boy') or simple, peasant adults ('The Forsaken Indian Woman', 'Goody Blake and Harry Gill'). The Edgeworths also carefully observed the language and mental habits of children, and recorded them in *Practical Education* (1798). They made the first sustained use in fiction of the language and beliefs of peasantry, in the Irish tale *Castle Rackrent* (1800), which was followed in 1801 by the *Essay on Irish Bulls* – an apology for Irish speech, ironic and Swiftian in manner, which in content echoes Wordsworth's case for the dignity and meaning of the vulgar idiom. When Francis Jeffrey saw a resemblance between some of Maria Edgeworth's stories and the *Lyrical Ballads*, however, he preferred the social usefulness, and safety, of her goals 'to the laudable exertions of Mr Thomas Paine to bring disaffection and infidelity within the comprehension of the common people, or the charitable endeavours of Messrs. Wirdsworth [sic] & Co. to accommodate them with an appropriate vein of poetry.'[4]

It is no wonder that Wordsworth made few converts in 1800 and 1802. His effort to exalt both the wisdom and language of the common man had precisely the disagreeable 'levelling' connotation that Jeffrey spotted, and this was never explicitly supported by the less democratically minded Coleridge, though at first Coleridge claimed to agree with the Preface. (The radical Hazlitt, on the other hand, warmed to precisely this aspect of the early Wordsworth – 'the political changes of the day were the model on which he formed and conducted his poetical experiments'.[5]) In developing and applying what had been half-formulated radical theories, Wordsworth did what Paine and Godwin had done in 1792, but 1798–1802 was tactlessly late. By now there was hardly a public for such experiments, and other intellectuals, notably Godwin and Coleridge, preferred to keep polite letters polite, and indisputably out of politics.

Presumably Wordsworth felt himself in active political disagreement with the literary men he knew, for in 1802 he revised his Preface to make even clearer the 'levelling' message with which it opened. The passages added in 1802 are marked in the following excerpt in square brackets. It should be said that some expert opinion holds that these additions show Wordsworth moving towards 'the poet as his own subject, as representative man; . . . the poet, rather than the rustic, is mankind's epitome, and in expressing himself he expresses all men'.[6] The reader must judge, but it is surely more natural to interpret the additional matter of 1802 very differently, as emphasising that we share our language and our profounder experiences with everyone – a fact denied, Wordsworth is saying, by the fashionable modern poetic language, which is capricious, over-personal, and narrowly confined to a narrow readership. Wordsworth urges the poet to identify himself with the common man, rather than let his superior education separate them. 'The Poet thinks and feels in the spirit of human passions. How, then, can his language differ in any material degree from that of all other men who feel vividly and see clearly? . . . the Poet must descend from this supposed height; and . . . express himself as other men express themselves' (p. 232). The anti-aristocratic animus of 1793 re-emerges here in a warning to literary men. Stylistically the 1802 Preface has become repetitive, but its repetitions add to its force, as a bold, eloquent statement of the radical interest in egalitarian writing.

There is no one unquestionably superior edition of the Preface, to which Wordsworth made changes on a number of occasions. The 1802 edition, rather than the last corrected edition of 1850, is preferred here because some of its wording ('low and rustic life' as opposed to 'humble and rustic life') is the version known to those contemporaries, such as Coleridge, who disputed with Wordsworth about the Preface.

The principal object then which I proposed to myself in these Poems was [to choose incidents and situations from common life, and to relate or describe them, throughout, as far as was possible, in a selection of language really used by men; and, at the same time, to throw over them a certain colouring of imagination, whereby ordinary things should be presented to the mind in an unusual way; and further, and above all,][7] to make these incidents and situations interesting by tracing in them, truly though not ostentatiously, the primary laws of our nature: chiefly as far as regards the manner in which we associate ideas in a state of excitement. Low and rustic life was generally chosen, because in that condition, the essential passions of the heart find a better soil in which they can attain their maturity, are less under restraint, and speak a plainer and more emphatic language; because in that condition of life our elementary feelings co-exist in a state of greater simplicity, and consequently may be more accurately contemplated, and more forcibly communicated; because the manners of rural life germinate from those elementary feelings, and from the necessary character of rural occupations, are more easily comprehended, and are more durable; and lastly, because in that condition the passions of men are incorporated with the beautiful and permanent forms of nature. The language, too, of these men is adopted (purified indeed from what appear to be its real defects, from all lasting and rational causes of dislike or disgust) because such men hourly communicate with the best objects from which the best part of language is originally derived; and because, from their rank in society and the sameness and narrow circle of their intercourse, being less under the influence of social vanity they convey their feelings and notions in simple and unelaborated expressions. Accordingly, such a language, arising out of repeated experience and regular feelings, is a more permanent, and a far more philosophical language, than that which is frequently substituted for it by Poets, who think that they are conferring honour upon themselves and their art, in proportion as they separate themselves from the sympathies of men, and indulge in arbitrary and capricious habits of expression, in order to furnish food for fickle tastes, and fickle appetites, of their own creation.[8]

I cannot, however, be insensible of the present outcry against the triviality and meanness both of thought and language which some of my contemporaries have occasionally introduced into their metrical compositions; and I acknowledge, that this defect, where it exists, is more dishonorable to the Writer's own character than false refinement or arbitrary innovation, though I should contend at the same time that it is far less pernicious in the sum of its consequences. . . .

[What is a Poet? To whom does he address himself? And what language is to be expected from him? He is a man speaking to men: a man, it is true, endued with more lively sensibility, more enthusiasm and tenderness, who has a greater knowledge of human nature, and a more comprehensive soul, than are supposed to be common among mankind; a man pleased with his own passions and volitions, and who rejoices more than other men in the spirit of life that is in him; delighting to contemplate similar volitions and passions as manifested in the goings-on of the Universe, and habitually impelled to create them where he does not find them. To these qualities he has added a disposition to be affected more than other men by absent things as if they were present: an ability of conjuring up in himself passions, which are indeed far from being the same as those produced by real events, yet (especially in those parts of the general sympathy which are pleasing and delightful) do more nearly resemble the passions produced by real events, than anything which, from the motions of their own minds merely, other men are accustomed to feel in themselves; whence, and from practice, he has acquired a greater readiness and power in expressing what he thinks and feels, and especially those thoughts and feelings which, by his own choice, or from the structure of his own mind, arise in him without immediate external excitement.

But whatever portion of this faculty we may suppose even the greatest Poet to possess, there cannot be a doubt but that the language which it will suggest to him, must, in liveliness and truth, fall far short of that which is uttered by men in real life, under the actual pressure of those passions, certain shadows of which the Poet thus produces, or feels to be produced, in himself. However exalted a notion we would wish to cherish of the character of a Poet, it is obvious, that, while he describes and imitates passions, his situation is altogether slavish and mechanical, compared with the freedom and power of real and substantial action and suffering. So that it will be the wish of the Poet to bring his feelings near to those of the persons whose feelings he describes, nay, for short spaces of time perhaps, to let himself slip into an entire delusion, and even confound and identify his own feelings with theirs; modifying only the language which is thus suggested to him, by a consideration that he describes for a particular purpose, that of giving pleasure. . . .

Nor let this necessity of producing immediate pleasure be considered as a degradation of the Poet's art. It is far otherwise. It is an acknowledgment of the beauty of the universe, an acknowledgment the more sincere, because it is not formal, but indirect; it is a task light and easy to him who looks at the world in the spirit of love; further, it is a homage paid to the native and naked dignity of man, to the grand elementary principle of pleasure, by which he knows, and feels, and lives, and moves. . . .

What I have thus far said applies to Poetry in general; but especially to those parts of composition where the Poet speaks through the mouths of his characters; and upon this point it appears to have such weight that I will conclude, there are few persons of good sense, who would not allow that the dramatic parts of composition are defective, in proportion as they deviate from the real language of nature, and are coloured by a diction of the Poet's own, either peculiar to him as an individual Poet, or belonging simply to poets in general, to a body of men who, from the circumstance of their compositions being in metre, it is expected will employ a particular language.[9]

It is not, then, in the dramatic parts of composition that we look for this distinction of language; but still it may be proper and necessary where the Poet speaks to us in his own person and character. To this I answer by referring my Reader to the description which I have before given of a Poet. Among the qualities which I have enumerated as principally conducing to form a Poet, is implied nothing differing in kind from other men, but only in degree. The sum of what I have there said is, that the Poet is chiefly distinguished from other men by a greater promptness to think and feel without immediate external excitement, and a greater power in expressing such thoughts and feelings as are produced in him in that manner. But these passions and thoughts and feelings are the general passions and thoughts and feelings of men. And with what are they connected? Undoubtedly with our moral sentiments and animal sensations, and with the causes which excite these; with the operations of the elements and the appearances of the visible universe; with storm and sunshine, with the revolutions of the seasons, with cold and heat, with loss of friends and kindred, with injuries and resentments, gratitude and hope, with fear and sorrow. These, and the like, are the sensations and objects which the Poet describes, as they are the sensations of other men, and the objects which interest them. The Poet thinks and feels in the spirit of the passions of men. How, then, can his language differ in any material degree from that of all other men who feel vividly and see clearly? It might be *proved* that it is impossible. But supposing that this were not the case, the Poet might then be allowed to use a peculiar language when expressing his feelings for his own gratification, or that of men like himself. But Poets do not write for Poets alone, but for men. Unless therefore we are advocates for that admiration which depends upon ignorance, and that pleasure which arises from hearing what we do not understand, the Poet must descend from this supposed height, and, in order to excite rational sympathy, he must express himself as other men express themselves. To this it may be added, that while he is only selecting from the real language of men, or, which amounts to the same thing, composing accurately in the spirit of such selection, he is treading upon safe ground, and we know what we are to expect from him.]

Notes

Introductory Essay

1 Alfred Cobban, *The Debate on the French Revolution, 1789–1800* (1950), p. 31.
2 Don Locke, *A Fantasy of Reason* (1979), publisher's advertisement.
3 E. P. Thompson, *The Making of the English Working Class* (1963), p. 107. It seems fair to notice in passing that here 'influence' is used loosely. Strictly speaking, it is so hard to assess the impact of a book on a single reader that we should be sceptical of claims that it has influenced many readers.
4 E.g., J. H. Tooke's Wilkite Society for Supporting the Bill of Rights of the late 1760s, or Christopher Wyvill's Yorkshire Association, 1780.
5 See J. G. A. Pocock, *The Machiavellian Moment* (Princeton, 1975) and Pocock, ed., *Three British Revolutions: 1641, 1688, 1776* (Princeton, 1980); Caroline Robbins, *The Eighteenth-Century Commonwealthman* (Cambridge, 1959); Bernard Bailyn, *The Ideological Origins of the American Revolution* (Cambridge, 1967).
6 Priestley, *An Essay on the First Principles of Government* (1768), cited in H. T. Dickinson, *Liberty and Property* (1977), p. 229.
7 Derek Roper, *Reviewing before the 'Edinburgh', 1788–1802* (1978), *passim*.
8 Quoted in A. Aspinall, *Politics and the Press, c. 1780–1850* (1949), p. 33.
9 H. T. Dickinson, *Politics and Literature in the Eighteenth Century* (1974), pp. xix–xx.
10 Quoted in A. Goodwin, *The Friends of Liberty: The English Democratic Movement in the Age of the French Revolution* (1979), p. 63.
11 'Down to the spring of 1797, when petitions were being sent up from many parts of England for the removal of the King's ministers, scarcely one of those persons who had declared themselves ardently and affectionately interested for the success of the French, deserted their cause' (Godwin, *Thoughts Occasioned by Dr. Parr's Spital Sermon* (1801), p. 4).
12 E. P. Thompson says that the ferment among industrialists and wealthy tradesmen belonged to 1791–2, and that disaffection among artisans was greatest in 1795 (*Making of the English Working Class*, p. 195). The sharpness of the contrast here tends to obscure the role of the middle-class writer, who, as these excerpts show, often remained attached to radicalism until the end of 1796, or later.
13 *Friends of Liberty*, pp. 223–4.
14 *The Enquirer*, pp. vi–ix. Cf. also Godwin's *Thoughts Occasioned by Dr. Parr's Spital Sermon* (1801). Godwin was not alone in representing his retreat from radicalism as an intellectual conversion to 'experiment' over 'system'. Arthur Young worded his recantation similarly some four years earlier: 'I am inclined to think the application of theory to matters of government, a surprising imbecility in the human mind; for men to be ready to trust to reason in enquiries where experiment is equally at hand for their guide, has been pronounced by various great authorities to be in every other science the greatest folly' (*The Example of France, a Warning to Britain* (1793), p. 2); see p. 102.

15 Quoted in Winifred F. Courtney, *The Young Charles Lamb, 1775–1802* (New York, 1982), p. 261.

16 It was Shelley, E. P. Thompson suggests, who transmitted Godwin's philosophic anarchism to the Chartists through the notes to his *Queen Mab (Making of the English Working Class*, p. 107n).

17 C. Lamb to Thomas Manning, 1 March 1800.

18 R. P. Knight (1750–1824) was a Foxite M.P. and a wealthy connoisseur, whose earliest work, a privately circulated essay on *The Worship of Priapus* (1786), became public knowledge and a source of scandal. In the mid 1790s his kind of sophisticated liberalism was considered more politically dangerous than it proved in reality to be, and a journal, the *British Critic*, was set up in 1793 to prevent 'the corruption, which prevails among scholars, and persons of the higher orders of life, from *evil principles*, and what may be called *a monopoly of the press*' (quoted in D. Roper, *Reviewing before the 'Edinburgh'*, p. 180).

19 See David Thomas, *George Morland*, catalogue for Arts Council exhibition, (1954), pp. 5–6, and John Barrell, *The Dark Side of the Landscape* (Cambridge, 1980), pp. 89–129. The contrast in the 1780s and 1790s between painters, dependent on patronage, and engravers, with their more varied and impersonal outlets, is made by Marcia Pointon in an unpublished lecture, 'The Uses and Abuses of Portraiture'.

20 Catherine Macaulay, *The History of England from the Accession of James I to that of the Brunswick Line*, 8 vols. (1763–83).

21 A much-amplified version of Millar's book appeared posthumously in 1803. For Millar as historian see Duncan Forbes, 'Scientific Whiggism: Adam Smith and John Millar', *Cambridge Journal*, vii (1954), 643–70. Cf. Christopher Hill, 'The Norman Yoke', *Puritanism and Revolution* (1968).

22 For the earlier-eighteenth-century background to the controversy about language, see M. Cohen, *Sensible Words: Linguistic Practice in England, 1640–1785* (Baltimore, 1977) and J. Barrell, 'The Language Properly So Called', in *English Literature in History*, 1730–80 (1983), pp. 110–75. Its progress after the French Revolution is given in Olivia Smith, *The Politics of Language* (Oxford, 1984).

23 John Thelwall, *The Fairy of the Lake and other Poems* (Hereford, 1801), p. 141.

24 Fox to D. O'Bryen, 29 July 1798; quoted in F. K. Prochaska, 'English State Trials in the 1790s: a Case Study', *Journal of British Studies*, xiii (1973), p. 71 n. 30.

25 In *The Enquirer* (1797), Godwin arrives at a half-way point in the adoption of a non-radical position on language. In his chapter on Style, he praises modern usage, but avoids committing himself to vulgar usage or the popular vernacular.

J. H. Tooke

1 Hans Aarsleff, *The Study of Language in England, 1780–1860* (Princeton, 1967).

2 M. Butler, *Peacock Displayed* (1979), pp. 14, 39–40.

3 E.g., William Hazlitt in *The Spirit of the Age* (1825; Everyman's Library edition, 1960): 'He kept repeating [at his trial in 1794] that "others might have gone on to Windsor, but he had stopped at Hounslow", as if to go farther might have been dangerous and unwarrantable' (p. 218).

4 'I . . . wonder much how, after you have expressed so much horrour at Mr. Harris's and Lord Monboddo's "words signficant without any signification", you could have the courage of placing a brace of these monsters . . . (neither of which can give the reader the least idea of the subject in question) . . . in your work, by way of frontispiece' ('I. Cassander' [pseud. of John Bruckner], *Criticisms on 'The Diversions of Purley' in a Letter to Horne Tooke, Esq.* (1790), p. 3). The Greek title, from Homer,

means 'winged words'. Tooke explains the subtitle by saying that Purley was the home of his friend William Tooke, and that the estate had previously belonged to John Bradshaw, presiding judge at the trial of Charles I.

5 Harris, *Hermes* . . . , p. 372.

6 William Tooke, political associate of J. Horne Tooke's from the era of the Wilkes controversy, and owner of the estate at Purley. J. H. T. took his friends's name in 1782 at the latter's request, presumably as an indication that he was to be made William Tooke's heir.

7 Sir Francis Burdett (1770–1844), radical politician, M.P. for Boroughbridge from 1796, supporter of reform and opponent of the war; M.P. for the popular seat of Westminster, 1807–37.

8 J. Horne Tooke himself, and the main exponent in the *Diversions* of his grammatical theories.

9 The youthful researches upon grammar to which Tooke refers were undertaken in prison after his trial in 1777. The case had turned upon a verbal quibble which led to some argument about the meaning of the conjunction 'that', afterwards amplified by Tooke in his pamphlet *Letter to John Dunning* (1778). This pamphlet first develops the iconoclastic, politicised view of grammar which is expanded in *The Diversions of Purley*.

10 A reference to James Harris's *Hermes*: see headnote to this chapter.

Richard Price

1 A revised edition, with Appendix containing the Declaration of Rights by the National Assembly of France. The edition used by Burke contained this Appendix.

2 D. O. Thomas, *The Honest Mind: The Thought and Work of Richard Price* (Oxford, 1977), pp. 286, 290.

3 Price, *The Evidence for a Future Period of Improvement in the State of Mankind, with the Means and Duty of Promoting It* (1787), p. 30.

4 Thomas, *Honest Mind*, p. 308.

5 Earlier in Burke's career he consistently advocated religious toleration, voting in 1779 for relief of Dissenters from subscribing to the Thirty-Nine Articles. He still urged relief for the Catholics of Ireland: cf. *A Letter to Sir Hercules Langrishe* (1792). His opposition now to the claims of Dissenters arises because he thinks them essentially political.

6 Cf. Burke on natural partiality to 'the little platoon we belong to' (pp. 39ff.), and Godwin's deprecation of partial attachments, e.g., within the family (pp. 156ff.).

7 Price's note: 'See the Declaration of Rights by the National Assembly of France, in the Appendix.'

8 Algernon Sidney (1622–83), republican, and author of the posthumous *Discourses concerning Government* (1698), which was reissued with additional material in 1763 and 1773. A prominent Puritan and supporter of the Protectorate, Sidney remained abroad for seventeen years after the restoration of Charles II, but after his return was implicated in the Rye House Plot and executed.

9 Benjamin Hoadly (1676–1761), Whig bishop; he was the leader of the early-eighteenth-century 'low church' divines who maintained 'revolution principles' against the champions of hereditary right and an authoritarian church.

10 Montesquieu, Charles Louis de Secondat (1689–1755), author of *L'Esprit des Lois* (1748), the comprehensive treatise on law and government which before the Revolution was admired by moderate reformers of all nationalities.

11 Fénelon, Francois de Salignac de la Mothe (1651–1715), Archbishop of Cambrai,

tutor to the eldest son of the *dauphin*, and author of *Télémaque* (1699), a didactic novel-epic aimed at his pupil which propagated the maxim 'that kings exist for the sake of their subjects, not subjects for their kings'. Fénelon had a high eighteenth-century reputation as a critic of courts, an advocate of religious toleration, Nature, and peace among nations.

12 Turgot, Anne Robert Jacques, Baron de Laune (1727–81), reforming French statesman and leading economist. A physiocrat and a contributor to the *Encyclopédie*, Turgot wrote in support of financial reform and religious toleration.

13 Price's Note: 'See articles III and VI of the Declaration of Rights by the National Assembly of France, in the Appendix.'

14 The illness of George III, Nov. 1788 to Feb. 1789, was a very public affair because it occasioned a constitutional crisis over the question of a Regency. Opposition politicians, headed by Charles James Fox, hoped to reap political benefits if their friend the Prince of Wales took over with full regal powers, while Pitt's ministry depended on preventing this, or on the King's recovery.

15 The characteristic positions of Tories or apologists for the Stuarts in the late seventeenth century.

16 The 'test' from which the Test Act takes its name was the receiving of the communion of the Church of England, as a precondition for taking office. See above, p. 4.

17 Here Price attaches a lengthy note which contrasts the current attitudes to reform of the Prime Minister, Pitt, with those of his father, William Pitt the Elder, Lord Chatham, from whom Price cites a personal letter to himself, favourable to toleration, of 16 Jan. 1773.

18 Jacques Necker (1732–1804), Louis XVI's Genevese-born minister, 1776–81, recalled in 1788 by popular demand, and in 1789 still regarded as a reformer, though in 1790 he was to lose credit, popularity, and office.

19 Price's note: 'Except in states so small as to admit of a Legislative Assembly, consisting of all the members of the State'.

20 William Pitt (1759–1806) began his parliamentary career in 1781 as a supporter of the liberal Whig Lord Shelburne. In the early 1780s he advocated peace with the American colonies, economic reform, and reform of parliamentary representation.

21 Price's note: 'A representation chosen principally by the Treasury, and a few thousands of the dregs of the people, who are generally paid for their votes'.

22 See Burke's description (p. 43) of events at Versailles on 6 Oct. 1789.

Edmund Burke

1 E.g., Godwin, when a Whig pamphleteer, praised Burke in *A Defence of the Rockingham party*. See also p. 149.

2 See James Boulton, *The Language of Politics in the Age of Wilkes and Burke* (Oxford, 1963), p. 95.

3 For Price on flattering kings, see pp. 27–8.

4 Charles, 3rd Earl Stanhope (1753–1816), scientist, radical Whig politician, and the Prime Minister's brother-in-law, though after the Revolution permanently estranged from Pitt by his strong pro-French sympathies. He was chairman of the Revolution Society which Price addressed.

5 Burke's note: 'Psalm cxlix'. The Rev. Hugh Peters (1598–1660), Independent divine and celebrated preacher of the Commonwealth, executed at the Restoration as an advocate of the execution of Charles I.

6 Declaration by Parliament, 13 Feb. 1689, to the Prince and Princess of Orange,

'on the rights and liberties of the subject, and settling the succession of the crown', the basis of the Bill of Rights passed by Parliament in Oct. 1689.

7 The 1789 voting system (enfranchising Frenchmen aged twenty-five and over) was elaborate, in two stages in country areas and three in the towns, and the final vote for a deputy took place in an electoral assembly, in which members of the middle class practised in public speaking dominated the discussion. Representatives of the Third Estate elected in 1789 were therefore drawn from the bourgeoisie. Almost half the five hundred seventy-eight members were lawyers; there were around one hundred businessmen, bankers, and traders, some fifty landowners, and a number of intellectuals (A. Soboul, *The French Revolution, 1787–99*, trans. A. Forrest and C. Jones (New York, 1975), pp. 124–9).

8 Marie Antoinette (1755–93), Queen of France, was the daughter of the powerful Empress Maria Theresa of Austria.

9 A notorious image, much resented and often recalled by radical intellectuals.

10 The most notorious phrase of the *Reflections*, for which see especially Eaton and Spence (pp. 185–9).

11 The notion that society originated in a combination for mutual protection. For radicals in the century following Locke, the principle implied that government rested on the consent of the governed – a notion salient in Rousseau, whose treatise, the *Contrat Social* (1762), may be in Burke's mind.

12 The French National Assembly spent some weeks in Aug. 1789 discussing their Declaration of the Rights of Man and the Citizen, on the American model; the claims of a state religion versus those of freedom of conscience made one of the most controversial issues. See chapter on Priestley, esp. n. 9.

13 When Burke retired from Parliament in July 1794, the government made generous arrangements designed to help him pay his large debts, estimated at £35,000, and to provide an income of £2,500. Since Burke had been an outstanding critic of pensions, especially secret, nominally court ones (see n. 22), he was promised that these proposals would be brought before Parliament. Instead of this, his annual pension was conferred direct by the Crown as a charge on the 4½% fund. This arrangement gave an opening to the parliamentary opposition, who seized the opportunity of the commotion over the Two Acts (see chapter on Coleridge, n. 16) to make capital out of it.

14 In the course of the third reading of Grenville's Treasonable Practices Bill, the Duke of Bedford suggested that the French *ancien régime* had fallen partly through the practice of giving 'exorbitant and lavish grants' to minions; he could not 'conceive what claims a man could have upon the country, whatever his merits may be, who by his writings could involve it in all the horrors of war'. The Earl of Lauderdale complained of 'an enormous pension, for endeavouring to inculcate doctrines, that tended to extinguish the principles of freedom' (*The Correspondence of Edmund Burke*, gen. ed. Thomas W. Copeland, 10 vols., Cambridge, 1958–78; vol. VIII (1969), pp. 342n., 400n.).

15 C. B. Macpherson, *Burke* (Oxford, 1980), p. 6.

16 Burke to Earl Fitzwilliam, 21 May 1797; *Correspondence*, vol. IX, p. 356.

17 Louis Philippe Joseph, Duke of Orléans (1747–93), 'Philippe Egalité', sympathised with the Revolution and in 1792 was elected a deputy for Paris to the Convention. He was guillotined in the Terror, 6 Nov. 1793.

18 Francis Russell, 5th Duke of Bedford (1765–1802), who attended Westminster School (see p. 52), became a Foxite Whig and steadily opposed the war with France. He was the immensely wealthy builder of Bedford Square and Russell Square in Bloomsbury, London.

19 Jacques Pierre Brissot (1754–93), one of the leaders of the Gironde party, with whom English radicals maintained close contact; he was guillotined when the Gironde fell.

20 James Maitland, 8th Earl of Lauderdale (1759–1839), a lawyer, former M.P., and now Scottish representative peer, was a vigorous opponent of Pitt's government in the Lords.

21 John Milton, *Paradise Lost*, Bk II, l. 625.

22 In Feb. 1780 Burke presented to Parliament his most elaborate legislative proposals under the title of A Plan for the Better Security of the Independence of Parliament, and the Economic Reformation of the Civil and other Establishments. His aim was to reduce the number of sinecure places and pensions, and to introduce tighter auditing of offices like the Paymaster's, which he himself currently held.

23 Though the addressee of the pamphlet, the 'Noble Lord', is not named, Burke earlier wrote a private letter, now lost, to Lord Grenville, who defended him on 13 Nov. in the Lords: material from this letter may be incorporated in the pamphlet. Burke to Windham, 17 Nov. 1795 (*Correspondence*, vol. VIII, p. 342).

24 M. Porcius Cato, who died about 150 B.C., rose to eminence and became proverbial during his long life for strictness and integrity. Publius Cornelius Scipio, surnamed Africanus, who came of a noble family, distinguished himself in battle against the Carthaginians so young that he was made an aedile in his twenty-first year.

25 *Paradise Lost*, Bk I, l. 196. Milton's Leviathan is an image for his fallen Satan.

26 John Russell, 1st Earl of Bedford (1486?–1555), an adroit courtier of Henry VIII who afterwards served both Edward VI and Mary. He profited greatly from the fall of others, for example receiving in 1539 estates in Devon forfeited by Henry Courtenay, Marquis of Exeter. For his grants of Church lands, see n. 34. The use of the word 'minion' for a Russell derives from the Duke of Bedford's speech (n. 14).

27 Burke's note: 'See the history of the melancholy catastrophe of the Duke of Buckingham. Temp. Hen. VIII' (Edward Stafford, 3rd Duke of Buckingham, 1478–1521, accused of disloyalty to the King and executed).

28 Boulogne, taken by siege in 1544, was restored to France by treaty in 1550. Russell took part in the siege and was one of the commissioners who negotiated the treaty.

29 When Burke retired from Parliament in July 1794, he vacated a seat at Malton owned by his friend Earl Fitzwilliam, who nominated Burke's only son, Richard, to the seat. Richard however died suddenly that August. The government's intention to make Burke a peer (Lord Beaconsfield) was shelved now that there was no successor to the title.

30 *The Whole Duty of Man* (1658), an often-reprinted devotional work, anonymous, but conjecturally by Richard Allestree.

31 Genesis x. 8–12. Nimrod is named as the first warrior in the Bible, a 'mighty hunter'.

32 *Macbeth* I.iv.45.

33 Joseph Priestley (see p. 83), the leading Dissenting polemicist, was also an eminent chemist.

34 Tavistock, Woburn, and Covent Garden were estates ceded to John Russell. The first two were spoils of their respective monasteries: the names remain associated with a Duke of Bedford because he lives at Woburn Abbey and his heir is the Marquis of Tavistock. Russell received Covent Garden and Long Acre, London, in 1552 when they were forfeited by the fallen Protector Somerset; in Burke's day, Covent Garden had been for a century past the site of one of London's principal theatres.

35 Purple, the ecclesiastical colour; blue and buff, electoral colours of the Whig party.

36 'Tonsor', hair cut in the monkish tonsure; and 'crop', the short revolutionary

hairstyle (see below, chapter on Cobbett, n. 4). On 30 Oct. 1795, Earl Fitzwilliam wrote to his wife, 'in our house for the first time the D. of B. [Bedford] appear'd a *round head without powder* – it will not add to the strength of Opposition that its leader to the House of Lords is dressing [as] a Bow-street runner' (Burke's *Correspondence*, vol. VIII, p. 377n.).

37 Louis Legendre (1752–97), French Jacobin orator, who before the Revolution kept a butcher's shop in the rue des Boucheries St Germain. After the fall of Robespierre, Legendre acted against the Jacobin Club, became president of the Convention, and helped to bring about the impeachment of the extremist J. B. Carrier.

38 Alexander Pope, *Essay on Man*, Ep. I, ll. 83–4.

39 The portrait of Keppel which Burke owned, one of several by Reynolds, is now in the National Gallery.

40 On 9 Dec. 1795, the brewer and philanthropist Samuel Whitbread introduced a Bill to regulate the wages of Labourers in Husbandry – i.e., to fix a minimum wage. It was defeated, on the grounds that government interference was a mistake, and that the desired ends 'would be better accomplished by the unassisted operation of principles' (*Parl. Hist.* xxxiii, 700–15). A Select Committee of the Privy Council sat during the year to report on the price of corn and on the measures to be taken – which included buying corn overseas; its report is summarised in the *Gent's Mag.*, LXV (Dec. 1795), 999–1009.

41 *Gent's Mag.*, LXV, 1004.

42 At a meeting of the day-labourers (not squires) of the small Norfolk parishes of Heacham, Snettisham, and Sedgford on 5 Nov. 1795, it was resolved that methods of lessening distress, such as selling flour under the market price through a subsidy from the parish rate, were insulting and inadequate, and that 'the price of labour should, at all times, be proportioned to the price of wheat' (*Annals of Agriculture*, xxv, 503, reprinted in *English Economic History: Select Documents*, ed. A. E. Bland, P. A. Brown, and R. H. Tawney (1914), p. 552).

43 The justices of the peace of the various counties met regularly at Quarter Sessions to discuss matters such as wages and poor relief (see above, p. 60). Though done early in the century, it had now become very uncommon to fix a minimum wage. To Burke, a legal requirement to farmers to raise wages amounted to a tax by the community on the farming interest; the opposing view was that the use of poor relief meant that the community was subsidising the farmer.

44 In Oct. 1795 the Secretary of State for Home Affairs, the Duke of Portland, sent a letter to the lords lieutenant of counties asking them 'to procure an account of the produce of the several articles of grain . . . comparing the same with the produce of a fair crop . . . in common years . . . and to report such account as quickly as possible'. Within the counties, the information was to be collected by J.P.s and the high constables of the hundreds (W. E. Minchinton, 'Agricultural Returns and the Government', *Essays in Agrarian History* (Newton Abbot, 1968), vol. II, p. 109). For Burke's comparison with requisitions in revolutionary France, see Young's comments two years earlier (pp. 102–6).

45 Proposals to set up granaries came from official and unofficial quarters: see, e.g., letter of 21 Dec., *Gent's Mag.*, LXV (Dec. 1795), 1006. In times of shortage throughout the eighteenth century granaries were a favourite target of mob violence (T. S. Ashton, *An Economic History of England: The Eighteenth Century* (1955), p. 227). Burke's attack on the scheme in this pamphlet was believed to have caused it to be dropped (Minchinton, 'Agricultural Returns', p. 111).

46 For Richard Burke, see p. 238 n. 29.

Mary Wollstonecraft

1 Claire Tomalin, *The Life and Death of Mary Wollstonecraft* (1974), ch.iv, pp. 29–44, 'Newington Green and the Dissenters'.

2 Johnson was the publisher of both of Wollstonecraft's books excerpted here, as he was the publisher of Tooke, of the less inflammable part (Pt I) of Paine's *Rights of Man*, and the London distributor of Priestley. His authors are the middle-class and intellectual radicals; D. I. Eaton (see p. 185) is a publisher more likely to handle actionable material, e.g., Godwin's *Cursory Strictures* (see p. 169), Paine's *Age of Reason*, and Thelwall's *The Tribune*.

3 Boulton, *Language of Politics*, pp. 167–8.

4 The practice of press-ganging or impressment was the eighteenth-century form of conscription or draft for the armed services. It fell particularly hard on experienced seamen, since the navy, with its appalling conditions, could not recruit enough men by other means. Pressing was intensely unpopular, and it was a practice not exercised after the end of the Napoleonic Wars in 1815, though the government did not give up its legal right. Like the Game Laws, which made game the property of landowners, and exacted stringent penalties for poaching, impressment was seen by radicals as a 'combination' of the rich against the poor.

5 See p. 83. The most influential of Priestley's works directly on education was *Essay on a Course of Liberal Education* (1768), which is based on his experience while teaching at the Dissenting Academy at Warrington.

6 A. L. Barbauld wrote *Lessons for Children* (from 1778), *Hymns in Prose for Children* (1781), and *Evenings at Home* (1796), as well as five radical pamphlets on political issues between 1790 and 1793. She was the daughter of John Aikin, another tutor at Warrington, where she lived 1758–73. After that she kept a school in Suffolk for eleven years with her husband, a Dissenting clergyman. From the late 1780s she lived at Hampstead and frequented the social circle of her publisher, Joseph Johnson.

7 In *Belinda*, Maria Edgeworth (1768–1849), like Wollstonecraft, puts the feminist case against Rousseau for making the passive, ultra-feminine Sophie his model woman (in *Émile*, 1762). Her anti-heroine Virginia is brought up on Rousseau's system, and grows up dependent and silly. The same novel satirises 'harum-scarum' women in the character Harriott Freke, who, though not a direct caricature of Wollstonecraft, reflects the genteel woman's distaste for the revelations of *Memoirs of Mary Wollstonecraft* (see p. 75 above). *Letters for Literary Ladies* (1795), Edgeworth's apprentice work for adults, contains three short works on feminist themes found in *A Vindication*, including Rousseau again. Other leading women writers who use fiction in this decade to explore the position of women, with greater or less radical commitment, include Fanny Burney (*Camilla*, 1796, but cf. *The Wanderer*, 1814), Charlotte Smith (*Emmeline*, 1788, *Desmond*, 1792, *The Old Manor House*, 1793), and Elizabeth Inchbald (*A Simple Story*, 1791, *Nature and Art*, 1796).

8 *The Cabinet*, ii (Norwich, 1795), 49.

9 For Rousseau's 'natural' scheme of education for a woman in *Émile*, see n. 7.

10 Joseph Gregory, *A Father's Legacy to his Daughters* (1774).

11 Experiences of the heroine of Wollstonecrafts's posthumous novel *Maria, or the Wrongs of Woman* (1798) develop the case against Rousseau, and other points in the excerpt. Maria is an unhappy wife and the mother of a baby. She is distracted from concern for her baby when she catches a glimpse of a young man, Henry Darnford, whom she identifies with another of Rousseau's characters – St Preux, the hero of

Julie, ou la Nouvelle Héloise. The love affair was to have ended unhappily, and in one of the projected endings to the unfinished novel, Maria was to have been left caring for her baby daughter.

Helen Maria Williams

1 Williams's note: 'As for me, I desired nothing better.'

Joseph Priestley

1 Priestley published an *Examination* of the Scottish psychologists Reid, Beattie, and Oswald (1774), and an edited version of David Hartley's *Observations on Man* (1749), entitled *Hartley's theory of the Human Mind, on the principle of the association of ideas; with essays by J. Priestley* (1775), to which Coleridge was indebted.

2 For a fuller account of the Birmingham riots, see pp. 136ff., and chapter on Cobbett, n. 7.

3 *Job* xxxi.35.

4 On 2 March 1790 Burke passionately opposed Fox's bill for the repeal of the Test and Corporation Acts (see p. 4), a speech which may have been decisive in securing the Bill's defeat.

5 For the view of Dissenters, that Burke's intervention helped them because it stimulated discussion, see p. 165. The point is also well argued by the unitarian Thomas Christie, *Letters on the Revolution of France* (1791), pp. 4–7, 48–50.

6 Burke was frequently accused by his opponents of being a covert Papist. Here, in accusing him also of sympathy with the exotic Eastern Orthodox Church (S. Sofia) and with ancient paganism, Priestley slyly returns upon Burke the insinuations Burke made against Price. See above , p. 38.

7 I.e., Burke's cult of Marie Antoinette (see above, p. 44) echoes his Catholic cult of the Virgin Mary. Burke's passage about Marie Antoinette drew ribald comment, since she was widely considered unchaste. See, e.g., James Mackintosh, *Vindiciae Gallicae* (above, p. 91), and, later, Byron: 'So much for chivalry. Burke need not have regretted that its days are over, though Marie Antoinette was quite as chaste as most of those in whose honours lances were shivered, and knights unhorsed'. *Childe Harold*, I and II, Addition to the Preface (1813).

8 Priestley here anticipates the classic study in the period of 'priestcraft' as a malign political influence throughout history, the Comte de Volney's *Ruins of Empires* (1791).

9 The First Amendment to the U.S. Constitution declared that no citizen could be compelled to support or attend any church not of his own choosing, nor suffer discrimination because of religious beliefs. Cf. also Thomas Jefferson: 'that the opinions of men are not the subject of civil government, nor under its jurisdiction' (Bill for Establishing Religious Freedom, brought before Virginia legislature, 1777).

James Mackintosh

1 Boulton, *Language of Politics*, p. 152.

2 Mackintosh was obliged to apologise for this passage in an Advertisement to the Third Edition, dated 28 Aug. 1791: 'I have been accused, by *valuable friends*, of treating with ungenerous levity the misfortunes of the Royal Family of France. They will not however suppose me capable of *deliberately* violating the sacredness of

misery in a palace or a cottage; and I sincerely lament that I should have been *betrayed* into expressions which admitted that construction.' For the reputation of Marie Antoinette, see chapter on Priestley, n. 7.

3 Charles Alexandre de Calonne (1734–1802), Louis XVI's minister (1783–7), lived in exile in England (1787–9) and, after being forbidden to return to France at the Revolution, joined the Comte d'Artois at the head of the *émigrés* who worked against successive revolutionary governments. The book Mackintosh attacks is *De L'État de la France, Présent et à Venir* (1790).

4 Mackintosh's note: *'Ce digne rejeton du grand Henri* [i.e., Henry IV of France] – Calonne, p. 413. *Un nouveau modèle de la Chevalerie Francoise. Ibid.* p. 114 [Mistake for 414]'. But Charles Philippe, Comte d'Artois (1757–1836), King of France as Charles X 1824–30, had, as Mackintosh insinuates, a reputation for dissipation rather than for chivalry. Together with Marie Antoinette he was the leader of the reactionary party at the French court. His base in 1791 was Turin, but he toured the courts of Europe seeking support for the French royalist cause. Pierre Terrail, Seigneur de Bayard (1473–1524), is the model of chivalry among historical French soldiers and courtiers, as is Sir Philip Sidney (1554–1586) among Englishmen.

5 For Montesquieu and his reputation as a liberal intellectual, see chapter on Price, n. 10. He was a practising lawyer, who in 1716 inherited from his uncle a high judicial office at Bordeaux, which he filled until 1728.

6 Mackintosh's spelling, repeated elsewhere in *Vindiciae* (p. 119).

7 Marchese de Beccaria (1735–94), Italian economist and penologist, whose most famous book, *Dei Delitti e delle Peni(On Crimes and Punishments)* (1764), helped to promote reforms in the penal codes of the major European nations.

8 For Turgot, see above, chapter on Price, n. 12.

9 Mackintosh borrows from Burke's armoury the image of a natural phenomenon, but applies it to the activities of philosophers, which Burke always represents as unnatural; Burke uses images from nature for unintellectual common life, and for the state.

Arthur Young

1 John Morley, *Burke* (1879; reprinted 1923), p. 236.

2 *Almanack of the Bishoprics* – viz., Metz, Toul, and Verdun.

3 The *Séance Royale* of 23 June 1789 was a formal meeting called by Louis XVI in an attempt to prevent the Tiers État and a few of the clergy from constituting themselves as a national legislature with full sovereign powers. At the *Séance Royale*, Louis declared that the Estates should deliberate apart, and that, if they refused to co-operate with him, he would act by his sole authority. Meanwhile, however, on 20 June, the deputies of the self-proclaimed National Assembly had sworn the Oath of the Tennis Court, by which they undertook not to separate until the Constitution was established.

4 Pierre Willemet (1735–1805), the author of botanical works, was director of the Jardin des Plantes at Nancy.

5 Diarbekr, Turkey, an inland town on the right bank of the Tigris.

6 France gained a large part of Alsace by treaty after the Thirty Years War (1648), and seized Strasbourg in 1681. But French administration of the province during the eighteenth century did not attempt to impose French language and customs and Alsace remained broadly German at the Revolution.

7 First edn, 'a mess for the devil'. A number of Young's emendations in 1793 involve the removal of vulgarities.

8 Young's anecdote is evidence of the suspicion and dislike in which Marie Antoinette was popularly held, as a secret, malign influence on policy.

9 Burke to Young, 5 Mar. 1793; *Burke's Correspondence*, vol. VII (1968), p. 356.

10 Young regularly cites as his source the French official newspaper, *Le Moniteur*: here, 18 Oct. (1792). 'Persons of fortune' and 'personnes aisées' are the same group: he precedes his French phrases with the English translation.

11 Young's note: '*Moniteur*, 17 Sept. [1792]'. On 9 and 16 Sept., the Assembly in Paris authorised the district administrations to take a census of the existing grain supplies in their areas, and to requisition corn where necessary in order to keep the markets supplied. See Burke, above, p. 68.

12 In Sept. 1792, Prussian and Austrian armies were advancing into France. On 4 Sept., the Executive Council ordered the requisition of grain and fodder for the armies at fixed prices laid down by the government. Requisitioning frightened the commercial middle classes, who believed in a free market economy, and deepened the division between the Girondins, representing the interests of the middle classes, and the 'Mountain', or Jacobins, who reflected the interests of the Parisian masses. Most English reformers communicated with the Girondins rather than with the Jacobins; Young's position on this question is not quirky.

Tom Paine

1 Noah Webster (1758–1843) had already published a *Grammatical Institute of the English Language* (1785) and *Dissertations in the British Language* (1789). In the latter, especially, he pointed to the gap between the common user of the language and a standard of correctness as learned as Samuel Johnson's.

2 Joseph Johnson published the first edition of Part I, but he then passed the book, presumably out of prudence, to J. S. Jordan, who also published Part II. For the mass distribution of *The Rights of Man* from May 1792, see above, p. 7.

3 Thompson, *Making of the English Working Class*, p. 108, and R. D. Altick, *The English Common Reader: A Social History of the Mass Reading Public, 1800–1900* (Chicago, 1957), p. 70.

4 Cf. *Autobiography of Francis Place*, ed. M. Thale (Cambridge, 1972), p. 198.

5 For critical discussion of Paine, see Boulton, *Language of Politics*, pp. 134–50; Eric Foner, *Tom Paine in Revolutionary America* (New York, 1976); and Olivia Smith, *The Politics of Language, 1790–1818* (Oxford, 1984).

6 *Rights of Man*, Pt II, ch. 4, 'Of Constitutions', pp. 68–9.

7 Abbé Emmanuel-Joseph Sieyès (1748–1836) was one of the chief theorists of the Revolution, and the author of the famous pamphlet, 'What is the Third Estate?' (1788).

8 The American President is not, however, a member of Congress.

9 Paine's note: 'Rev. William Knowles, master of the grammar school of Thetford, in Norfolk'. Paine's account of his seafaring curiously resembles Defoe's description of his hero's going to sea, against advice, in *Robinson Crusoe*, an extremely popular book throughout the eighteenth century.

10 Paine appends a long autobiographical note, which begins:
Politics and self-interest have been so uniformly connected, that the world, from being so often deceived, has a right to be suspicious of public characters: but with regard to myself, I am perfectly easy on this head. I did not, at my first setting out in public life, nearly seventeen years ago, turn my thoughts to subjects of government from motives of interest; and my conduct from that moment to this, proves the fact. I saw an opportunity, in which I thought I could do some good, and I followed

exactly what my heart dictated. I neither read books, nor studied other people's opinions. I thought for myself. The case was this:

   During the suspension of the old governments in America . . . I was . . . impressed with the idea, that a little more than what society naturally performed, was all the government that was necessary; and that monarchy and aristocracy were frauds and impositions upon mankind. On these principles I published the pamphlet *Common Sense*.

The long account which follows of his role in American politics includes a letter of testimonial from George Washington.

11 Paine's note: 'See Sir John Sinclair's *History of the Revenue* [i.e., *History of the Public Revenue of the British Empire* (2 vols., 1784)]. The land-tax in 1646 was £2,473,499.'

12 The previous two paragraphs are omitted in editions of 1793, along with other paragraphs singled out for particular criticism by the prosecution at Paine's trial in Dec. 1793. Publishers evidently hoped in this way to avoid prosecution, but in May 1793 H. D. Symonds, who had published an expurgated *Rights of Man*, received a four-year sentence in Newgate for the offence. See also p. 8.

13 Paine's note:
   Several of the court newspapers have of late made frequent mention of Wat Tyler. That his memory should be traduced by court sycophants, and all those who live on the spoil of a public, is not to be wondered at. He was, however, the means of checking the rage and injustice of taxation in his time, and the nation owed much to his valour. . . .
   Tyler appears to have been an intrepid disinterested man, with respect to himself. All his proposals made to Richard, were on a more just and public ground, than those which had been made to John by the Barons; and notwithstanding the sycophancy of historians, and men like Mr Burke, who seek to gloss over a base action of the court by traducing Tyler, his fame will outlive their falsehood. If the Barons merited a monument to be erected in Runnymede, Tyler merits one in Smithfield [in London, where he was murdered in 1381].

14 Paine's note: 'Poor-rates began about the time of Henry the Eighth, when the taxes began to encrease, and they have encreased as the taxes encreased ever since.'

15 This list of the oppressors of humanity includes the European crowned heads, the Emperor Leopold II of Austria (1747–92), King Frederick William II of Prussia (1744–97), the Empress Catherine II of Russia (1729–96); Lord Cornwallis (1738–1805), who, after commanding the British forces in America, had become commander in India, and was currently fighting Tippoo Sahib; and Tippoo Sahib (1753–99), the Sultan of Mysore, who fought a series of campaigns against the British, and had a reputation for cruelty.

16 See chapter on Priestley, n. 8.

17 See chapter on Priestley, n. 9.

18 Paine was reissued in the post-war period of Cobbett's greatest influence. See above, p. 19.

19 Paine was the friend of the Girondin party, which fell in June 1793.

20 Paine was arrested on 27 Dec. 1793. (For the imprisonment of H. M. Williams, another friend of the Girondins, earlier that autumn, see p. 80.) Paine remained in prison for ten months, during the Terror of 1794: he believed that he owed his life to an illness which prostrated him for a month, and to once being accidentally overlooked. He made use of his time in prison to write *Age of Reason*, Part II.

21 Joel Barlow (1754–1812), American poet and political writer, spent the revolutionary period in Europe. In London he was a member of the S.C.I., and published a

celebrated pamphlet, *Advice to the Privileged Orders* (1792). He was ardently pro-
French and republican.

22 Paine's note: '[It] is, however, necessary to except the declaration, which says, that
God *visits the sins of the fathers upon the children.* (Second Commandment.) It is contrary to every principle of moral justice.'

23 This connection between heathen religions and Christianity closely resembles the
account given by Volney (for whom see chapter on Priestley, n. 9.) and by Charles
Dupuis, whose *Origine de tous les cultes, ou religion universelle* (7 vols., 1795) makes
many of Paine's points in more detail.

William Cobbett

1 Cobbett's reappearance with Paine's remains was the subject of much contemporary
amusement. The monument was never raised and the relics disappeared.

2 From the speech of the Secretary at War (Sir George Yonge, Bart.) during the
debate on the Army Estimates, 15 Feb. 1792 (*Parl. Hist.* xxix, 811).

3 *Twelfth Night* IV.ii. 114.

4 Army uniforms continued extravagant into the nineteenth century, and officers
especially were frequently satirised for 'foppery'. The old-fashioned practice of
powdering the soldiers' hair was especially vulnerable to criticism in a decade in
which it became fashionable, particularly in republican circles, to wear the hair loose
and natural, or cut short in the Roman manner.

5 '*some purpose* or other': the endemic popular and radical suspicion that governments
were warmongers.

6 George Spater, *William Cobbett: The Poor Man's Friend* (2 vols., Cambridge, 1982),
vol. I, pp. 48–51.

7 Dissenters believed, with some evidence, that men in authority locally were behind
the mob. (1) On the evening of the dinner to mark Bastille Day, an inflammatory
handbill appeared on the streets purporting to be by the radicals. They maintained
that it was a forgery (later in his pamphlet, Cobbett claims it was genuine). (2) The
mob was extremely well informed, singling out for destruction three Unitarian
meeting-houses, one Baptist chapel, and the homes of twenty-seven prominent and
prosperous citizens, almost all Dissenters. (3) Three magistrates have been identified by a modern historian, R. B. Rose, as orchestrators of the rioters. They and
others were at best inactive, and it was three days before troops were brought in
from outside Birmingham to quell the riots.

8 Unitarianism, as opposed to Trinitarianism, implies the humanity rather than the
divinity of Jesus. Those professing it tend to minimise the essential elements in
religion, and to approach the scriptures historically and critically. Unitarianism had
become the intellectually dominant strain in Dissent in the late eighteenth century,
taking over the role of Deism earlier, and it was not always easy to distinguish
between the two positions. On this and other points, Cobbett is unsympathetic but
not necessarily incorrect. It was indeed a middle-class, intellectual type of Christianity, without a wide popular appeal.

9 'Unluckily' is the doubtful word here. See n. 7.

10 See n. 7.

11 Evidence was collected against about fifty rioters; seventeen were tried at the
Summer Assizes at Warwick and Worcester; of the four found guilty, one was
reprieved, three hanged (R. B. Rose, 'The Priestley riots of 1791', *Past and Present*,
xviii (Nov. 1960), 82).

12 10 Aug. 1792: the insurrection in Paris which overthrew the monarchy: i.e., the

second, more popular revolution which followed the 'bourgeois revolution' of 1789.

13 Cobbett's footnote:

Let us hear the Doctor again. "My second son, who was present both at the riot, and the assizes, felt more indignation still, and willingly listened to a proposal to settle in France; and there his reception was but too flattering." It is useless to ascertain the time of this flattering reception, in order to prove that it was in the midst of massacres; for the revolution has been one continued scene of murder and rapine. . . .

Priestley's second son William became a naturalised French citizen on 8 June 1792.

Samuel Horsley

1 The anniversary of the death of 'Charles King and Martyr' was at least as sacred an occasion to the Tory and High Churchman as the anniversary kept by the Revolution Society, so that Horsley's use of the occasion to reply to Price's now notorious *Discourse* is apt.

2 *Sermon* (1793), pp. 6–7.

3 *Ibid.* p. 19.

4 For the Social Contract, especially Rousseau's version of it, see chapter on Burke, n. 11.

Richard Watson

1 *A letter to his Grace the Archbishop of Canterbury* (1783), p. 20, quoted in Richard Allen Soloway, *Prelates and People: Ecclesiastical Social Thought in England, 1783–1852* (1969), p. 3.

2 See *Ibid.* p. 30.

3 See Paine's *Rights of Man*, above, pp. 116ff.

William Godwin

1 Some literary critics, from Leslie Stephen on, dissent from this view and see *Caleb Williams* as essentially unpolitical. But see Boulton, *Language of Politics*, pp. 207–49, Gary Kelly, *The English Jacobin Novel, 1780–1805* (Oxford, 1976), pp. 179–208, and M. Butler, 'Godwin, Burke and *Caleb Williams*', *Essays in Criticism*, xxxii (July 1982), 237–57.

2 See p. 156. It is interesting that Godwin here places himself and his readers in the servant class, as he also seems to do when he narrates the story of Caleb Williams in the first person.

3 Godwin was caricatured in the editorial matter of *The Antijacobin*, where he is alluded to as 'Mr Higgins of St Mary Axe', and in many satirical novels of the late 1790s, such as Isaac d'Israeli's *Vaurien* (1797) and George Walker's *Vagabond* (1799). Parodic versions of the fire and of the philosophising are more or less obligatory in such novels.

4 *Political Justice*, Bk III, ch. VI.

5 See below, chapter on Thelwall, n. 16.

6 Toronto, 3 vols., 1946.

7 1793; the chapter then was numbered Bk I, ch. V.

8 The chapter was considerably expanded in 1796, from the original Bk I, ch. III, 'The Moral Characters of Men Originate in their Perceptions'.

9 For Fénelon, see above, chapter on Price, n. 11.
10 Godwin's note: 'The question, how far impartial justice is a motive capable of operating upon the mind, will be found examined at length, Bk IV, ch. X.
11 Substantially 1793, but for change from 'wife, mother' to 'brother, father', with subsequent modifications, see above, p. 150.
12 1796, substituted for a 1793 chapter now omitted.
13 Godwin's note: 'Bk IV, ch. II.'
14 Godwin's note: 'The Spartan. [John] Logan's [*Elements of*] *the Philosophy of History* [1781], p. 69.'
15 One of the many passages in which Godwin's ideas and vocabulary echo Burke's *Reflections*.
16 1796, substituted for a 1793 chapter now omitted. Of this and the previous chapter, F. E. L. Priestley notes that both were entirely re-written, but says (of III.VI especially) that the contents are largely the same. These chapters now have, however, a close affinity with *Caleb Williams*, and they are the prime example of how the novel, as in effect a series of case studies in class relationships, enabled Godwin to improve his theoretical discussion of that topic in *Political Justice*.
17 Godwin's note: 'Bk I, ch. VI'.
18 Substantially new in 1796.
19 New in 1796. The last paragraph of the excerpt clearly alludes to the lecturing of Thelwall, which Godwin criticised elsewhere in 1795: see chapter on Thelwall, n. 16.
20 Godwin's note: 'This argument is the great common place of Mr. Burke's Reflections on the Revolution in France, and of a multitude of other works, ancient and modern, upon the subject of government.'
21 Godwin's note: 'Bk I, ch. VII.'
22 The closing pages of this chapter were modified at different times. The last four paragraphs were added in 1796. A long footnote protesting at the imposture advocated in Burke's *Reflections* was cut in 1798.
23 1793.
24 Godwin's note: 'Bk IV, ch. III'.
25 Originally ch. VI. Until 1798 the Appendix was not separated from the chapter. There are a number of excisions and re-writings in both 1796 and 1798, on points of delicacy and probably in response to adverse criticism of Godwin's handling of sexual matters.
26 Joseph Gerrald (1763–96) was sent to the Edinburgh convention of Scottish radicals in 1793 as a delegate from the London Corresponding Society, tried by the notorious Scottish Judge Braxfield, and sentenced to fourteen years' transportation for sedition. He died five months after his arrival at Botany Bay.
27 For a similar phrase applied to freedom of the press, see above, p. 6.
28 Sir James Eyre (1734–99) also played a part in an earlier political struggle, for he acted as Wilkes's counsel in the Wilkes v. Wood case (1763). But in 1770, when Tooke drew up for the corporation of London a remonstrance to the king on the subject of Wilkes's exclusion from Parliament, Eyre caused offence to the corporation by refusing to present it. He was knighted and raised to the exchequer bench two years later, having won ministerial approval over this episode. He encountered Tooke again, as a judge of the court which fined and imprisoned him for his libel after the Battle of Lexington (see above, p. 18).
29 Godwin's note to *Charge* (see above), 'p. 2'. For the unusual practice of publishing the Charge in advance, see Godwin's explanation in an Appendix to *Cursory Strictures*:

The law of High Treason differs from our other criminal laws, by allowing the persons accused an interval of ten days, between the delivery of the indictment and list of witnesses, and the day of trial. The object of the law apparently is, that he may have adequate time, in a matter of so extraordinary magnitude, to prepare his defence (p. 29).

The first trial, Hardy's, opened on 28 Oct. 1794.

30 Sir Michael Foster (1689–1763), judge, was praised by Charles Churchill in *The Rosciad* (1763) as impartial.

31 Sir Matthew Hale (1609–76), judge, served both the Stuarts and the Commonwealth.

32 Godwin's note to *Charge*, 'p. 5'.

33 *Charge*, 'p. 4'.

34 *Charge*, 'p. 6'.

35 *Charge*, 'p. 6'.

36 *Charge*, 'p. 8'.

37 *Charge*, 'p. 9'.

38 Godwin's note: '*Hume* [*History of England*], vol. vi. ch. liv, p. 404'.

Hannah More

1 More's note: 'Lord Ferrars [Laurence Shirley, 4th Earl Ferrers, 1720–1760] was hanged in 1760, for killing his steward.' The evenness of the law, in respect of well-defined crimes, was a proud boast of English eighteenth-century conservatives: see also Watson, p. 146.

2 For *The Whole Duty of Man*, conjecturally by Allestree, see chapter on Burke, n. 30.

3 The description of kings as 'crowned ruffians' originated in Paine's *Common Sense* (1776; Harmondsworth, 1976, p. 81), but by now was almost proverbial.

4 Matthew xxii.21.

5 First Epistle General of Peter ii.17.

6 The Sunday School educational movement was founded in 1780 by the Gloucester newspaper proprietor, Richard Raikes. The National Sunday School Society was formed in 1785; by 1797, 1086 schools and 69,000 pupils were affiliated. In 1789 Hannah More and her sister moved to Cheddar, in the Mendip Hills, Somerset, where they found thirteen adjoining parishes without a single resident curate; they set up a series of Sunday schools and superintended them vigorously, to the great disgust of many neighbours.

7 Psalms xxvii.1.

Daniel Isaac Eaton

1 'The story was aptly introduced to answer the purpose of the moment, in reply to a preceding speaker' (from Mr Gurney's speech for the defence, *Trial of D. I. Eaton for Publishing a Supposed Libel at the Old Bailey, Feb. 24, 1794* (1794), p. 36).

2 Caractacus was the British chieftain who led the resistance to Roman invaders A.D. 48–51, and was sent as a captive to Rome (Tacitus, *Annals*, xii.33).

3 Such tales of atrocities to slaves were common currency in newspapers in the early 1790s, when Wilberforce and others repeatedly brought up the issue of emancipation of the slaves in the Commons, and it was supported by passionate rhetoric from many of the leading orators, including Pitt, Burke, Fox, and Windham.

Thomas Spence

1 This paragraph, 'O hearken! . . . under foot', does not appear in the 1775 lecture or in reprints derived from it.

2 Cf. Spence's *Rights of Infants* (1797), which demands that the weak (i.e., women and children) should have an equal share of the fruits of the earth.

Samuel Taylor Coleridge

1 The King proclaimed special fast-days to ask for God's blessing and assistance for Britain's cause in the war with France. To unitarians and Dissenters generally, fast-days were doctrinally obnoxious.

2 This passage was quoted, with modifications, as a footnote in Southey's *Joan of Arc* (1796), p. 150.

3 Quoted from a poem by William Crowe, first published anonymously in the *European Mag.*, xxvii (June 1795), 418–19.

4 Richard Watson, Bishop of Llandaff, spoke in support of the motion, moved by the Duke of Bedford in the Lords on 27 Jan. 1795, 'that the existence of any particular form of Government in France, ought not . . . to preclude negotiation, which might procure peace'.

5 The see of Canterbury yielded an annual income of £17,000, Durham of £17,500.

6 See Horsley's sermon of 30 Jan. 1793, above, p. 143.

7 George Pretyman (1750–1827), Bishop of Lincoln, *A Charge Delivered to the Clergy of the Diocese of Lincoln . . . 1794.*

8 Patton and Mann cite Coleridge's note in the margin of the Norton Perkins copy of *Conciones*: 'Parody on Burke's celebrated passage in "Letter on the French Revolution"'. See above, p. 44.

9 For the frequent insinuation that Burke was secretly a Jesuit, trained at the seminary at St Omer in France, see also above, p. 87.

10 Matthew Prior, *Henry and Emma*, l. 453, slightly misquoted. New Holland is the name given to Australia by the Dutch seamen who first explored the West Coast.

11 Joseph Addison, *The Campaign*, l. 291.

12 James Macpherson, *Poems of Ossian, Fingal*, Bk I.

13 William Paley, *The Principles of Moral and Political Philosophy* (2 vols., 1794), vol. II, pp. 224–31.

14 A remark of Samuel Horsley in the House of Lords, 11 Nov. 1795, which is reported with some significant variations. E.g., *Parl. Hist.* xxxii, 258: 'In fact, he did not know what the mass of the people in any country had to do with the laws but to obey them' – a remark plainly in keeping with his sermon (above, p. 143).

15 Cf. William Windham in the House of Commons, 23 Nov. 1795: 'ministers . . . were ready to exert a vigour beyond the law, as exercised in ordinary times and under ordinary circumstances' (*Parl. Hist.* xxxii, 386).

16 On 6 Nov. 1795 Lord Grenville in the Lords introduced an Act for the Safety and Preservation of His Majesty's Person against Treasonable and Seditious Practices and Attempts (Grenville's Bill or the Treason Bill). By its terms, treason need no longer consist of overt acts, but might include inciting the people to hatred or contempt of the King, and printing, writing or malicious speaking with intent to harm the King. On 10 Nov. 1795, Pitt in the Commons introduced an Act for the More Effectually Preventing Seditious Meetings and Assemblies (Pitt's Bill or the Convention Bill). This forbade meetings of fifty or more without the consent of a magistrate, who could disperse meetings at discretion.

17 On 29 Oct. 1795 a mob attacked the King in his coach on the way to open Parliament. The government linked the assault with the huge but peaceable mass meeting in a field behind Copenhagen House, Islington, on 26 Oct. The object of the meeting, organised by the London Corresponding Society and addressed by Thelwall, was to demand annual parliaments and universal suffrage and to protest against the war.

18 Here Coleridge quotes from the preamble to the *Treason Bill* (printed in, e.g., *Morning Post*, 9 Nov. 1795). Some of his later 'quotations' are paraphrases.

19 On 30 Dec. 1794, Windham made a bitter riposte to Opposition references to the Treason Trials earlier that month: 'He wished them joy of the innocence of an acquitted felon' (*Parl. Hist.* xxxi, 1029).

20 *Hosea* viii. 7.

21 George III was also Elector of Hanover, an absolute monarchy, the doings of which could sometimes be an embarrassment to his British government. A Hanoverian decree of 19 Dec. 1793 brought libraries and reading societies under strict police supervision.

22 James Harrington (1611–77), the author of *Oceana*, is one of the libertarian political thinkers most cited and reprinted in radical journals; Milton, Locke, and Algernon Sidney are also standard names. See above, pp. 11 and 26.

23 Thomas Walker (1749–1817), cotton merchant and founder of the Manchester Constitution Society, was charged in 1794 with treasonable conspiracy, but Erskine, defending counsel, proved that the state's witness had manufactured evidence at the behest of a local magistrate. Walker was acquitted, and the witness tried and convicted of perjury, but the magistrate was not prosecuted. Fox brought up the scandal of Walker's trial in the parliamentary debate of 16 May 1794; *Parl. Hist.* xxxi, 923.

24 Matt. xxvi. 60.

25 An argument used in the Commons, and attacked by the Whig Opposition, including Fox.

26 Pitt on his day was a fine orator, but Coleridge was given to ridiculing his speeches for empty verbosity; he uses the legal language of the Bill as an occasion for teasing Pitt. Patton and Mann point out that Coleridge was taught at school by the Rev. James Bowyer that certain images were clichés: Bowyer used to give the example of the poisonous manchineel fruit; thus in finding a resemblance between the fruit and the over-luxuriant Bill, Coleridge develops a private joke. (Cf. *Biographia Literaria*, ed. J. Engell and W. Jackson Bate (Princeton and London, 1983), vol. i, ch. i, p. 10.)

Joseph Ritson

1 Ritson gives a learned note on the implications in medieval times of being outside the law.

2 Ritson's note:

In the first volume of Pecks intended supplement to the *Monasticon*, consisting of collections for the history of Præmonstratensian monasteries, now in the British Museum, is a very curious riming Latin poem, with the following title: "*Prioris Alnwicensis de bello Scotico apud Dumbarr, tempore rigis Edwardi I. dictamen sive rithmus Latinus, quo de* WILLIELMO WALLACE, Scotico illo ROBIN WHOOD, *plura sed invidiose canit:* " and in the margin are the following date and reference: 22. *Julii* 1304. *32. E.* 1 *Regist. Prem. fol.* 59. a." This, it may be observed, is the first known instance of our heros name being mentioned by any writer whatever; and affords a strong and respectable proof of his early popularity.

3 Ritson's note on pampered clergymen refers to a portrait of one in Holcroft's novel *Hugh Trevor* (1794–7), and to some ancient anti-clerical verses, one concerned with Robin Hood, the other a ribald squib against bishops of Durham.

4 Ritson's note turns into a twenty-nine page essay on dramas about Robin Hood.

5 What should have been a separate seven-page essay on Robin Hood songs was inadvertently added to the essay mentioned in the previous note.

6 Ritson's example is from Bishop Latimer's sixth sermon before Edward VI, in which Latimer complains that he could not get a congregation to hear him when he visited a church to preach on a saint's day because, he was told, it was also Robin Hood's day.

7 Ritson describes how Robin Hood is associated with 'druidical monuments' near Halifax, and how another group of standing stones in Derbyshire is named after him.

8 Ritson gives a thirteen-page note on the historical connection of Robin Hood with May Day and May games, and of the efforts of magistrates in England and Scotland during the sixteenth century to suppress these festivals, both because they were often accompanied by riots, and because of their 'irreligiousness'. Scott has clearly used some of Ritson's material in his novel *The Abbot* (1820), ch. XIV, and, especially, note G, 'Representation of Robin Hood and Little John', which borrows the anecdote from Latimer given in n. 6 above.

John Thelwall

1 *Parl. Hist.* xxxi, 1029; see chapter on Coleridge, n. 19.

2 See n. 16, below.

3 Thelwall supplied a somewhat embittered Prefatory Memoir to *Poems Written Chiefly in Retirement: The Fairy of the Lake*, etc. (Hereford, 1801), which gives the details of his experiences at Llyswen. He had to take one neighbour to Brecknock sessions 'for ferociously assaulting him with a pickaxe'. During another hue and cry, he defended 'his house from the last extremities of outrage, by causing it to be publicly known, that he would put to death the first unauthorized individual who should presume to set foot on his premises' (p. xxxvii). Rousseau before him and Shelley after him (also in rural Wales) were attacked by peasants outraged by their advanced politics.

4 Hazlitt, *Works*, ed. P. P. Howe, 21 vols. (1930–4), vol. XII, p. 264.

5 *Fermes ornées*: cf. the description in Jane Austen's *Persuasion*, ch. V, of the elegant conversion (*c.* 1814) by Charles and Mary Musgrove of a farm in, supposedly, Dorset, on the southern English mainland (*Persuasion*, ed. Chapman, Oxford, 1954, p. 36).

6 Homer, *Odyssey*, Bk IX. 369.

7 See above, pp. 163ff., and below, n. 17.

8 *Letter*, above, p. 59.

9 By the Treaty of Pillnitz in Aug. 1791 the Emperor Leopold II of Austria and King Frederick William II of Prussia agreed to take common action against any attack by France. This was the basis of the first coalition of the European *anciens régimes* against revolutionary France, and it led to the Austrian and Prussian invasions of the following year (for which see above, p. 105).

10 Robert Banks Jenkinson, afterwards 2nd Earl of Liverpool (1770–1828), had just succeeded to the courtesy-title Lord Hawkesbury with the elevation of his father to

the earldom. In 1792 he visited Coblenz and met the leading French *émigrés*. He made his parliamentary reputation Dec. 1792–May 1793 with vigorous speeches against reform and in favour of war with France. Thelwall had a personal grievance against him, since it was Jenkinson who hired 'bludgeon men' to break up his meetings. (See above, p. 206.)

11 In one of his most exaggerated parliamentary performances, much caricatured and ridiculed by the Opposition and by radicals, Burke on 28 Dec. 1792 announced that an order had been given at Birmingham for 3,000 daggers. He produced one and threw it down on the floor of the House, exclaiming, 'This is what you are to gain by an alliance with France' (*Parl. Hist.* xxx, 189).

12 *Letter*, above, p. 58.

13 For the *True Briton*, see p. 214. *The Times* also received government subventions.

14 *Letter*, above, p. 52.

15 John Reeves (*c.* 1752–1829), founder of the Association for the Defence of Property against Republicans and Levellers (see above, p. 179), and author of the originally anonymous pamphlet *Thoughts on the English Government* (1795). On 23 Nov. 1795 the Whip M.P. Charles Sturt contrasted this pamphlet unfavourably with an allegedly seditious speech by Thelwall, and Reeves was afterwards prosecuted (20 May 1796) for a libel on the Constitution.

16 A reference to Godwin's pamphlet on the Two Acts, *Considerations on Lord Grenville's and Mr. Pitt's Bills* (1795), in which Godwin calls Thelwall an 'impatient and headlong reformer', and adds, apostrophising Reform, 'How often has thy standard been unfurled by demagogues, and by assassins drenched and disfigured with human gore!' (*Uncollected Works*, ed. J. Marken and B. Pollin (Gainesville, 1968), pp. 211–12). Thelwall's note:

> It is painful to see such a name, in such a list. But if men of great powers, however sincerely attached to liberty, voluntarily, by cold abstraction and retirement, cherish *a feebleness of spirit*, which shrinks from the creations of its own fancy, and a solitary vanity, which regards every thing as vice, and mischief, and inflammation, but what accords with its own most singular speculations; and if, under these impressions, and regardless of the consequences to an isolated individual, assailed already by all the malice and persecutions of powerful corruption, they will send such bitter defamations into the world, as are contained in the first 22 pages of "Considerations on Lord *Grenville's* and Mr. "*Pitt's* Bills," they must expect to be classed with other calumniators. The bitterest of my enemies has never used me so ill as this *friend* has done. But nothing on earth renders a man so uncandid as the extreme *affectation* of candour.

17 'The counsels of the lecturers, those wicked panders to avarice and ambition . . .' (Burke, *Letter to a Noble Lord*, 2nd edn, 1796, p. 47).

The Antijacobin

1 A. Aspinall, *Politics and the Press, c. 1780–1850* (1949), p. 69.

2 *Ibid.* p. 78. See below, chapter on Wakefield, n. 1, for the recurrent assertion during the 1790s that some English newspapers were in the pay of the French government.

3 Southey used all these themes, and at this stage led the way in establishing them, though the pantheon of democratic heroes is common property: e.g., for Wat Tyler, see chapter on Paine, above, n. 13.

4 George Canning (1770–1827) entered Parliament in 1794 as a friend of Pitt; he was Under-Secretary for Foreign Affairs, 1796-7; Foreign Secretary, 1807-9 and, creatively and importantly, 1822-7; Prime Minister, 1827.

5 William Gifford (1756-1826), self-made son of a glazier, and a former shoemaker's apprentice, made his name with the anti-sentimental satires *The Baviad* (1794) and *The Maeviad* (1795), and 1809-24 was first editor of the *Quarterly Review*.

6 The hostile summary of Jacobin ethics in the last two paragraphs sounds familiar to readers of Wordsworth's tragedy *The Borderers*, in which the actions of the two leading characters, Marmaduke and Oswald, reflect virtually all the notions which Canning lists. *The Borderers* was written between late 1796 and early 1797, and remained unpublished until 1842. For a similar passage by Burke, see p. 57.

7 A parody of the opening couplet of Richard Payne Knight's *Progress of Civil Society* (1796) (for which see p. 13):
> Whether primordial motion sprang to life
> From the wild war of elemental strife. . .
Knight's poem was imitated at length in *The Antijacobin*, nos. XV, XVI, and XXI, Feb.–Apr. 1798.

8 Gaspard Monge (1746–1818), French mathematician, geometrician, and keen supporter of the Republic. He was briefly Minister of the Marine (1792-3), contributed to military research and to the founding of the école normale and the future polytechnic, and in 1796 went to Italy, following Bonaparte's army, as one of a committee of intellectuals which received the art treasures levied from Italian towns.

9 Published 1795. The third stanza was the work of Coleridge.

10 For Cobbett's pamphlet of the same name, reissued 1797, see p. 129.

Gilbert Wakefield

1 From 1791 French militancy was fed by the assurances of British radicals that an invasion of England would be matched by a popular insurrection. In 1798 there was a renewed call for censorship. It was stated in the French legislature, and repeated in the Commons, that the French government had some English newspapers in its pay. A newspaper (the *Morning Chronicle*?) found on board a neutral vessel bound for France in 1798 contained one item surely meant for the French: 'The outward-bound fleet which has been collecting near six weeks, and is allowed to be the most valuable that ever left our ports, is about to sail under the convoy of two frigates! How easy would it be for the French to detach two or three sail-of-the-line from Brest, and give our commerce an irretrievable blow!' (Reported in the *Antijacobin*, 23 April 1798; quoted in Aspinall, *Politics and the Press*, p. 34 and n.)

2 Milton, *Paradise Lost*, Bk X, ll. 300–2.

3 In 1745–6 the Jacobite army, led by Charles Edward Stuart, 'Bonnie Prince Charlie', penetrated into England, almost unresisted, as far south as Derby.

4 Samuel Croxall (d. 1752), outspoken miscellaneous writer of the reign of George I, produced a popular translation of the *Fables of Aesop* (1722), written primarily for children in a naive, clear English. Thomas Creech (1659–1700), translator of Lucretius and Horace, was mimicked by Pope in the opening of Pope's imitation of Horace, Bk I, ep. VI. Pope then added the couplet,
> Plain truth, dear Murray, needs no flowers of speech,
> So take it in the very words of Creech.

William Wordsworth

1 Michel Gérard (1737–1815), deputy from Rennes to the Estates-General, who gained much popularity by wearing peasant garb, though he voted with the bourgeois leader Le Chapelier. Wordsworth's idealised impression of him may

derive from paintings by Jacques-Louis David or from Collot d'Herbois's *Almanach du père Gérard pour 1792* (Paris, 1792).

2 The fullest account of the writing of the *Lyrical Ballads* is Coleridge's, in *Biographia Literaria*, ch. XIV.

3 W. J. B. Owen cites as a primitivistic commonplace a passage from Hugh Blair's *Lectures on Rhetoric and Belles Lettres* (1767), which is about poetry 'in its ancient original condition', when it 'spoke . . . the language of passion and no other' ('The Preface to *The Lyrical Ballads*', *Anglistica* ix (1957), Appendix, p. 192). For further discussion he refers the reader to L. Whitney, 'English Primitivistic Theories of Epic Origins'. *Modern Philology*, xxi (1924), 337–78, and M. H. Abrams, *The Mirror and the Lamp* (New York, 1953), pp. 78–84.

4 *Edinburgh Review*, iv (1804), 329–30.

5 'Mr. Wordsworth', *Spirit of the Age* (Everyman, 1960), p. 253.

6 W. J. B. Owen, *Wordsworth as Critic* (Toronto and London, 1969), pp. 106, 104.

7 The bracketed part of the sentence was added in 1802. For Coleridge's criticisms of this paragraph in 1817, see *Biographia Literaria*, ch. XVII: 'a rustic's language, purified from all provincialism and grossness, and so far reconstructed as to be made consistent with the rules of grammar (which are in essence no other than the laws of universal logic applied to psychological materials), will not differ from the language of any other man of common-sense, however learned or refined he may be, except as far as the notions which the rustic has to convey are fewer and more indiscriminate' (vol. II, p. 52). The wording of this defence of correct grammar is specifically anti-levelling and anti-Tooke. But cf. Wordsworth, in his *Essay Supplementary to the Preface* (1815), on his desire to divest his (middle-class) reader 'of the pride that induces him to dwell upon those points wherein men differ from each other, to the exclusion of those in which all men are alike, or the same' (*Prose Works*, vol. II, p. 426).

8 Authors' note (in Coleridge's hand in MS.): 'It is worth while here to observe, that the affecting parts of Chaucer are almost always expressed in language pure and universally intelligible to this day.'

9 Wordsworth here touches on traditionally poetic characteristics such as metre, which he deals with elsewhere in the Preface at greater length. His comparison of poetry and prose may be indebted to the article by the leading Dissenting critic, William Enfield, 'Is Verse Essential to Poetry?', *Monthly Mag.*, ii (1796), 455–6. Enfield's arguments seem mostly compatible with Wordsworth's, but they are by no means as wide-ranging or as implicitly democratic.

Select bibliography

1. Primary sources

Analytical Review, 1788–99

Annual Register, a view of the History, Politics and Literature, 1758 onwards

Association for Preserving Liberty and Property Against Republicans and Levellers, *Proceedings* [1793]
  Liberty and Property preserved against Republicans and Levellers. A Collection of tracts [1793]

Bage, Robert, *Man As He Is*, 1792
  Hermsprong, or Man As He Is Not, 1796

Barlow, Joel, *Advice to the Privileged Orders*, 1792
  The Conspiracy of Kings; a Poem, 1792

[Belsham, William] *Historic Memoir on the French Revolution*, 1791

Boothby, Sir Brooke, *Observations on the Appeal from the New to the Old Whigs, and on Mr Paine's Rights of Man in two parts*, 1792

British Critic, 1793–1825

Burke, Edmund, *An Appeal from the New to the Old Whigs*, 1791
  A Letter to Sir Hercules Langrishe, on the Subject of the Roman Catholics of Ireland, 1792
  Thoughts on the Prospect of a Regicide Peace, 1796
  The Correspondence of Edmund Burke, gen. ed. Thomas W. Copeland, 10 vols., Cambridge, 1958–78

Burnett, James (Lord Monboddo), *On the Origin and Progress of Language*, 6 vols., 1773–92

Butler, John, *Brief Reflections on the Liberty of the British Subject*, Canterbury [1791]

[Callender, T. J.] *The political progress of Britain; or an impartial account of the principal abuses in the government of this country from the Revolution in 1688. The whole tending to prove the ruinous consequences of a popular system of war and conquest* [1792]

Calonne, A. de, *Considerations on the Present and Future State of France*, 1791

Cartwright, John, *Take your choice! Representation and respect: imposition and contempt. Annual parliaments and liberty: long parliaments and slavery*, 1776
  The commonwealth in danger; with an introduction containing remarks on some late writings of Arthur Young, 1795

Christie, Thomas, *Letters on the Revolution of France*, 1791

Coleridge, Samuel Taylor, *The Watchman*, 1796
  Collected Letters, ed. E. L. Griggs, 6 vols., Oxford, 1957–71
  Notebooks, ed. K. Coburn, 3 vols., 1957–73

The Critical Review, 1756–1817

Darwin, Erasmus, *The Botanic Garden*, 1789–91
  The Golden Age: a Poetic Epistle to Thomas Beddoes, 1794
  Zoonomia, or the laws of organic life, 2 vols., 1794–6

Select bibliography

Phytologia: or the philosophy of agriculture and gardening, 1800
The Temple of Nature, or the Origin of Society: a poem, 1803
Collected Letters, ed. D. King-Hele, Cambridge, 1982
d'Israeli, Isaac, *Vaurien, or Sketches of the Times*, 1797
[Dyer, George] *The Complaints of the Poor People of England* [1793]
Edgeworth, Maria, *Letters for Literary Ladies*, 1795
    with R. L. Edgeworth, *Practical Education*, 1798
              Essay on Irish Bulls, 1801
European Magazine, 1782–1824
Gentleman's Magazine, 1731–1833
Godwin, William, *Caleb Williams, or Things As They Are*, 1794
    Considerations on Lord Grenville's and Mr. Pitt's Bills, 1795
    The Enquirer. Reflections on Education, Manners and Literature, 1797
    St. Leon: a Tale of the Sixteenth Century, 1799
    Thoughts occasioned by the perusal of Dr. Parr's Spital sermon . . . being a reply to the attacks of Dr. Parr, Mr. Mackintosh, the author of an Essay on Population, and others, 1801
Hamilton, Elizabeth, *Memoirs of Modern Philosophers*, 1800 [Satirical novel]
Harris, James, *Hermes, or a Philosophical Inquiry concerning Universal Grammar*, 1751
Hays, Mary, *The Memoirs of Emma Courtney*, 1796
Holcroft, Thomas, *Anna St. Ives*, 1792
    Hugh Trevor, 1794–7
    Memoirs, written by himself, and continued to the time of his death from his diary, notes, and other papers, by William Hazlitt, 3 vols., 1816
Horsley, Samuel, *The Charge . . . Delivered at his Primary Visitation . . . in 1796*, 1796
    The Charge . . . Delivered at his second General Visitation . . . in 1800, 1800
    The Watchers and the Holy Ones, 1806
Inchbald, Elizabeth, *Nature and Art*, 1796
Jones, Sir William, *The Principles of Government, in a Dialogue between a Gentleman and a Farmer*, new ed., 1797
Knight, Richard Payne, *The Landscape*, 1794
    The Progress of Civil Society, 1796
Lofft, Capel, *Remarks on the Letter of Burke*, 1790
London Corresponding Society, *Address . . . to the other societies of Great Britain*, 1792
    Correspondence, revised and corrected, with explanatory notes [1795]
    To the Parliament and People of Great Britain. An explicit declaration of the Principles and Views of the L.C.S., signed by J. Ashley, 1795
[Mackenzie, Henry], *The Letters of Brutus to Celebrated Political Characters*, 1791
Mackintosh, James, *The Law of Nature and of Nations*, 1798
Mathias, Thomas James, *The Pursuits of Literature*, A Satirical Poem in Four Dialogues, with Notes. 1794–7
Monthly Magazine, 1796–1843
Monthly Review, 1749–1845
[More, Hannah], *Cheap Repository Tracts*, 3 vols., 1798
    The Shepherd of Salisbury Plain, Pts I and II, n.d., signed 'Z'
Oldys, Francis, *The Life of Thomas Pain*, 1792
Paley, William, *The Principles of Moral and Political Philosophy*, 1785
    Horae Paulinae, 1790
    A View of the Evidences of Christianity, 1794
[Parkinson, James] *An address to the Hon. Edmund Burke from the swinish multitude*, 1793, signed Old Hubert, secretary, n.d.

Select bibliography

The village association or, the politics of Edley containing the soldier's tale; the head-borough's mistake; the sailor's tale; the curate's quotations; and Old Hubert's advice [1793]

Mast and acorns: collected by Old Hubert [1794]

Revolution without bloodshed; or, Reformation preferable to revolt, 1794

Parliamentary History of England from the Earliest Period to the year 1803, from which last-mentioned epoch it is continued downwards in the work entitled 'Hansard's Parliamentary Debates' [edited by William Cobbett], 1818

Parr, Samuel, *A Spital Sermon preached upon Easter Tuesday, April 15 1800*, 1801

Pigott, Charles, *A Political Dictionary* (1795)

Polwhele, Richard, *The Unsex'd Females: a poem addressed to the author of The Pursuits of Literature*, 1798

Priestley, Joseph, *An Appeal to the public, on the subject of the riots in Birmingham*, 1791

Reeves, John, *Thoughts on English Government. Addressed to the quiet good sense of the people of England*, 1795

Reid, William Hamilton, *The rise and dissolution of the infidel societies in the metropolis: including, the origin of modern deism and atheism; the genius and conduct of those associations; from the publication of Paine's Age of reason till the present period*, 1800

Robison, John, *Proofs of a Conspiracy, Against All the Religions and Governments of Europe, Carried on in the Secret Meetings of Free Masons, Illuminati, and Reading Societies*, Edinburgh, 1797

[John Scott] *Letter by a member of the Revolution Society*, 1790

Southey, Robert, *The Fall of Robespierre*, Cambridge, 1794 [Act I by Coleridge]

Joan of Arc: an Epic Poem, Bristol, 1796

Poems, Bristol, 1797

Wat Tyler: a Dramatic Poem, 1817

Spence, Thomas, *The Grand Repository of the English Language*, Newcastle, 1775

A supplement to the history of Robinson Crusoe, being the history of Crusonia, or Robinson Crusoe's island, down to the present time. Copied from a letter sent by Mr Wishit, captain of the good-intent, to an intelligent friend in England, after being in a storm in May, 1781, driven out of his course to the said island. Published by the said gentleman, for the agreeable perusal of Robinson Crusoe's friends of all sizes, new edition, Newcastle, 1782

The case of Thomas Spence, book-seller, the corner of Chancery-Lane, London, who was committed to Clerkenwell Prison, on Monday the 10th of December, 1792, for selling the second part of Paine's Rights of man. And a bill of indictment found against him [1792]

The rights of infants; or, the imprescriptable right of mothers to such a share of the elements as is sufficient to enable them to suckle and bring up their young. In a dialogue between the aristocracy and a mother of children. To which are added, by way of preface and appendix, strictures on Paine's Agrarian justice, 1797

The restorer of society to its natural state in a series of letters to a fellow citizen, 1801

The important trial of Thomas Spence for a political pamphlet, entitled "The restorer of society to its natural state", on May 27th before Lord Kenyon and a special jury [1801]

Trial of Thomas Spence in 1801 together with his Description of Spensonia, End of Oppression, Recantation of the End of Oppression, Newcastle-on-Tyne Lecture Delivered in 1775, also, a Brief Life of Spence and a Description of his Political Token Dies, ed. Arthur W. Waters, ltd edn, Leamington Spa, 1917

Thelwall, John, *The Peripatetic; or, Sketches of the Heart of Nature and Society in a series of Politico-Sentimental Journals in verse and prose of the eccentric excursions of Sylvanus Theophrastus*, 3 vols., 1793

Select bibliography

Peaceful discussion and not tumultuary violence, the means of redressing national grievance. The speech of John Thelwall at the general meeting of the friends of parliamentary reform. October 26, 1795. Taken in short-hand by W. Ramsey [1795]

An appeal to popular opinion against kidnapping and murder. Including a narrative of the late atrocious proceedings at Yarmouth, 1796

Prospectus of a Course of Lectures, 1796

Poems, chiefly written in retirement. With a Prefatory Memoir of the Life of the Author, Hereford, 1801

Towers, Joseph, *Thoughts on the Commencement of a New Parliament,* 1790

Trimmer, Sarah, *Reflections upon the education of children in charity schools with outlines of a plan of appropriate instruction for the children of the poor . . .,* 1792

Wakefield, Gilbert, *The defence of Gilbert Wakefield, B.A. late Fellow of Jesus College, Cambridge; on an official information from the attorney-general for a reply to the Bishop of Landaff's Address to the people of Great Britain: delivered in the Court of King's Bench, on February 21, 1799* [1799]

Watson, Richard, Bishop of Llandaff, *The Wisdom and Goodness of God in Having Made Both Rich and Poor,* 1793

Apology for the Bible, in Answer to Thomas Paine, 1796

Address to the People of Great Britain, 1798

[John Wolcot] *Odes of Importance. By Peter Pindar,* 1792

Young, Arthur, *An enquiry into the state of the public mind amongst the lower orders and into the means of turning it to the welfare of the state. In a letter to William Wilberforce,* 1798

Secondary sources

General histories of the period include Ian R. Christie, *Wars and Revolutions: New History of England,* vol. 7 (1982); Clive Emsley, *British Society and the French Wars* (1979), J. Steven Watson, *The Reign of George III* (Oxford, 1960), and the relevant volumes, VIII and IX, of the *New Cambridge Modern History,* especially vol. VIII: *The American and French Revolutions, 1763–1793,* ed. A. Goodwin (Cambridge, 1971).

The following treat radicals and the radical movement more directly: Eugene C. Black, *The Association* (Cambridge, Mass., 1963); Colin Bonwick, *English Radicals and the American Revolution* (Chapel Hill, 1977); Asa Briggs, 'Middle-class Consciousness in English Politics, 1780–1846', *Past and Present* 9 (1956), 65–74; P. A. Brown, *The French Revolution in English History* (1914); Carl B. Cone, *The English Jacobins: Reformers in Late Eighteenth-Century England* (New York, 1968); J. E. Cookson, *The Friends of Peace: Anti-War Liberalism in England, 1793–1815* (Cambridge, 1982); A. Goodwin, *The Friends of Liberty: The English Democratic Movement In the Age of the French Revolution* (1979); J. Ann Hone, *For the Cause of Truth: Radicalism in London, 1796–1821* (Oxford, 1982); Frida Knight, *The Strange Case of Thomas Walker* (1957) and *University Rebel: The Life of William Frend, 1757–1841* (1971); S. Maccoby, *English Radicalism, 1786–1832* (1955); J. G. A. Pocock, *The Machiavellian Moment* (Princeton, 1975) and, as editor, *Three British Revolutions: 1641, 1688, 1776* (Princeton, 1980); R. B. Rose, 'The Priestley riots of 1791', *Past and Present* 18 (1960), 68–88; E. P. Thompson, *The Making of the English Working Class* (1963); G. A. Williams, *Artisans and Sansculottes* (1968).

For the agrarian background to excerpts (5), by Burke, and (12), by Young, see T. S. Ashton, *An Economic History of England: The Eighteenth Century* (1955); W. E. Minchinton, *Essays in Agrarian History,* 2 vols. (Newton Abbot, 1968); Walter M. Stern, 'The Bread Crisis in Britain, 1795–6', *Economica,* 31 (1964), 168–87; and

Select bibliography

various studies by G. E. Mingay, notably the selections from Arthur Young listed under Young below.

On French history in the revolutionary period, major work by French historians is now available in translation, especially Georges Lefebvre, *The French Revolution*, 2 vols., (trans. 1962 and 1964); A. Soboul, *The French Revolution, 1787–1799*, trans. A. Forrest and C. Jones (New York, 1975); and J. Godechot, *The Counter-Revolution: Doctrine and Action, 1789–1804* (1972). Albert Goodwin's *The French Revolution* (Hutchinson University Library, 1953) remains a good introduction; M. J. Sydenham's *The First French Republic* (1974) is useful for its narrative and bibliography, and there are bibliographical essays in A. Cobban, *A Short History of Modern France*, 2 vols. (Harmondsworth, 1961).

On radical writings, the readership, and the press, the following can all be recommended: R. D. Altick, *The English Common Reader: A Social History of the Mass Reading Public, 1800–1900* (Chicago, 1957); A. Aspinall, *Politics and the Press, c. 1780–1850* (1949); James Boulton, *The Language of Politics in the Age of Wilkes and Burke* (Oxford, 1963); Alfred Cobban, *The Debate on the French Revolution, 1789–1800* (1950); H. T. Dickinson, *Politics and Literature in the Eighteenth Century* (1974), and *Liberty and Property* (1977); M. Dorothy George, *English Political Caricature: A Study of Opinion and Propaganda, 1793–1832* (Oxford, 1959); A. Lincoln, *Some Political and Social Ideas of English Dissent, 1763–1800* (Cambridge, 1938); Derek Roper, *Reviewing Before the 'Edinburgh', 1788–1802* (London, 1978); Olivia Smith, *The Politics of Language, 1790–1818* (Oxford, 1984); R. K. Webb, *The British Working-Class Reader, 1790–1848* (1955).

There are very few studies of the Revolution debaters as a group, except for James Boulton's (see paragraph above), but some of the individual writers have acquired a flourishing secondary literature. On Tooke, there is a rather unsympathetic chapter in Hans Aarsleff's *The Study of Language in England, 1780–1860* (Princeton, 1967). For Price, see D. O. Thomas, *The Honest Mind: The Thought and Work of Richard Price* (Oxford, 1977). On Burke, apart from his *Correspondence* (for which see Primary Sources), two good short introductions can be singled out, Frank O'Gorman's *Edmund Burke: His Political Philosophy* (1973), and C. B. Macpherson, *Burke* (Oxford, Past Master series, 1980). J. G. A. Pocock's 'The Political Economy of Burke's Analysis of the French Revolution', *Historical Journal* 25 (1982), 231–49, is a highly suggestive discussion of *The Reflections* and, by implication, of *Thoughts on Scarcity*. Claire Tomalin is not primarily concerned with the writings, but she sets Mary Wollstonecraft interestingly in her social context in *The Life and Death of Mary Wollstonecraft* (1974). G. E. Mingay's *Arthur Young and his Times* (1975) is a useful selection from Young's writing, with introductory matter. Eric Foner's *Tom Paine in Revolutionary America* (New York, 1976) has relevant points to make about his prose techniques. Cobbett awaits the literary treatment his style deserves, but George Spater's biography, *William Cobbett: The Poor Man's Friend* (2 vols., Cambridge, 1982), is informative about the circumstances in which the works were produced. Richard Allen Soloway discusses the Church's response to the Revolution in *Prelates and People: Ecclesiastical Social Thought in England, 1783–1852* (1969). Though much interest has been shown in Godwin of recent years, it is hard to pick out a good introduction. Two older books are still valuable, C. Kegan Paul's *William Godwin: His Friends and Contemporaries*, 2 vols. (1876), and H. N. Brailsford's *Shelley, Godwin and their Circle* (1913); Don Locke's *A Fantasy of Reason* (1979) is both a biography and a discussion of Godwin's philosophy. For More, Eaton, Spence, and Thelwall, see the following: M. G. Jones, *Hannah More* (Cambridge, 1952); Daniel McCue, 'The Pamphleteer Pitt's Government Couldn't Silence', *Eighteenth-Century Life*, 5 (1978), 38–54; Olive Rudkin, *Thomas Spence and his Connections* (reprinted New York, 1966), and Thomas R. Knox, 'Thomas Spence, the Trumpet of a Jubilee', *Past and Present*, 76 (1977), 75–98; J. Cestre, *John Thelwall* (1906).

The two major poets among the prose writers have attracted so much good critical writing that selection is invidious, but the following variously treat the 1790s: M. H. Abrams, *The Mirror and the Lamp* (New York, 1953); R. D. Mayo, 'The Contemporaneity of the *Lyrical Ballads*', *PMLA*, 69 (1954); Mary Moorman, *William Wordsworth: The Earlier Years* (Oxford, 1957); F. M. Todd: *Wordsworth: Politics and the Poet* (Oxford, 1957); John Colmer, *Coleridge: Critic of Society* (Oxford, 1959); E. P. Thompson, 'Disenchantment or Default? A Lay Sermon', in *Power and Consciousness*, ed. Conor Cruise O'Brien and W. D. Vaneck (New York, 1969); Carl Woodring, *Politics in English Romantic Poetry* (Cambridge, Mass., 1970); Mary Jacobus, *Tradition and Experiment in Wordsworth's Lyrical Ballads* (Oxford, 1976); Kelvin Everest, *Coleridge's Secret Ministry: The Context of the Conversation Poems, 1795–8* (Hassocks and New York, 1979). For the decade's creative writing other than its prose non-fiction, see Gary Kelly, *The English Jacobin Novel, 1780–1805* (Oxford, 1976), and M. Butler, *Romantics, Rebels and Reactionaries: English Literature and its Background, 1760–1830* (Oxford, 1981).